The Templar Mission

To Oak Island and Beyond

Search for Ancient Secrets:
The Shocking Revelations
of a 12th Century Manuscript

By

Zena Halpern

The Templar Mission to Oak Island and Beyond

1st edition

ISBN: 978-1544744513

Cover by Betsy and Jeff Brewster (The Brewster Studio), and Kimberly Scott

Printed in USA

Dedicated

To

Ralph de Sudeley

The Unknown English Templar Knight Who Led a Mission and Voyage to America in the 12th Century

Acknowledgments

William David Jackson, MD, discoverer of the 12th century Knights Templar Document and compiler of the collection of research notes, sketches and artifacts related thereto

Professor Cyrus H. Gordon, scholar extraordinaire who set in motion a lifetime of search for lost history of pre-Columbian America

Dr. Elisha Linder, pioneering maritime archaeologist, and P'nina Linder

Dr. Uzia Avner and Rina Feldman Avner, for their enduring friendship

Betsy and Jeff Brewster of the Brewster Studio, for their maps, cover design and support

David S. Brody, author, whose patience and assistance with editing made this book possible

Doug Crowell, who shared all his knowledge of the Oak Island story with me

Steve St. Clair, my stalwart supporter and marketing expert

Richard Moats, Archaeoastronomer, whose discoveries have opened a new era in Oak Island studies

Judi Rudebusch, for her support and devotion

Don Ruh, who shared Dr. Jackson's materials with me

Rick Lagina, whose interest and support opened a new chapter in the Oak Island mystery

The Curse of Oak Island team and Prometheus Entertainment

Ron Richards, computer lifesaver

Gerard Leduc, Ph.D., Templar researcher

Chris Finefrock, script writer

Kimberly Scott, for her work on cover design

Nancy Kimmel, for her proofreading assistance

Harry and Melanie Weymer, for their enduring friendship

Elena Bellomo, Ph.D., Jessica Black, Philip Bayley, Col. USAF (Ret.), Dr. Salvatore Tancredi, Tim Loncarich, Alessandra Nadudvari, Professor Richard Freund, Professor Jim Scherz, Dan Spartan, Jay Wakefield, Janet and Scott Wolter, Gloria Amendola, Stacey Lynn Hirshman, and Jerry Lutgen.

My grandsons Jason Halpern for his graphics and William J. Halpern for his music. Marc and Kristi for their love and caring. Last but not least, to my son Dr. Davin Halpern for his never-ending devotion and love.

Contents

[Note: High resolution images of the maps and artifacts
shown in this book can be found at the author's website:
www.zenahalpern.info]

Introduction

Part I

Bannerman Island and the Jackson Search

A discovery of mysterious artifacts on a deserted island in the Hudson River led one man on a search that ended with his purchase of an eight hundred year old Knights Templar Document. Part I traces Dr. William D. Jackson as we follow his leads through an intricate maze of clues. These are the events, discoveries and connections that played out over centuries, resulting in a historical drama that involved kings and queens in Europe, a secret society, and shadowy paramilitary groups—all maneuvering to obtain a document that would lead them to wealth and power.

By sheer accident, on a mundane fishing expedition in 1968, four men visiting an abandoned island in the Hudson River in New York State found something that would set off a chain of events leading to the discovery of this Templar Document. At the time of this fishing trip, one man, William D. Jackson, found artifacts that changed his life forever. We will discuss these artifacts and how they ultimately led Jackson to the Templar Document located in the Church of San Sigismundo, in Italy. This historic church held the Templar Document for centuries. The document was sold to Jackson by Gustaveste Benvenuto, whose ancestors had been involved with the document as far back as the 15th century.

The chapters of Part I will take the reader through a labyrinth of leads, coincidences, mysterious events and, above all, secrecy, featuring encoded documents with invisible ink, strange connections, and shocking revelations.

Part II

The Templar Discovery in Jerusalem

Players in this drama move in and out over the centuries, emerging and vanishing. Tracking this saga has been an enormous undertaking, and there still remain some unanswered questions. We look forward to taking the reader on this incredible journey. Our ultimate prize will be in revealing the images and explanations of the Templar Document.

Jerusalem was captured in 1099 during the First Crusade. A Templar team in 1104 was headquartered in the Al Aqsa Mosque and began explorations below the Temple Mount in an area of subterranean tunnels. They made an earthshaking discovery of four ossuaries hidden in a chamber. What was hidden in these ossuaries is a history changer.

Numerous accounts have been published regarding the Templars and what was believed to have been found beneath the Temple Mount. Books on this subject have been rife with speculation, suggesting that the Ark of the Covenant, temple treasures and ancient scrolls had been discovered. Since the 1980s, a profusion of books have dealt with the subject of the Templars with no definitive evidence of any written document having been found. Until now.

The contents of these ossuaries were taken to Castrum Sepulchri, a Cistercian Abbey in Italy, some time in the early 12th century. This abbey was a rich repository for archives brought from the Holy Land during the Crusades and was consecrated by a famed figure, Bernard of Clairvaux.

The provenance of the Templar Document has been established by extensive investigation, tracking it from Castrum Sepulchri to the Church of San Sigismundo in Cremona, a Templar city, where it was eventually moved. This city and northwest Italy had an extensive Templar presence from the 12th to the 14th centuries and was where the Templar Document was kept in secrecy for five hundred years until Dr. Jackson purchased it from Mr. Benvenuto.

PART III

Templar Voyage and Mission to Land of Onteora

When Dr. Jackson bought the Templar Document from Mr. Benvenuto, a separate journal entitled *A Year We Remember* was part of the document. I have separated *A Year We Remember* into subparts in order to give it more direct attention and explain its significance to the reader. This account of an unknown voyage by an English Templar, Ralph de Sudeley, is told in his own words, recounted to a monk and recorded in Castrum Sepulchri.

De Sudeley's mission of 1178-1180 was to recover secret scrolls kept on Hunter Mountain in New York. The mission was planned and set in motion by Templar Grand Master Odo de St. Amand at a crucial time in the 12th century. An assassination in England in 1170 that shook Europe and the Church is connected to and may have triggered de Sudeley's mission.

PART IV

Templars, Oak Island and Gold

While on his way to Hunter Mountain in New York, the de Sudeley team made a stop on Oak Island, Nova Scotia. In Part IV we examine ancient maps which indicate where specifically the Templars visited: the famous Oak Island, of Money Pit fame. Many historians believe that whatever treasure was buried on Oak Island is related to the Templars. The information in this section confirms those beliefs and provides additional details. Two maps are shown and discussed, as is a document called the *La Formule* Cipher. These documents turned up unexpectedly while writing this book and add a new chapter to this ever-evolving story.

Author Statement

I have spent the past 10 years chasing down a fascinating story, a story that could change history as we know it. It is the story both of a secret 12th century Knights Templar mission to Oak Island and a mountain range in New York State, and of the efforts made by various secret societies over the centuries to either conceal or uncover the reasons for this mission.

It is also my story over the past decade, pulling together disparate evidence from somewhat shady characters and looking for other sources to prove or disprove this strange story.

Here, then, is the culmination of a decade of work. Read my story. Read of the amazing journey to America by the medieval Templars. Read of the fascinating efforts over the centuries to both conceal the journey and later uncover its secrets. Read about the Vatican and the Freemasons and the CIA—they all play a part in this adventure. Read about treasures and ciphers and betrayals, as well as a newly uncovered chapter in the Oak Island mystery which was presented in 2016 on the History Channel's *The Curse of Oak Island*.

My research is not complete, unfortunately. There are still questions unanswered, which I plan to address in Volume 2 of this work. But 90% will have to do. I can wait no longer to share this with the world.

PART I

Bannerman Island and the Jackson Search

CHAPTER 1

A Mysterious Brass Device is Found

Bannerman Island, Hudson River, New York State, 1968

A deserted island in the Hudson River is where this adventure began almost fifty years ago. This is the true story of William D. Jackson's unrelenting search which began with an accidental find on Bannerman Island and ended in Rome and the Vatican Library. Dr. Jackson's search led him through a maze of events, leads and clues and ultimately to a history-changing discovery. At some point I became involved—because of my expertise in ancient Middle-Eastern history, I was asked for help deciphering some of the clues in this mystery. Going forward, as others aged, my involvement grew. Now it falls on me to tell this story.

In the summer of 1968, Dr. Jackson and three friends decided to go fishing and explore Bannerman Island in the Hudson River, about fifty miles north of New York City. Dr. Jackson (writing in 1984) recalled that fateful day in the summer of 1968:

> *When I first went on a diving trip in the Hudson River near Cold Springs, N.Y., I never dreamed that events would unfold that has encompassed almost twenty years of my life. My three friends and I went for two weekends diving in the*

Hudson River in May and June in 1968. Between Pollepel Island (aka Bannerman Island) and the mainland there are very shallow areas and we anchored the boat upstream. We walked through the ruins of Bannerman Castle. We then went to the mainland and tied up to the shore using a skiff to reconnoiter the banks and do a little fishing. There were several pieces of cement we located two of which were shaped as ornaments on the island with the ball on the top orange size. Two of these I felt would look good on the stone pillars of the gate posts for my wife's flower garden and I took them.

Bannerman Island, Hudson River with View of Arsenal and the Castle

Map Showing Bannerman Island (see arrow)

The Bannerman Connection:
The First Bannerman and the Battle of Bannockburn
in Scotland: 1314

The MacDonald Clan fought in the epic Battle of Bannockburn in 1314, Scotland's battle for independence from England. During this battle, an outnumbered Scottish army fought a far superior English army under Edward II and won Scottish independence.

The name Bannerman was bestowed on Francis of Clan Mac-Donald by Robert the Bruce for bravery in rescuing the king's banner in this battle. It is said that the king cut off a streamer from the national St. Andrew's Cross and proclaimed Francis a "Bannerman" and thus the name became a badge of honor. For seven hundred years the Bannerman family has honored this event by naming a son Francis.

Francis Bannerman VI came to this country from Dundee, Scotland in 1854 with his father when he was three years old. His father began a business in surplus military equipment in Brooklyn, New York. Francis Bannerman VI inherited the business and expanded it to be a worldwide business in armaments during the Spanish-American War. At the end of the Spanish-American War in 1897, Bannerman bought arms and military supplies, including captured Spanish equipment.

In 1890, Bannerman manufactured the repeating shot gun and in 1897 the business was relocated to 579 Broadway in Manhattan. The City of New York would not allow him to store 30 million ammunition cartridges within city limits and a new facility was needed. In 1904, Bannerman bought Pollepel Island in the Hudson River where he built an arsenal which became known as "Bannerman Island Arsenal." The huge sign on the arsenal could be seen by boats sailing north on the Hudson River.

He then built a replica of a Scottish Castle for his family and constructed gardens on the island, decorated with many stone garden ornaments. Frances Bannerman VI died suddenly in 1918 after gall bladder surgery. In 1920 there was an explosion in the arsenal of 200 pounds of gunpowder stored in the powder house. After this event the island lay deserted except for occasional visitors who took photographs or collected items strewn around the island.

View of Sections of the Arsenal and the Scottish Castle (modern)

Bannerman Island Arsenal (historic)

The island is less than ¼ mile from the eastern shore of the Hudson River and passengers on Amtrak travelling north or south can see the castle through their windows. Today it is a historical landmark rescued from years of neglect and decline and managed by The Bannerman Castle Trust, part of New York State Office of Parks and Historic Preservation. Tours are presently available.

Did the Templars Come to the Rescue?

The historic Battle of Bannockburn in 1314 was a defining and critical battle in Scottish history for it overthrew the yoke of English rule and was the beginning of Scottish independence. This battle took place just seven years after the expulsion of the Templars from France by King Philip in 1307 and months after the torture and burning of Grand Master Jacques de Molay in Paris in 1314. There is a document in the Paris Bibliotheque in Latin referring to Templars leaving with carts filled with documents and possibly treasures. Some authors believe that Templar ships sailed to Scotland with the treasure from Paris. It is further believed by some that the Templars were involved in the Battle of Bannockburn and that their arrival at the conflict marked the turning point in the battle.

In the 12th century Hugh de Payens, the first Templar Grand Master (1119–1136), visited and received land from King Henry I of England to build a Templar preceptory in London, England, now called the *Temple Church*. He then visited King David I of Scotland. There is no doubt that the Templars were a force in both Scotland and England in the 12th century and that they received support from the English and Scottish monarchies. For example, in 1127, King David I of Scotland gave land to the Templars to build Balantrodoch, a Templar preceptory. It is now known as Temple Midlothian and is located on the South Esk River in Lothian, in eastern Scotland. This location is close to where Rosslyn Chapel was later built in 1446.

The proud Scottish heritage of the MacDonalds/Bannermans was preserved for hundreds of years. Francis Bannerman VI so loved his Scottish heritage that he built a replica of a Scottish castle here in New York, as pictured above. In the early 20th century, Francis Bannerman VI travelled to various countries related to his business and bought materials for the Scottish castle. He may have been in England or Scotland in the very early 1900s. Did he visit with Liam MacDonald, of the aforementioned Clan MacDonald, whom we will meet later? That is just one of many unanswered questions.

1969: Mysterious Artifacts are Found Inside One Garden Ornament

Francis Bannerman VI was a student of antiquities and was an avid collector. This may explain part of the mystery of what he hid on the island. He placed many of his antiques in a small museum next to his store in New York City, including his collection of rare military memorabilia.

In 1968, Dr. Jackson took the two garden ornaments from Bannerman Island to his garden on eastern Long Island, where they remained untouched for a year. In 1969, his five-year-old son, Mark, broke off the top of one ornament, exposing hidden items. In his own words, Dr. Jackson described what happened: *"A year later I was mortified that my son had damaged one by removing the ball atop it. It was then that I noticed that the ball was in fact a sort of key fitting a keyway in the base and locking a cover in place."* (Jackson Commentary p. 32, 1984) He then describes what he found inside the garden ornament: *In the cavity of the iron box was a green metal round object about one inch thick. This cleaned up to be the Brass Seal. I was not familiar with the markings either on the papers or the seal but when I knew that the language was Theban I tried to locate any information on this strange language and this led to a lengthy search.*

Dr. Jackson later sketched his find:

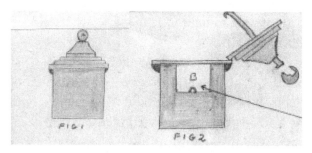

The Garden Ornament from Bannerman Island

Figure 1, on the left, shows the garden ornament. This held the brass device and a clay tube. The small ball on top is marked "A." Figure 2, on the right, shows where the "brass seal" (marked "B") was hidden inside.

Francis Bannerman VI & Scottish Templars Timeline

- Templars in Scotland. King David I in Balantrodoch, early 12th century
- MacDonald/Bannerman tradition traced to Battle of Bannockburn, 1314

- Francis Bannerman VI born in Dundee Scotland, 1851
- Francis Bannerman VI buys Bannerman Island, 1904
- Francis Bannerman VI buys brass device, 1906
- Francis Bannerman VI hides brass device & clay tube in Garden ornament, ca. 1906-1918
- Frances Bannerman VI dies suddenly, 1918

Mysterious Brass Device

This mysterious brass device, discovered by accident, intrigued Dr. Jackson. There is a center disk on the upper section which can be removed. The upper section is inscribed with a pentagon, Theban letters (which we will explain in detail, below), Roman numerals, and symbols for constellations. On the lower section Jackson discovered an inscription in Theban; it turned out to be instructions on how to remove this disk.

**Upper Section of the Brass Device; this Angle
Shows the Removable Disk**

Inscribed around the edge of the device are symbols for constellations, moon settings, Theban letters, and Roman numerals. There are four Theban letters in the center and four at each point of the pentagon.

Enlarged View of the Upper Section of the Brass Device

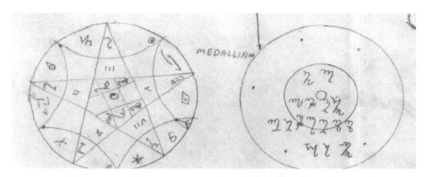

Dr. Jackson's Sketches of the Upper and Lower Section
Left: Symbols Showing Constellations and Moon Positions
Right: Theban Letters Tell How to Open the Device

Dr. Jackson left no notes or comments that would be helpful to explain the upper section of the device. I consulted with Richard Moats, a retired US Air Force remote image analyst, aircraft accident investigator, and instructor. He specializes in aerial image interpretation and archaeoastronomy. He has published many papers on Adena and Hopewell sites, including discovery of a Hopewell Celestial Observatory in central Ohio. Mr. Moats is currently an associate member of the Midwestern Epigraphic Society (MES) and the Archaeological Society of Ohio (AASO). He was the 2015 Converse Award winner for outstanding contributions to Ohio archaeology. The following are his notes:

> *General Device Description: The device is a container comprised of a top/lid made up of a disk and a lower hollow vessel with a hollow center. The disk is engraved on both sides with symbols to include an early form of Theban script, geometric symbols, Roman numerals and lines that are straight and curved to form a symmetrical geometric pattern across the circular disk. The upper section of the device has a removable disk, a central hole and five holes at the apexes of the curved lines that intersect the perimeter of the device. The device is made of brass with a patina that appears to have significant age.*

A Secret Compartment is Found in the Mysterious Device

Upper section opened with disc removed, small triangle shown on the edge

Hollow center, which held 3 small coppe: discs and a small gold triangle

Side view of the device, 1" thick

Another view of the device, 3" diameter

Dr. Jackson figured out how to open the brass device by following the instructions on the lower section. If lines were drawn connecting the Theban letters "C A M" they would meet in the center. Dr. Jackson tapped this center mark with a fine punch and a hammer, causing the center disk to fall out, revealing a secret compartment. It measures as 1 and ¼ inches in diameter and 1 inch deep. Within it he found four objects inside: one round copper disk, one rectangular object, one L-shaped object, and one small gold triangle.

Each of the four objects told a different story. Three of the objects have been lost but luckily Jackson had sketched them and they are shown below. Fortunately the small gold triangle was saved and we were able to analyze it in person along with the device.

What Was the Purpose of the Device?

Richard Moats gives us his answers to this question:

> *I have evaluated all of the available data on this device. I have chosen to use only the most visual and tangible elements of data to form a logical conclusion as to its purpose. In taking this course I intentionally steer clear of the chain of custody and evaluations of others but at the same time use only the most pertinent bits of data. By taking this approach I believe this evaluation will adhere to scientific principles and sets the foundation for deeper study into the origin, dispersion and operation of this device. Without having the device in my possession or making an ocean voyage using it for navigation, it is impossible to give a complete evaluation of all the nuances of the device. By studying all the available data there is no doubt that this device, in the hands of a navigator familiar with the creation and application of this and like devices of the era could have used it to make a transatlantic voyage from Western Europe or Africa to the Americas and return home to sail another day.*

Symbols of Constellations and Moon Settings

The ten symbols etched onto the perimeter of the device, when read clockwise, are deciphered as follows: "Full Moon Rising, Corina, Lyra, Ara, Cygnus, Full Moon Setting, Aquarius, Gemini, Full Moon at Mid Arc, Lupus." These indicate the device is most likely intended to be used in navigation.

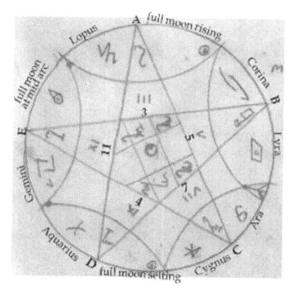

Device Markings Deciphered

Theban Alphabet

Theban is not a language. It is an alphabet developed for cryptic purposes and may date back as early as the 1st century CE:

Theban Alphabet with English Correspondence

The first appearance of the Theban alphabet appears in a book by Heinrich Cornelius Agrippa (1486-1535), entitled *de Occulta Philosophia*. Agrippa wrote three books on occult subjects and the Theban alphabet was included in the third of these books. He referred to Pietro de Abano, 1250, of Padua, as the source of his knowledge of Theban. Padua was an important city in northern Italy and the site of one of the earliest universities in Europe. It was a Templar city in the 13th century. It is possible that Theban was brought to Padua by the Templars.

Agrippa was a student of Johannes Trithemius, who referred to Agrippa's work in his book in German, which was not published until 1609. After the publication of the book by Trithemius, it took years for this knowledge to circulate and eventually become adopted by devotees of magic and the occult. Agrippa and Trithemius wrote about cryptography and occultism, and their books deal in part with the sending of secret messages. Trithemius' book was thought to be about magic but was in reality a highly sophisticated system of cryptography.

The Objects Inside the Brass Device

As stated above, inside the brass device, Dr. Jackson found a number of mysterious objects: one round copper disk, one rectangular object, one L-shaped object, and one small gold triangle.

Copper Disk

The first object was a copper disk. The markings on this disk (both sides) clearly portray a voyage:

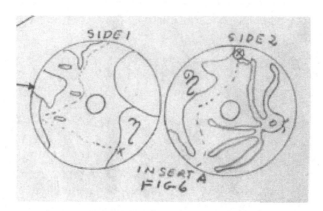

Jackson's Sketch of Round Copper Disk

Left, Side 1: A voyage is clearly traced with a dotted line, beginning at the "X" in Africa. The Theban letter "A" is shown in southern Africa. Africa is separated from the upper part of Africa where there is a Theban letter, "O." The dotted line crosses the Atlantic and makes a stop on land. It continues close to the coast of Florida. The region and the three islands are identified based on new evidence. Please see Epilogue after Part IV.

Right, Side 2: The dotted line continues up the coast of Florida, ending at a circle with an "X" marking Nova Scotia. (In light of evidence later discussed in the Epilogue, I believe the "X" marks the famous Oak Island off the southern coast of Nova Scotia.) There is a Theban "E" drawn below an indentation, which remains a mystery. The right half of side 2 is dominated by the octopus with five arms.

The octopus with five arms appears throughout this mystery. The octopus symbol is associated with the French Merovingian kingdom of the 5th to 8th centuries. Legend states that a sea creature called the *Quinotaur* impregnated the matriarch of this family. The Latin name Quinotaur translates to "bull with five horns." The *Quinotaur* was a water beast similar to Neptune. It appears that the octopus (sea creature) symbol with the five arms is meant to symbolize a legacy with and connection to the Merovingians.

Rectangular Object

The second copper object Dr. Jackson found is rectangular. This, too, features an octopus with five arms (on Side 2):

Dr. Jackson's Drawing of the Copper Rectangular Object

[We will examine the word *QUETZLCOATL* and the *312/356 SW* markings below in the Epilogue. These marking were not understood until this book was being edited in February, 2017.]

I believe that whoever inscribed side 1 made an error and reversed latitude and longitude. The "W" mark is, I believe, meant to indicate North Latitude 42 degrees 27 minutes 30 seconds. The "N" mark is meant to indicate West Longitude 70 degrees 60 minutes. These coordinates point just north of Boston, to the Saugus River. This is a mystery that requires further research, though Ohio researcher Richard Moats believes this location may have been a stop-over point along the coast to allow the voyagers to obtain fresh water and food and to make needed repairs to their ships. It is important to understand that ancient sailing ships required thousand of iron nails to hold the wooden planks together. Many of these nails broke or shook loose during the pounding of the cross-Atlantic voyage. It was necessary, therefore, to forge new nails upon arriving in America (archeologists confirm that iron was forged at the Viking site at L'Anse Aux Meadows circa 1000 CE). The choice of the Saugus River area as a stop-over point makes perfect sense in light of the history of the area as a leader in the production of iron. The oldest iron works in America, founded in 1646, is located in Saugus on the banks of the Saugus River. The location was ideal (both in Colonial times and medieval times) for iron production owing to 1) to its proximity to the coastline, 2) the existence of a shallow, navigable river which could be damned to create dry docks, 3) adequate supplies of timber to make charcoal, and 4) the vast amounts of bog iron which existed in nearby ponds and swamps. This last factor is the most essential, as many coastline areas of New England boast forests and navigable rivers but are lacking in the supply of bog iron.

The words at the bottom of side 2 read, *Altomra de Leon's Tomb*. This is striking, for it tells us that whoever carved this knew about the Templar voyage and the names of two important people mentioned in the Templar Document: Altomara (correct spelling) and de Leon. As we shall learn later, Altomara's tomb was on Hunter Mountain; her ashes were interred in a cave there. Again, whoever inscribed this object knew the name ***Altomara,*** which appears prominently in the Templar Document. It follows therefore that the inscribers must have had access to the Templar Document at some point.

I believe that whoever inscribed these objects was part of a secret group who used the five arm octopus as their symbol. More will be discussed of this later, when we focus on references to the Goddess and how these references relate to another mysterious document known as the MacDonald Journal. Furthermore, the inscribers of the three objects knew the latitude and longitude of Hunter Mountain. They knew the names Altomara and de Leon, people named in the Templar Document. Who this group was that inscribed these inserts has remained elusive and is one of the biggest mysteries in this story.

L-Shaped Object

The third object is an L-shaped object, here:

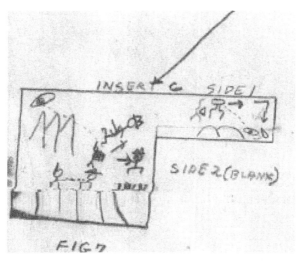

Dr. Jackson's Drawing of the L-Shaped Object

The left side depicts a battle involving two or three figures, one with a feather. Three mountains are shown on the upper left, with an eye above them; the eye has dots apparently leading to one of the mountains. The right side shows two mountains: Hunter Mountain and the opposite peak, Plateau Mountain. Above them, left to right, we have a stream, a rock formation with a flat table or ledge on top, two arrows, and a dotted line going to a cave. "Table Rock" is a distinguishing land mark on Hunter Mountain even today. We will return to this drawing (and battles in this area) in our discussion of "Hunter Mountain—Modern Day Search," below.

Triangular Object

The fourth object found in the brass device actually was a narrow gold triangular wedge, drawn by Dr. Jackson here:

Dr. Jackson's Drawing of the Triangular Wedge

Dr. Jackson named this the "nail." The triangle was inscribed on both sides with these words: ***Quetzalcoatl*** and ***Angra Pequena***. The triangle measures 1 inch long, 1/4 inch wide and 1/8 inch thick.

Quetzalcoatl was the Mayan deity and was worshipped by the Aztecs. *Angra Pequena* is Portuguese; it means "small cove" and was the name of an ancient harbor on the West African coast.

The names *Quetzalcoatl* and *Angra Pequena* raise some very intriguing questions. Dr. Jackson, in one of the letters, wrote that he had the triangle tested in 1970 and it was 800 to 1,000 years old. If

An up close view of the gold triangle. The letters are
Q (u,e,t,z,) A L C O A T (l)

it is 800 to 1,000 years old, then it was used for some purpose some-time in the 11th to 12th centuries. The inscriptions could have been added by those who inscribed the other copper objects, which were also tested and dated to the year 1700 CE, + or – 50 years.

Angra Pequena was supposedly named by Bartolomeu Diaz in 1487 when he sailed down the west coast of Africa to find the route to India for Portugal. Diaz was blown off course into a small cove and took shelter in *Angra Pequena*. But the fact that Diaz explored the area does not mean he named the harbor. The Portuguese explored this coast before Diaz and likely named this small harbor in their early explorations. There were Portuguese voyages down the coast of West Africa as early as the 14th century.

Why Angra Pequena?

A n g r A p e q E N A
[Angra **is on the upper part and** *Pequena* **is below it]**

Angra Pequena is on the western coast of Namibia, a country with a desert region rich in diamonds and minerals. The National

Geographic Atlas states that the area is known for gold, silver and uranium.

Gold and diamonds are part of this story and may explain why the name of an ancient harbor was inscribed on the gold triangle hidden inside the hollow center of the brass device.

A Clay Tube Was Also Found in the Garden Ornament

Dr. Jackson also found a small clay tube at the bottom of the stone ornament with the brass device. The clay tube had a single piece of paper which Jackson separated into two fragments: 4 inches long by 2 inches wide. Below are Jackson's own words describing this find:

In the other [ornament] however was a layer of hard earth either clay or dried mud under which was some more dried seaweed and a small clay tube about 4 inches long by ½ inch wide sealed with a zinc or lead seal having a coat of arms on it on with a ship and an anchor and a hand holding a flag with an "X" on it was barely visible. Below this was a layer of beeswax and a cork stopper. Inside was a piece of oiled cloth holding what I originally believed to be a single sheet of paper with strange markings on it and a red wax seal with a Fleur-de-Lies on it. Later I was able to separate this into two separate fragments about 4 inches long by 2 wide.

Two Fragments from Clay Tube

There are burn marks on the fragments, caused by Jackson when he applied heat to see if there was any invisible writing. Note that on the bottom left of this fragment is a barely visible round seal. This tiny fragment had Theban letters written on it that needed to be translated. Although not believed to be discovered until the 16th century, Theban in actuality was used in the 12th century by the Cistercian monks in Castrum Sepulchri. Its origins prior to the 12th century are shrouded in mystery. It may have been used as an ancient cipher as early as the 1st century CE. Also note there was a red wax seal with a fleur-de-lis on the fragment.

Dr. Jackson worked for the Spartan Agency, an intelligence agency sometimes hired by the CIA to perform covert operations. A member of the Spartan Agency, Alex C. in Lisbon, was contacted for translation. Alex C. liked to work on decipherment and translation as it was an interesting challenge for him. He enlarged the fragments and sent three emails explaining what they revealed. (Letters written by Alex C. are dated Nov. 24, 2008, Dec. 20, 2008 and Feb. 12, 2009; all are shown in the online appendix.) There were strange names written in these fragments relating to a major historical event in the 1st century CE: Arimathea, Magdela, and Yohanan.

Alex C. analyzed the fragments and commented on the language, the shape of the fragments, the double encoding, and the fragments' appearance. The darker marks were from iron rust staining the paper indicating that it had been in an iron container for a long time. (The clay tube was in the ornament with the brass device. The ornament was iron, with plaster on the outside.)

In a letter written on Feb. 12, 2009, Alex C. made the following comments on the supposed heretical nature of the translation and that it would be academic suicide to acknowledge such a theory. I sent a letter to Alex C. via a friend in which I asked if I could communicate further with Alex as I had a lot of questions and my background in this area was limited. I received a negative reply from Alex C., which I've shown below:

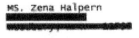

untitled   JULY 1, 2009

MS. Zena Halpern

Dear MS. Halpern

I am most gratified that my work on the documents presented
to me was of help to you.

My sole and primary interest was in the cryptography as this
is my hobby and your documents posed an interesting problem for me.

I have no further interest however in the results of this work and
must therefore decline u\your request for future contact. Anything
I have told you concerning my association with Mr. Spartan and
Mr. Jackson is the extent of our prior relationships. I have
no further infirmation to shed on your problem. I am sorry.

very truly yours,

Extract of One of the Letters from Alex C.

One letter from Alex C. translated a portion of one fragment to read: *"placed him on a stretcher, remove the head cloth and fold it alone."* Alex C. then referred to John 20:6-7, but did not elaborate. On July 28, 2013, an article on the internet by Professor James Tabor caught my eye, entitled, *The Earliest Account of the Discovery of Jesus' Empty Tomb: What it Says and What it Does not Say!* Essentially, Tabor analyzed the Biblical passage referred to by Alex C. and concluded that Joseph entered the burial tomb of Jesus and removed the body. This, of course, directly contradicts conventional Christian belief that Jesus was resurrected. This perhaps explains why Alex C. chose to distance himself from these writings.

Obviously this clay tube with the two fragments was meant to be kept in great secrecy. The fragments contain information that could be heretical and highly controversial, and the explosive nature of them precludes further discussion at this time. Possibly scholars with specialties in this subject will comment on the fragments after publication of this book.

Francis Bannerman hid these mysterious objects in a garden ornament. He even went so far as to devise a specially fitted key to prevent the ornament from being opened. His plans were to retrieve it at some future time. He never did, dying in 1918; his secret died with him until fifty years later when two of these garden ornaments were taken from Bannerman Island and placed in Dr. Jackson's garden on eastern Long Island. They remained in his garden for a year until his son broke off the key on one of them and Jackson found the brass device and a clay tube inside. An astonishing story thus unfolded.

Getting a Better Understanding of Dr. Jackson

As I began to examine the brass seal and the four inserts, I quickly came to realize that I had a massive mystery on my hands. Jackson left the sketch, but there were very limited explanations regarding the objects. In order to understand these items and unravel all of the mysteries here I had to start from square one. In 2011, I began to search more deeply into the life of Dr. Jackson, initially with the help of my friend Judi R. We scoured the internet for anything we could glean about William D. Jackson and tracked down people from his past who could provide us with some answers. Here is what we discovered:

Bill Jackson was born in Yonkers, New York, probably in 1933. I say probably because while we searched for records for his birth and high school, we found no mention anywhere of someone named Bill Jackson. The information we have gathered is mostly based on personal communications with his past co-workers at the Spartan Agency and old friends of his.

At age 18, after graduating from high school, he enlisted in the Korean War and served as a medic from 1951 to 1953. After the war ended in 1953, he went to medical school and was an intern in a Bronx hospital. He married a nurse and had two sons and one daughter.

In the early 1960's, during the post Cold War era, Dr. Jackson began working for the Spartan Agency as a contractor, working with the military and the CIA until the 1990s. During his years at the Spartan Agency, Dr. Jackson worked on Plum Island in Long Island Sound, where the army did biological chemical testing. His medical training was used there. What we know about the Spartan Agency is rather limited due to its secretive nature; however, we do know that they had at least twenty-four people working for them. During his obsessive search for answers regarding his historical findings, Jackson turned to these contacts for help in photography, chemical testing and cryptography. Jackson shared what he learned with his boss, the CEO of the Spartan Agency, Dan Spartan. Dan became interested in the mystery and began to help Jackson with his research.

A Disconcerting Message

Through the course of writing this book, unexpected letters, some covertly delivered to me through a complex layer of secrecy, have turned up from people who were connected with the Spartan Agency. Some have added to the understanding of the Jackson story and other mysterious connections have emerged. Every possible shred of evidence was pursued about Dr. Jackson's activities and his purchase of the Templar Document. While writing this book, certain documents and letters turned up sent to me by Dan Spartan and others connected with the Spartan Agency that were unexpected and extremely tantalizing. One of the most interesting things I learned was that Dr. Jackson was involved in the mysterious Oak Island treasure in Nova Scotia.

My research into Dr. Jackson's purchase of the Templar Document and his thirty years of involvement with it and his Oak Island ventures is based on a collection of over twenty-five letters, artifacts, and photographs.

While searching the internet for anything related to Dr. Jackson our searches apparently alerted someone to our investigation. I received an alarming letter sent to my home address. I have kept the original envelope with its postmark. It is dated April 26, 2011:

I do not think there is any way that the writer of this note can be identified. It has come to my attention that you have, with the assistance of others both in Minnesota and South Dakota, initiated a computer search for persons that could have detrimental results. Just how is what I shall try to explain to you now. Once, a long time ago, a man believed he was doing his religious and civic duty by providing information concerning members of a group to which he belonged that had caused the deaths of other individuals and engaged in illegal acts. Arrests were made and indictments obtained. The man came forward in good conscience and testified against those persons so putting his life at great risk. Much later it was learned that associates of those sentenced sought to kill both the man and his family so he decided with his wife that they would divorce. She took one son and went her way while he took the other. Bothe were independently entered into the Federal Witness Protection Program. The man was moved with his son to New York and they started a new branch of the family while the wife started anew outside the United States. That man's son became aware that persons that sought his father had become aware of him and his family through some of his work and they had long vindictive memories. It was decided to move both him and his family again in 1994 with another new identity, this time outside the confines of the U. S. While I can not provide a name here you knew that man's son and his initials were W. D. J. I hope you will see why you should desist in your line of research. These people do not want to be found and others will stop at nothing to find them. Further they will NEVER give up.

A Letter of Warning

The initials W.D.J. (second line from bottom) identify William David Jackson. Whoever wrote this letter knew that I was being helped by my friends in South Dakota and Minnesota and had given my name and address to certain Spartan operatives. The message explained a great deal and was also a warning; we immediately stopped searching the internet or public records for any information specifically related to Jackson. It may be that Dr. Jackson's father was involved in the struggle for Irish independence in the 1940's. I never found out who sent this message but the person who wrote this was very familiar with the details of Dr. Jackson's life.

My search was initially focused on the recovery of thirty years of Dr. Jackson's work, letters, documents, photos and any records he may have left with coworkers over the years. It then grew to become a search within a search. Jackson's connections were turning out to be intensely interesting and far reaching, including connections to secret, powerful groups bent on discovering the hiding place of lost documents and treasures in North America.

CHAPTER 2

Searching for a Needle in a Haystack

In order to establish provenance, it was vital to find evidence establishing that the brass seal at one point belonged to Francis Bannerman VI, who presumably hid it in the garden ornament sometime between 1906 and 1918, when Bannerman died. Dr. Jackson went to the Westchester Historical Society to find information about Bannerman in 1969 and found Bannerman records at the society. He found one very interesting entry that indicated a 'brass artifact' had been sold to Mr. Bannerman in 1906. I then began my investigation to verify what Jackson had seen in the Bannerman records. I contacted the Westchester Historical Society (now the Tarrytown Historical Society) and was told that all Bannerman records had been transferred to the Hagley Museum and Library in Wilmington, Delaware.

No stone could be left unturned to find whatever possible to support that the brass seal existed and that Francis Bannerman owned it.

The Search Within a Search: Forty Years Later
Hagley Museum & Library in Wilmington, DE

In August, 2010 I contacted the Hagley Museum and Library in Delaware. The librarian informed me that the Bannerman archives were available to researchers and made recommendations about how to locate the materials. I enlisted my friend Don Ruh to go to Delaware and he drove to the Hagley Museum and Library and met the librarian, who brought out the old boxes of Bannerman records.

The Hagley Museum & Library collection included a chrono-
logical file from 1870-1950's, an alphabetical file from 1898-1904,
Armory sales, Catalogs, arms, a list of dealers in antiquities and
curiosities, names of arms dealers Bannerman had dealt with, and
travel records from 1900 and the countries he visited. This was
a huge collection covering every aspect of Francis Bannerman's
business and interests. One ledger alone had 400 pages. After
looking through several boxes, Don found "Accession 2185,"
which documented Bannerman's purchase of military goods from
state and federal arsenals and also purchases of arms and military
antiques made on buying trips to Europe. Accession 2185 consisted of 118 volumes of older books and a massive amount of
material and files including Bannerman's famous catalogs dating
back to 1886.

Amazingly, after going through the boxes and ledgers containing endless receipts and bills, Don Ruh discovered the receipt
from 1906 between two pages of a journal. Here was a key piece
of evidence: A vital part of the puzzle now established that Francis Bannerman VI bought the brass device on April 22, 1906
from a "J. Roche." The receipt listed the Bannerman business
address, 105 Broadway New York, NY. The receipt described the
brass device as "three inches round by one inch thick," a match
to the one Jackson had found in the garden ornament. More specifically, it was described as having "a five pointed star with odd
characters on it." This was the pentagon and the *odd characters*
were the symbols on one side. The receipt even recorded information about the other side as, "the obverse had strange letters."
The *strange letters* were the Theban characters. This was a perfect description of the brass device! It even recounted that the
brass device came with "a parchment compiled by G. Benvenuto of Italy dated 1820 written in Latin describing how to make
the object and explaining the markings, their meanings and use
as a navigational tool." Francis Bannerman's initials are on the

receipt, with the price "$3.65" marked "Pd" (paid). The exact receipt is shown below:

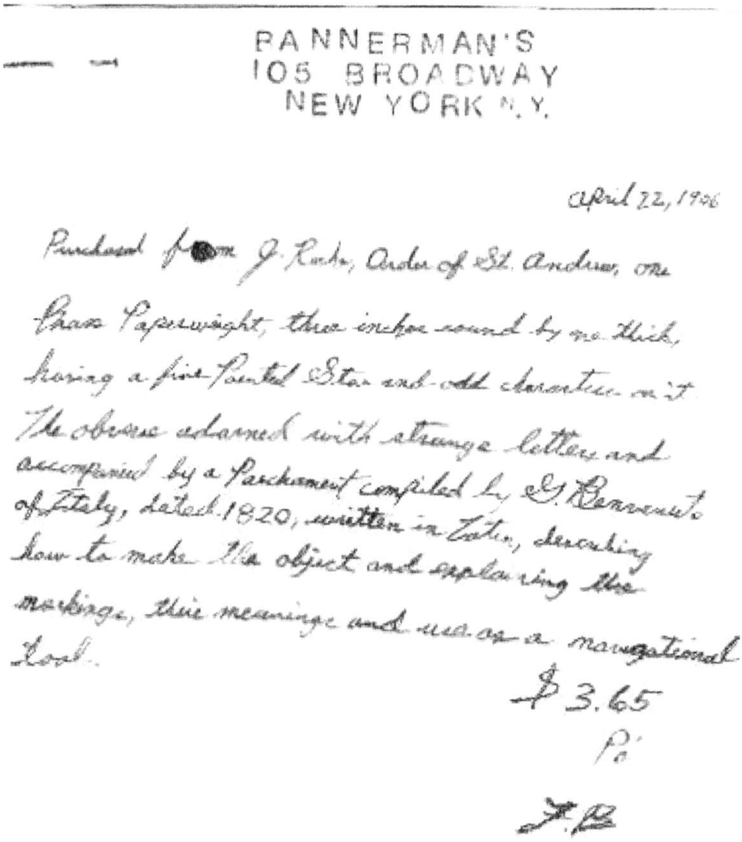

BANNERMAN'S
105 BROADWAY
NEW YORK N.Y.

Bannerman Receipt—Purchase of Brass Device
[Courtesy Hagley Museum and Library, Wilmington, Delaware]

There are many key facts worth summarizing from this receipt:

*J. Roche sold the brass paperweight (brass device) to Francis Bannerman on April 22, 1906.

*J. Roche belonged to the Order of St. Andrew.

*The brass "paperweight"/device featured odd characters, strange letters and a five pointed star.

*It was sold with a parchment written in Latin compiled by G. Benvenuto, an Italian, in 1820.

*The parchment explained how to make a brass device and what the markings meant.

*The brass device was a navigational tool.

A Parchment in Latin

There was another important clue on the receipt, a phrase stating that a "parchment compiled by G. Benvenuto of Italy, dated 1820, written in Latin, describing how to make the object..." Would the Latin parchment help solve the growing mystery? It became a major objective of our search at the Hagley Museum and Library to find the Latin parchment. Disappointingly, we were unable to find the Latin parchment in the Bannerman archives.

Startling Twists Were Turning Up

The receipt shockingly confirmed what the brass device was used for: navigation. This raised a multitude of questions: When was it used? Who used it? How was G. Benvenuto in 1820 involved? Who was J. Roche, the man who sold it to Francis Bannerman, and what was the "Order of St. Andrews?"

Who Were These Mystery Men?
G. Benvenuto of Italy and J. Roche?

I now had two mystery men: J. Roche and G. Benvenuto. First, J. Roche: From whom did he get the brass device? What was his relationship to Francis Bannerman? How did the Order of St, Andrew figure in this? Could anything about J. Roche be found? An internet search on the Order of St. Andrew revealed that St. Andrew was one of the twelve apostles and was revered in Scotland, which indicated the Order was some kind of religious group.

A host of unsolved questions revolved around J. Roche and how he obtained the brass device and the clay tube. Did he know the meaning of the fragments in the clay tube? Did Bannerman meet Roche during his trips to England and Europe? How did G. Benvenuto in 1820 learn the meaning of the markings on the navigation device?

These questions kept me up at night. As the investigation moved ahead pieces of this massive puzzle began to come in.

As I wrote this book, I would make new discoveries, forcing me to update previous chapters as more and more information was revealed within this mystery. One example: the man who sold the 12th century Templar document to Dr. Jackson in 1971 was Gustaveste Benvenuto. His ancestors turned out to be a genealogical treasure going back hundreds of years.

Benvenutos: A Family Mystery

A one-hundred-fifty-year link connected two Benvenutos. One in 1971 sold the Templar Document to Jackson. The other in 1820 wrote the parchment describing the mysterious brass device. This clearly was no mere coincidence. Later, more startling information turned up connections to other Benvenuto family members from 1778, 1715, and even the 14th century. How far back did the Benvenuto involvement go? Was it possible that they were connected to the 12th century Templar Document in the church in Cremona in the 15th century? Could the Templar Document have been acquired by a Benvenuto and became part of a collection of medieval documents passed down to members of their family?

Amazing Connection!
Benvenuto and Prince Henry Sinclair, 14th Century

Unexpected historical materials kept appearing in my research. An important document was found by sheer luck. I saw the name Benvenuto in the archives of the University of Michigan, tracked it down, and found a document entitled, *Dialogues to Prince Henry.* This document described a "Benvenuto of London" living in the 14th century and writing to Prince Henry Sinclair, aka the Earl of Orkney, the man who legend claimed sailed to America in 1398. Sinclair's grandson built Rosslyn Chapel in 1446 in Scotland, where carvings of American corn and aloe are found, paying homage to his grandfather's visit to America.

What was being unraveled here? What was the Italian connection to Scotland? These letters written to Prince Henry Sinclair are evidence linking Scotland, Italy and London in the 14th century. During this time Prince Henry Sinclair was not only the earl of the Orkney Islands but he was also deeply involved with Queen Margaret of Denmark (1353-1412). She is known for her success in forming the Kalmar Union as a buttress against the Hanseatic League. Furthermore, Sinclair was believed to have employed a Venetian admiral, Antonio Zeno, to lead his voyage to America.

Furthermore, during my research, two letters turned up from the Jackson collection that showed a Benvenuto family member had written in 1778 to certain parties, referencing the "year we remember paper" and discussing the brass navigational device. Two of the other parties to this correspondence—"M. Vauxhall, Esq." and A. Carlile—have been tracked to Philadelphia. Dr. Jackson's transcription of these letters is shown below:

10 March 1778

M. Vauxhall, Esq.

I have this day received a letter from the Italian, M. Benvenuto, explaining the third and forth pages of the year we remember paper. He describes a system of ancient navigation by means of an odd device. This device having a wire basket upon it receives the metal plate engraved with the simbols for A, B, E, T, and O besides various constellations. The plate is retained in the wire frame with four small brass nail like pieces of triangular shape much as a common nail. These are placed into similar cuts in both the plate and the base below the wire basket. The top of the device is aligned with simbols to the sthd. and port of each letter by which the navigator has in his head certain stars of each that will reveal through the center hole a star that will guide the course across the waters from the dark continent to our home shores. The base of this device rests in some recess upon the deck of the vessel all so secured to prevent movement from the sway of the vessel upon the sea. The triangle shaped cuts are so arranged as to be one compass point apart thus making 32 cuts about the circle and a point due north. No variation for the angle of the sun is so allowed thus making for significant error over the long voyage yet owing to the size of the land mass it could little be missed. Page three also shows the device with a smaller disk centered about a central pin with 40 lines radiating from the center culminating in small circles in which a pin is placed in accordance with the cycle of Venus.

Shall I replace this with the cryptic form to be included with the other pages you have sent me? I await your reply before continuing with my commission.

Your servant, CCCCP member

A. Carlile

The First Vauxhall Letter

MAGNA EST VERITAS

17 May 1778

M. Vauxhall, Esq.

In accordance with your commission I have discovered the ciphers solution as the Veritas Vos Liberabit phrase. I have duly translated the document as requested and have replaced the translation again in the cryptic form. I have further replaced the wording of all measurements with those of the common hand. The following consists of an explanation of the terms used in the document:

Term	feet	Inches
Finger		.79
Hand or Palm		3.17 to 4
Span		9.32
Cubit	1	7.05
Reed- 6 Cubits	9	6.31
Stadium	606	9.00
Mile	4857	
Sabbath Day Trip 2000Paces		
Standard Day Trip	about 22 miles	
Cab	1Qt plus .37 pints	
Noon Mark	sixth Hour from 11 to 12 noon	
Gerah	12.62 grains	
Firkin	8 Gallons 2 Quarts 1 Pint 1 Gill.	

The above I have replaced with the common use of measure such as hand, rod , link and chain.

For the trouble at hand I must ask for an addition of 7s. 6d.

Your servant, CCCCP member
A. Carlile

The Second Vauxhall Letter

The second letter appears to be a decipherment of the code in the Templar Document. The caption of the second letter, *Magna Est Veritas,* is Latin meaning, *Great is the Truth*. More work needs to be done on these letters, but they verify the ongoing connection of the Benvenuto family to this mystery.

Tracking Benvenutos

1971 – Gustaveste Benvenuto sold the Templar Document in 1971 to Dr. Jackson in Rome.

1820 – A "G. Benvenuto in 1820" is referenced in the receipt from the Hagley Museum and Library; he knew the meaning of the markings on the brass device.

1778 – The Italian Benvenuto wrote two letters to M Vauxhall, Esq. in Philadelphia about the brass navigation device.

1715 – Men with the names "Benvenuto" and "Roche" co-authored a pamphlet with Native American names translated into Italian, French, and Gaelic, which Jackson obtained in Paris from a rare book dealer. The pamphlet also had the name of the Church of San Sigismundo and the name of a document there.

15th century – Benvenuto was involved with the Templar Document in the Church of San Sigismundo; furthermore, as the ancestor of the Duchess of Milan, Maria Bianca Visconti, he likely would have had access to Templar documents.

14th century – A Benvenuto was an expatriate in London and wrote a series of letters to Prince Henry Sinclair.

Every Possible Clue is Followed

This was just the beginning of a very complex mystery that stretched back centuries and the Benvenutos were proving to be inextricably connected. Although what we found raised a lot of questions, we knew that the evidence from the Hagley Museum of the receipt was solid and would eventually lead us to the answers we sought.

What we know: Bannerman owned this brass device/navigation instrument and the clay tube sometime between 1906 and 1918 (1918 being the year he died). World War I began in 1914 and ended in 1918; this is relevant as Bannerman was involved in his armament business and the war effort until his sudden death in 1918.

Bannerman was a well-known man internationally and a collector who met many people in his travels; he had wide connections through his business. He had contacts here and in Europe and it is plausible that he was involved in more than we will ever know. There were travel records at the Hagley Museum showing that Bannerman traveled to Europe in 1900 and 1903 and that he was in England in 1911, 1912 and 1915-16. Who did Bannerman have contact with when he was in England?

I was finding myself being plunged deeper and deeper into this labyrinth.

CHAPTER 3

Century Old Journal Leads to Medieval Church

Word spread quickly through Westchester Historical Society as Dr. Jackson inquired about Bannerman Island and the mysterious brass device. It did not take long for Dr. Jackson to be contacted by someone who had important information. David Whittles, of a law firm located in Yonkers, New York, represented an anonymous client (a relative or close friend of the Bannerman family) who was offering to sell an old journal they thought Jackson would be interested in. On April 16, 1981, Jackson wrote to his friend Dan Spartan, excerpted here:

> *When I requested information on the Seal from the Westchester Historical Society someone there contacted another individual whose Attorney sent me an offer to purchase the Journal said to have been given to the unnamed individual by a member of the Bannerman family. Why? Obviously Bannerman was also a Macdonald and thus perhaps related to Liam MacDonald who most likely originally wrote the Journal. Who the unknown owner of the Journal was and why they parted with it is unknown. It was purchased through David Whittles Attorney at Law of Yonkers N.Y. for $400.00*

The "seal" Jackson referred to is the brass device found in the garden ornament. Jackson made an important point here: Bannerman VI was a MacDonald and may have been related to Liam MacDonald, "who most likely originally wrote the journal."

Skillful Sleuthing to Uncover the 'Anonymous' Owner

When Jackson wrote his letter in 1981, he did not know who the anonymous owner of the MacDonald Journal was and asked Dan Spartan to look into it. To find out who the anonymous person was, Dan Spartan visited the law office surreptitiously and obtained a file that led him to the owner. It turned out that the anonymous seller was Ms. Bertie MacDonald of Irvington, New York.

Dan Spartan met with Ms. Bertie MacDonald and learned some very interesting information. She recalled that she had seen the journal with a brass seal affixed to it with strange writing on it. She relayed that her husband and Francis Bannerman VI were close friends. She also mentioned a "Mr. Delores" who was supposedly involved with this affair, but all she knew for certain was that he died in New York City. I later learned more about "Mr. Delores."

The MacDonald Journal

The journal Jackson obtained from Ms. MacDonald is a first-hand account of two British prisoners' planned escape from jail, written in 1913. We are not told why they are in prison, but we learn that their names are Liam MacDonald and Hank Roche. Of note, this is the second "Roche" in this mystery, the first being J. Roche, who sold the brass device to Bannerman.

Cover of the MacDonald Journal, 1913

The men planned their escape for January 1, 1914. Liam Mac-Donald is the journal writer and he describes how they made the articles necessary for the escape and how they passed through the guard post in disguise with a forged pass. Guards found out about the escape and chased after them. MacDonald describes how they killed their pursuers and rowed in a snow storm to a harbor where a skiff was waiting.

The escapees had help from two outside men: Lewellyn Deloros and Etienne Lintot. Every detail of the escape had been planned out precisely. Liam MacDonald and Hank Roche travel to the English Channel and cross to France.

The journal then explains their mission: They were to go to the Church of San Sigismundo in Cremona, Italy and locate a document with a mysterious "key." This document was the primary motivation behind their escape, of such importance that they risked death if they were caught. We never learn who enlisted Deloros and Etienne to assist them in their escape. The only name mentioned is the "Order." Who the mysterious Order was that provided them with a ship, weapons and supplies is never revealed.

Uncovering Mysteries with Help of Dan Spartan

The journal gave Jackson the tantalizing lead to the church in Cremona, Italy which had the "key" that held the location of where, as we shall learn, secret knowledge was hidden in North America. There were many questions in attempting to uncover who these men were and their backgrounds. But one thing was sure-- Liam Mac-Donald, the writer of the journal, was related to the MacDonald/Bannerman family and that is how the journal became a family heirloom and was in the possession of a MacDonald descendant in 1969 when Jackson began his investigation at the historical society. The seller, Ms. Bertie MacDonald, never truly knew of the importance of this journal which had been handed down as simply a treasured family heirloom.

As more and more information came to light from the journal, Jackson knew he needed some help, so he turned to one of his most trusted friends: Dan Spartan. Dan learned of my interest in Jackson's research through a friend who also worked at the Spartan Agency, and it was from Dan himself that I received letters and documents over a time period of two years. He sent me Jackson's pictures, maps, original notations, research, and even the journal.

Dan Spartan did not provide a return address during our correspondence. All I knew was that he was living in Southeast Asia and used a mail service. I want to emphasize that although I never met Dan Spartan, he generously gave me as much as he had of Jackson's materials because this book is not only Jackson's story, but his also. On April 6, 2008, I received a four page letter from Dan Spartan. I have kept the postmarked package. Inside there was a packet and four maps. On July 14, 2009, I received the MacDonald Journal from Dan Spartan, but after a cursory reading I put it on a shelf.

Another letter from Dan Spartan arrived March 14, 2011. It showed a map of France with four signatures on the back. Sent with the map and the copy of the journal were two original handwritten pages from the journal, written on both sides. In the first letter, Dan Spartan explained:

> The map of France is the older of the pages sent to you. It has been made of paper of European origin possible French or Swiss and is about 50 to 100 years old. Due to the variety in the shape of the letters written upon it, it is considered to have been done with a steel rib fountain pen with a rubber bladder and written in a black India ink of a manufacture that dates to the turn of the century. The signatures on the back however are more uniform and may have been added at a later date with a ball pointed pen.

Dan Spartan also wrote that he had chemical testing done on the map. Dan Spartan's Agency had many contacts and was able to get expert help in identifying the paper, the ink and the pen. He wrote that neither the chemist nor the writing experts would reveal their identities *due to their employer.* The Spartan Agency did covert work for the government and the *employer* was most likely the CIA.

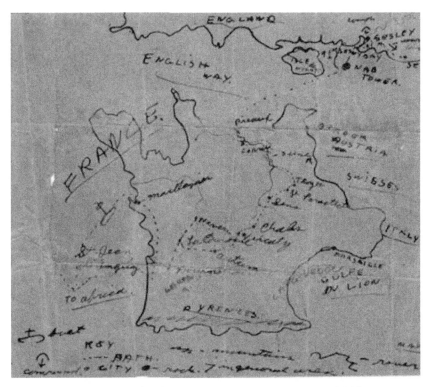

Map I Received from Dan Spartan April 6, 2008

The map shows the southern coast of England and specific places that show the MacDonald and Roche escape route from *Chichester* to *Nab Tower.* The prison they were in existed in Dorchester. They identified *Sessy*, and the *Isle of Wight.* Note the dotted line across the English Channel to *Preuex* in France. They were joined by the two outside men, Lewellyn Deloros and Etienne Lintot in France. Lewellyn Deloros met them in Vezaley. Deloros' name is in the code in the journal and he signed his name on the back of the map. Every name across France is identified in entries in the journal. Note the key at the bottom of the map.

The MacDonald Journal describes their route across France. It was arranged for them to stay at Benedictine monasteries in towns across France. It was January, 1914, just after World War I had broken out in September, after the archduke of Austria was assassinated. The escaped prisoners arrived on the west coast of France near Maillezais (near La Rochelle), where they boarded a ship for the island of Madeira, Hank Roche's home. There is evidence that they sailed to the west coast of Africa based on an invisible ink section in the journal that Jackson found with chemical tests. This entire mission was executed with precision planning. One entry in the journal (#8) explains their goal. Hank Roche tells Liam MacDonald that he had been commissioned by members of his Order to recover secret knowledge hidden in North America and the "key" to this recovery can be found in the Church of San Sigismundo, in Cremona, Italy.

There is a key at the bottom of the map, and dotted lines which likely plotted their travels. As I mentioned previously, the dotted line went from Nab Tower in England across the English Channel to Preaux, France. In the upper right corner the map identified places on the southern coast of England: Sesley, Nab Tower, and the Isle of Wight. These places can be found on modern maps. From Preaux, France the dotted line continues south to Troyes, Vexaly and then turns northwest to Maillezier. Then the dotted line travels into the Atlantic, passing by a drawing of what appears to be a ship and the name St. Jean de Imaguaz.

On the right, the map reads, "Gulfe du Lion, Marseille," and a faint word in the gulf, "Languedoc." Languedoc in southwest France is associated with a great deal of mystery and is where Renne le Chateau is located, home of a mysterious saga.

The phrase, "to Africa," on the map indicated their intention to sail to the west coast of Africa. Below I discuss why they may have been traveling to the west coast of Africa.

It appears that the map is written in at least two different styles of handwriting, and a third differentiation in the heaviness of the ink. The back of the map contains four signatures, at right, each with different handwriting:

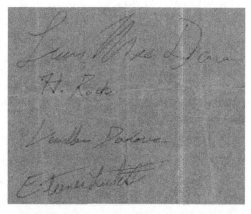

The Names on the Back of the Map

The burning question was, who were the four men in the Mac-Donald Journal? And how did Hank Roche know about a secret document in a medieval church? Lintot and Deloros seemingly must have been members of the same secret Order and also knew about the document in the church. Amazingly, I came to learn, this knowledge had been passed down for five hundred years from the time of a Milanese nobleman by the name of Francesco Sforza, who lived in the 15th century. Hank Roche, Lewellyn Deloros and Etienne Lintot all knew that the "key" was in a document in the Church of San Sigismundo. Their mission was to get to the church and retrieve the document. Who were these men?

Liam MacDonald

His signature is the first one, and the largest. His name had already turned up as related to the MacDonald/Bannerman clan--an American relative of Francis Bannerman, the writer of the journal. What was he doing in an English prison? It is possible he was imprisoned because of activities related to the Irish independence movement in the early 1900s. Many Irish Americans had traveled to the British Isle to fight during this time.

Hank Roche

Hank Roche was the chief architect of the escape and somehow he was related to J. Roche and the Order of St. Andrew. St. Andrew was a first century disciple of John the Baptist and was one of the apostles of Jesus. An apocryphal book, *The Acts of Andrew,* is considered an agnostic work. The flag of Scotland features the St. Andrew cross, an "X" in a square. In the Battle of Bannockburn, King Robert the Bruce carried the St. Andrew's cross. I sensed there was a special meaning to the choice of St. Andrew as a symbol for Scotland, beyond that he was one of the apostles. But what was it?

Hank Roche had connections to a secret "Order," for he states in the journal he was sent to retrieve "clay jars of knowledge" on orders from the "lodge," hidden in North America. The "lodge" that sent him on this mission may have originated in the 15th century. Much later, as a result of connecting a multitude of dots, I discovered that it was possible that this "Order" or "lodge" went back much further and could be part of the legend of the origin of the Merovingian kingdom in France. But I was getting into unknown territory which needed extensive research. Every piece of evidence or lead that I found had to be researched; clues became facts only with supporting historical data.

Lewellyn Deloros

Lewellyn Deloros was one of the outside men that helped with the escape, whose name turned up many years later, mentioned by Bertie MacDonald when Dan Spartan interviewed her. This man turned out to have a notorious history, working undercover for certain officials in the Vatican. These connections became apparent after some research into his involvement with a secret organization known as Propaganda 2 (P2). Information turned up about him which placed him in 1948 in India and connected him to a famous Italian scandal involving the Vatican's Banco Ambrosiano. Mr. Deloros bought antique swords, known as "swagger sticks," in India for high officials in the Catholic Church. On two of the swords, he inscribed directions to a cave on Hunter Mountain, in the Catskills. Here is where this story took another fantastic turn. The cave had a document pertaining to Nova Scotia's Oak Island, which I will examine in full later within the Oak Island section of this book (Part 4).

Etienne Lintot

When researching "Etienne Lintot," I found that there was a Lambert de Lintot who died in 1775. In 1743 he had been a grand master of the Masonic Lodge, St. George de' Observance. He was an artist and had done engravings relating to Masonic legends about the "Royal Arch of Enoch" and its nine crypts. My knowledge of Masonic history was nil at the time and so this meant nothing to me. But later, I noticed that photos which Jackson had taken of the Templar Document contained the name "Book of Enoch." How did this book from the bible connect with the Templars? It suggested that secret knowledge about lost documents were being passed down to key people. Was there a core group? There were more questions than answers at this point in time.

These four men were not fools and the Order backing them meant business. They were involved in a dangerous mission. They would not undertake this mission unless it was believed that the documents were preserved and retrievable. I also wondered whether there could be other valuable objects hidden in the cave or caves.

Exploring the Physical Characteristics of the Journal

Accompanying the map were two original pages of the journal, handwritten on both sides. In Dan Spartan's letter to me he went into considerable detail to explain these pages:

> *...it is further written with the letters while thin in some places and thicker in others reveals it had not been done with a modern pen and that the journal was written with a purpose to convey covertly to some party unknown that this was a copy of an original document with some parts added or subtracted with it's sole purpose being to convey secret information to a part or parties unknown. Also it should be of some note that maybe the total number of pages or entries had to be controlled to convey meaning-ful numbers.*

Dan Spartan had the paper tested and the paper used in the journal had a watermark from the turn of the 20th century. Dan Spartan's information turned out to be very important in explaining certain words used that revealed a code in the journal. Every 12th line contained certain words to construct the code. But there is more to this journal than just a code. When Jackson examined it, he suspected it contained invisible ink in sections. Not only was the journal made to convey secret information but it had a built-in code with the names of two places in America. Jackson copied the journal from the original pages sometime in 1970. The two original pages I have are very fragile, and I preserved them in non-acidic plastic covers.

There were 52 handwritten entries on seventeen original pages of the journal. Jackson copied each page of the original handwritten journal on a typewriter. Jackson searched the entries and pages and tested the pages under special lighting and used a hair dryer on sections of the journal. He applied Sodium Ferrocyanide, Ferric Ammonium Sulfate, Sodium Carbonate and used black light to reveal hidden secrets of the journal. He photographed and enlarged sections of the drawings. The results were startling. What emerged from the handwritten pages was a code that contained the name of a mountain in New York State. In addition, the invisible ink portions contained a strange passage about a country in West Africa where there were known deposits of gold and diamonds. Was this where Hank Roche and the others were heading when they wrote "to Africa" on the map? The MacDonald Journal presented a tangled web of intrigue and a trail of secret searches dating back to the 15th century. The journal was so gripping and tantalizing that it became a compulsion of mine to try to untangle the strands.

It wasn't just the story that the journal was telling of the prisoners' escape that intrigued Jackson. Even more so, he was fascinated by the covert aspects of the mystery: the embedded codes in the entries and the invisible ink. This is why he obsessively pursued research on the journal and doggedly hunted for answers around the world. He possessed the brass device, the clay tube, the original journal with the code, the names of the four men involved in the escape from the prison, specific references to places in England and France, and invisible ink messages referencing a country in West Africa.

More Shocking Information about this Journal

In this letter Dan Spartan refers to the invisible writing in the journal and explains that Dr. Jackson used his wife's hair dryer, chemicals and black light to bring out invisible ink in the journal. He also sheds light on his career in the intelligence field by using a fake home address.

March 14, 2011

Dear Mrs. Halpern

The last time I communicated with you I told you I would send your way anything else I had concerning material passed to me by my late friend Bill Jackson if I came across it. My wife has found among our old computer records the enclosed documents. I am not exactly sure how they figured into his research but I do know they come from Bill's work on the journal he acquired, through a Mrs. McDonald, though the sale was handled by a law firm and supposed to be anonymous. There was a lot of cryptic stuff connected with that Journal I recall and he did a lot of chemical tests on it as well as giving it to Dave Rian who did some cryptanalysis of its contents. There were a lot of places where concealed writing was revealed throughout the journal. Bill used his wife's hair drier on it much to her annoyance I remember and it brought out some writing. He also used Sodium Ferrocyanide, Na4Fe(CN)6.1OH2O, Ferric Ammonium Sulfate, AL2(NH4)2 (SO4)4. 24H2O, Sodium Carbonate, NA2 CO3.1OH2O and Black Light too. What was revealed by these tests I do not remember and all I have of the results is herein enclosed. Bill also took enlarged photographs of sections of the journal's drawings. Those that we have found depict a route through France and places where the escapees would seek refuge. Also whether these places were Monasteries or Bishoprics. There is also a diagram of the prison grounds and a sample usage of an improvised device to stamp the initials of a personage, Lawrence Vine, on some document used in the escape. Why he took these enlargements we don't know.

With regards to the one chemical result I do have Bill determined it was written with a strong tea solution as would have been available in a prison. In fact this type of ink was used in a prison escape from Champ Dollon Prison in Geneva Switzerland. It was made in the prison kitchen where the man worked and used to send secret messages to a confederate outside the prison. It is developed by placing a moistened blotter over the page, having been moistened with the Ferric Ammonium Sulfate solution. If you are interested in this subject I would suggest a book by Mr. Samuel Rubin, "The Secret Science of Covert Inks" Loompanics Unlimited 1987, as a good reference.

I hope these pictures are still of interest to you. If not just discard them. We have access to Adventures Unlimited, Barnes & Nobel and Amazon dot Com but have not seen anything yet in print by you.

My son has just shot with a blow gun his first monkey and we are having it with rice on the bar-b-que. Lialla likes it done this way. We are cooking on a floating deck as the river is up this time of year. Lialla goes to work by boat like Bill used to do. I take my son to school that way too, catch fish on the way home.

Due to the paranoia in America a return address on any first class mail is now required. As a result I would be very surprised to find that there is a 200 Aaquinah Drive in Pooler Georgia. I think it would be astrotronomically improbable if there were a person by the name of Murry living there. I am sure you understand. Best wishes.

Sincerely,

P. Spartan

Dan Spartan

Second Letter from Dan Spartan to Me, March 14, 2011

Decoding the MacDonald Journal

Forty years ago, Dr. Jackson did remarkable detective work. He figured out the key to the code in the journal and typed it out to show a cleverly concealed code in each page. When I received the journal from Dan Spartan I saw many spelling errors and corrected them. Little did I know that the code was in the spelling errors; I had to go back through the entire journal and reinsert the spelling errors exactly as meant to be on every twelfth line.

As I said, every twelfth line in the handwritten diary contained a misspelled word. The third letter of each misspelled word was the key letter. I have put the code word in bold to assist the reader as we examine the journal entries below.

Dan Spartan's Letter to Me Regarding the Coded Journal

Below is an excerpt from a letter written to me by Dan Spartan:

I have found the entire translation of the Journal I sent you and some pictures. This requires some translation in itself. Murial would have been proud of this work but Bill typed it all by himself. Why would she have been proud of it? Because of all the misspelled words of course. But Bill is not that bad a speller you see. It is because they are supposed to be misspelled as in the original work. If you can replace the right letter but write the wrong one you see that the writer of this journal was sending a cryptic message to someone. Denton hit on the key first when he thought it was in the title. It is. 12 letters to a line equals 12 lines down omitting the I sleep lines. Then 3 lines of the Title equals three letters in on the 12th line and a wrong letter usually though not always results. Ingenius. It reads as near as Dave Rian can figure out "New Amsterdam North America Hunter Mt." These guys were up on their spy stuff before we were born.

"Murial" is Jackson's wife, "Bill" is Jackson, "Denton" is Jackson's friend Denton Maier, and Dave Rian worked for the Spartan Agency. Dan Spartan's last remark is on the 'mark' in that the Spartan Agency was involved in covert activities, working on behalf of certain agencies of the U.S government.

Jackson wrote re the Journal:

This journal was originally written in black ink and then written again in blue ink adding the misspelled words to convey the secret message to someone unknown. There may be other cryptic messages hidden within the wording of this document that we have not uncovered.

CHAPTER 4

Prison Break: A Reading of the Journal

The Journal is written in a cryptic form to disguise its true purpose. Three lines begin the journal:

The Journal of
Sir Caradas du
Doloros Tower

The three lines are the key to deciphering the code in the journal. The name "Sir Caradas du Doloros Tower" is a clever combining of names to create the key to the code. The three short lines each have twelve letters. All of the letters form a 12 by 3 rectangle. It means that every third word on every twelfth line in the journal is a code word. The name "Doloros" is, not surprisingly, a reference to Lewellyn Deloros, referenced above.

The journal was handwritten so that every twelfth line would have the code word. This cannot be easily reproduced on a modern computer so I have instead placed each code word at the beginning of a line (flush left) and highlighted it in bold so that the reader can follow the code. Many code words are intentionally misspelled, presumably to highlight them further. In addition, certain choices of words do not fit with English usage of the early 1900's. These anomalies were caused by the needs of the cryptographer.

Four entries contain words in capital letters—#12, #39, #44 and #52. They are part of a code which leads to a numerical table. They will be highlighted in the journal.

The MacDonald Journal contains 54 entries. I have added my comments at the end of each entry.

THE MACDONALD JOURNAL
THE JOURNAL OF
SIR CARADAS du
DOLOROS TOWER
Dated October, 1913

Entry 1

I Sir Caradas du Dolorous Tower being taken prisoner by the enemy of Sir Lionel and friend of the Late Sir Sagimare le Desirious and put in prison in the dungon of King Agwisance of Ireland as a hold for the cousin of Sir Dinadain, Sir La Cote. I having no recollection of date, see a cell with four walls, a straw bed, one loose rock to see light, a small fireplace never of late lit and the sundry bones of the last resident of this place Sir John W. Merlin Paine de la Paix. I have on the person of me this paper, pen and a flask of wine, also coin, my shirt, pants, shoes and a small dirk hidden in the fold of my leg and attached with a string to my penal organ.

In nhe *room was a tin plate, plaster boal and the human bones of the fingers and chest. Also a piece of metal I used later. Mixing charcoal from the walls of the fireplace which gathered for centuries and some wine I write this journal of my stay so the next follower will know me. Using metal and strength I brake the chain that binds me. The guard brings food which is a pottery bowl of slop and four pieces of bread of morsel size. I eat slop and save the bread. I also hide under the straw the other bowl for he takes the one I have and also hide metal. Guard check is one hour after the food is served and 15 times til morning at seven bells.*

Comments on Entry 1

"*In nhe*" is the code word. The key is "**n**," the third letter.

The section beginning with "I Sir Carradas du Delorous Tower" recites names taken from Arthurian legends. These names appear in the book, "Le Morte de Arthur," by Sir Arthur Mallory, written in the 1450s. The book is a compilation of tales about the legendary

King Arthur and the Knights of the Round Table. "Sir Caradas" is Edmund Carradas, a commander in one of the battles in Hadrian's War, in the 2nd century CE. "Delorous Tower" is a reference to Lewellyn Doloros, one of the men in the journal. "Sir Lionel" is one of the Knights of the Round Table, referenced in "Le Morte de Arthur." "Sir Sagimore le Desirious" and "King Agwisance" are figures in the Arthurian legends. "Sir Dinadain" was a Knight of the Round Table. Regarding "Sir John W Merlin Paine de la Paix," Paine is an English name from Kent and Sussex. "De la Paix" is from a French medieval poem. It may be a secret reference to Thomas Paine's writings.

The names make up the twelve lines to give the first letter of the code.

The letter "n" is the third letter and begins the secret message.

Entry 2

I mark days on the wall with a metal bar. One meal a day and peace to work I remove the loose stone today and see the

fae reaching ocean. I chip out a place in the crumbling stone for pen, ink, journal, shirt, soles and buckles of shoes, pants, 2 buttons, 3 coins, flint tin cup small using my tool. In replacement tool breaks leaving appointed end and a dull end. In the straw I find a hollow reed with which I make a rope 14 inches long, I eat slop and save bread. I am tired.

Comments on Entry 2

"*fae*" is the code word. The key is the third letter, "e."

The "far reaching ocean" is the English Channel. The prison was located in the Chichester/Dorchester area near the English Channel coast.

Count from one 12th line to the next.

We now have **N E** making up the beginning of a code word.

Entry 3

Today I make 3 days. I hollow out bed leg for my tools then make a needle from bone of man. Guard then removes all but one bone and I hide it in the cache. I put point on needle rubbing it on the wall. Put in cache. Eat. Save bread and I sleep heavy.

Comments on Entry 3

There is no code in entry 3.

Entry 4

I awake this morning to find new rushes on the floor. Paper is hard to write on. Cold. Find that rushes soaked in

wiwe *make good rope. Have found new and better paper, wood for a calendar. I compile a time schedule when I am free. They are ten in the morning, in Lav enroute to compound and Thursdays on the rock pile to strengthen the outer wall of the fortress from a bombing.*

Comments on Entry 4

"wiwe" is the code word. The key is the third letter, "**w**."

This was prior to the beginning of WWI and the Germans were first using zeppelins to bomb the English coast.

Entries #1, 2 & 4 spell out the word **N E W**.

Entry 5

Postpone fire for lack of tinder. Times changed. Meet French Man that speaks English in cell 4420. I am in 4488. He thinks that is under me. Start to dig.

400	1	2	3	4	5	6	7	8	24	50	25
100	19	20	21	50	54	55	54	55	52	42	9
90	89	88	87	86	85	84	83	44	81	74	12

*I **start** tonight. He has some tools and contact 3 times a year with outside. He can get wine money steel but no messages so far. I must get guard to let letters H. R. through. He might accept a 16f bribe. No bread tonight. Visited barber. Found 31 October 2 weeks away now.*

Comments on Entry 5

"**start**" is the code word. The key is the third letter, "**a**."

In addition to the code word, the three rows of the numerical table contain a code. I recalled a letter Jackson had written that mentioned the fifth entry in the journal, which explained the numerical table. He thanked Dave Rian for bringing this to his attention. Dave Rian was an associate of Dr. Jackson and a cryptographer. I have underlined the numbers referenced by Jackson below. Jackson's Notes regarding Entry 5 (these notes discuss several items which I have not yet discussed, but which will become known to the reader later):

> *There is one final note to which I have to thank Dave Rian for bringing to my notice. That is that there is at the fifth entry a notation that one cell is under the other, 4420 is under 4488. A numerical table follows to show this. However the numbers in the table do not follow any prescribed sequence. Next it should be noted that there are certain words that are printed in capitals in my typing as they are in the journal. Dave points out that PAIN the "t" was missing and I added it in: but let us omit that now. Thus PAIN=4. MAA BALCARDS plus the word LONG = 15. And the word ORDER = 5 letters totaling 24 letters.*
>
> *If we look at the number 24 in the table we find that below it 55 and 44 below that. It was at 55 degrees W Longitude by 44 degrees N Latitude that the ships keel was located with the Tanit and the Octopus carving on the stone. Further the words WARNING LINES 1000 TIMES =21 plus the word NOIR =4 giving a total of 25. Looking under #25 in the table we see 42 with a 9 next to it. Is it by*

> *coincidence that at 42.9 degrees N. Latitude by 74.12 deg.*
> *W._Longitude [author note: see the numbers 74 and 12*
> *below the 42 and 9] there is a stone on Hunter Moun-*
> *tain in New York state that has carved on it a triangle*
> *often associated with the Mother Goddess and sometimes*
> *referred to as a Tanit symbol. The last entry in the journal*
> *mentions 'THE GODDESS.'"*

In entry #5, Liam MacDonald meets the Frenchman Hank Roche in cell **4420**. MacDonald is in cell **4488**. MacDonald says Roche can make contact three times a year with the outside but has been unable to send messages. MacDonald needs to get the guard to send letters to H.R. (Hank Roche), perhaps by bribing the guard.

We now have **N E W** and **A.**

Entry 6

I awake at 5 or so and start digging as instructed. Hear noise from floor. My friend later says that he started it with men making noise on bars with tin cups. I asked how they knew

to mo *it and he tells me they have a code system on that floor and that is how he contacts his friend Etienne on the outside. Digging possibly complete tomorrow. I am P and must contact C according to the code system of alphabetical letters. Guard took bribe and will pay half tonight. I got cigarette from him which will make good tinder when I get it started. I go to work now lots of repair work. Our guys are doing a great job on the walls. I wonder if they know this is a prison. I steal a small metal disk to fool the guard with a future bribe. Try………………chisel………… tools at…………tonight.*

Comments on Entry 6

"to mo" is the code word. The key is the third letter, "**m.**"

"Etienne" is *Etienne Lintot,* one of the men whose signatures is on the back of the map. He is the outside man who will assist them in

their route across France. They have a code system on the floor and that is how the prisoners contact Etienne on the outside.

We now have **N E W A M**.

Entry 7

I awake early and start to dig further. The stone is under my bed and I must be careful not to make noise. The taps say

I as *digging in the right place. Tomorrow I will try to move the stone. I have not seen him all day and not tomorrow for I am to go to cambers so my cell can be inspected. I am not afraid for not even Lord Dudley could trace my work the last time I broke from his bitch of a place called Hell Stone and well named. I in the compound area have found a piece of sheet steel and it is very flexible and bendable also a piece of leather from a belt. It is the 11th day of the 10th month being here since the 4th and should leave if all goes well by the 4th of January. There is some sap leaking into my cell from above and it smells and burns. This may be light. I'll ask my friend A. about it tomorrow. I got bread today and some*

water *for the first time. Bread I keep and now I sleep.*

Comments on Entry 7

"I as" is the code word. The key is the third letter, "**s**."

"water" is another code word. The key is the third letter, "**t**."

We do not know who Lord Dudley is.

We now have **N E W A M S T**.

Entry 8

I awake early and must postpone the stone moving until tonight as the guards made a check of the cell but found nothing as I predicted. Tonight I move the stone the tobacco with flint and steel and light the liquid which burns also. It is some liquid of oil and see what I have come upon. Tomorrow an inspector comes and are fed meat a rare treat and hope it has a bone to replace my broken needles. No bread. Now I sleep and work. I meet Hank Roche through the stone in the floor being here 3 and one half years. We get acquainted and I tell of my plan to escape and he tells me a strange story of secret knowledge hidden by members of his Lodge in the dim past that he was commissioned to recover for them before he was captured and put here. Then we go to his cell

where *he has a cache in the side of the wall. He has a knife, large bottle of cheap wine, money, razor, punch tool some wire and a candle. Also a brass bolt, chisel. Tin cup, and a cloth like me. He says that by widening the wall we would have a 5 foot cache between stones. No bones in the meat but Hank has a steel needle. I find a bunch of metal washers and steal a light from the guard while showing them to him.*

Comments on Entry 8

"**where**" is the code word. The key is the third letter, "**e**."

This passage is one of the most critical to understanding the significance of what Hank Roche told Liam MacDonald, who describes it as a "strange story" of secret knowledge hidden by members of Roche's lodge in the dim past. Jackson must have been convinced that he was on the brink of uncovering a complex and fascinating mystery. What was the secret knowledge? How far back did this mysterious Lodge go? How were the secrets passed down over centuries? How did Hank Roche play into this story? Much of the historical background pertaining to the identity of these men has been lost or hidden. Why they were in prison is unknown.

We can glean some sparse background from the journal as Mac-Donald reports the building of fortifications along the coast. The diary was written in 1913, a year before World War 1 began. By 1914, Germany was bombing English installations along the coast and prisoners were working on fortifications of buildings, such as the prison, near the English Channel. Hank Roche was captured in

1909, as evidenced by the statement that he has been in prison for 3½ years. What was Hank Roche involved in and did this result in his imprisonment? The statement that he was *"commissioned to recover secret knowledge for members of his lodge"* opens up a connection to a secret group. But which group?

We now have **N E W A M S T E.**

Entry 9

I awake early and start plan for big cache. If we remove section we may succeed.

[There is a blank space here in the Journal which holds a concealed message.]

I sreal a small bag from work house toilet for small equipment. Needs some sewing on it. We make plans for escape in January, late December or in March. No meeting tonight for inspections are changed. Have some tools lined up for tomorrow. No bread just slop and water. Now I sleep and tomorrow we try for oil for the guard took back the light and a bribe to shut up.

That was a close one.

Comments on Entry 9

"*I sreal*" is the code word. The key is the third letter, "**r.**"

A word is building up: **N E W A M S T E R.**

Entry 10

I awake late. Whipped. Brought to group late. Found out that confinery is always full on Thursday and Friday men are put in compound until Sunday. Compound is at front gate where it can't be reached from the side gate. I take Bakers hat that delivers bread to officers. Many coins in hands so plan to

stdrt work on Monday.

Comments on Entry 10

"stdrt" is the code word. The key is the third letter, "**d.**"

Word is now: **N E W A M S T E R D.**

Entry 11

I awake for a normal day. Guard last night was paid half his bribe. For 2 day extension and two cigarettes I will pay 1 ½ pence more the ½ pence to before a 1 pense coin that a writ will be the change worth ½ pense thus we get a piece of paper that is the same as that of a pass for plan which was the object of the exercise anyway. Also Hank showed me brass metal made on his floor stone from metal works where he is put to work. We need a substantial soap so guards won't see ink on our fingers. We gather mud tomorrow. Now I sleep

Comments on Entry 11

No code word in this entry. Plans are developed to obtain paper to create the pass. They bribe the guard to get the paper. Ink on their fingers must be washed off. The purpose of the brass metal Hank made is unknown.

Entry 12

I awake and day is normal. Cache is coming along nicely. The ½ pense I have and the back can be used for the Pass.

Moaday may get a bit of green PAIN(t).

Hank tells me the secret knowledge is cached in 12 scrolls in clay jars hidden in a cave in North America for over a thousand years and the key to its location is in a document kept in the Church of San Sigismundo Cremona built by Francesco Sforza, duke of Milan in the fifteenth century.

Comments on Entry 12

"Moaday" is a code word. The key is the third letter, "**a.**"

"PAIN" is also a code word, in capitals. It equals the number four. Refer to entry #5 for explanation.

This entry is a bombshell. Hank tells Liam MacDonald that secret knowledge is hidden in a cave in North America. This entry in the journal focused me on the Church of San Sigismundo and the city of Cremona, Italy. The church held the "key" to a secret document kept in the church. The entry refers to a cache of ancient scrolls, hidden for over a thousand years in a cave in North America. It also offered another clue—the name of a 15th century historical figure, Francesco Sforza, the Duke of Milan.

I had never heard of this church or of Francesco Sforza, and Dr. Jackson had apparently not researched these matters. Research into the Sforza name led me to an avalanche of history connected to the Templars in northwest Italy. Sforza's marriage turned out to be a key factor in this developing mystery and revealed far reaching connections across centuries. I devote a full section to Sforza later in this book; I briefly discuss him below.

Francesco Sforza was the Duke of Milan in 15th century Italy. His closest associate was Cosimo de Medici; he also associated with Rene de' Anjou popes and European royalty. Francesco Sforza's son, Ludovico Sforza, was the patron of Leonardo da Vinci. The descendants of the Sforza family were connected by marriage to two Queens of France: Catherine de Medici (1519-1589) and Marie d' Medici (1573-1642). [Genealogical charts are set forth in the appendix.]

The Church of San Sigismundo in Cremona, Italy is one of the finest examples of Renaissance architecture. It was ordered re-built over the older church by Francisco Sforza in celebration of his marriage in 1441 to Maria Bianca Visconti, who was of the ancient noble Visconti dynasty. Their marriage produced eight children, who in turn spawned the famous Sforza/Visconti/ Medici lines. These families were ruling dynasties in Milan, Cremona and Florence and were interconnected by marriage with other royal families in England, France and Spain.

My research has led me to conclude that Francesco Sforza, his wife Maria Bianca Visconti, and his close associates Cosimo de Medici and Rene de' Anjou, all knew of the secret Templar Document which recounted the voyage to America in the late 12th century.

The code word is now almost complete: **N E W A M S T E R D A**.

Entry 13

Hard work at the stones today. I get pick and watch the sparks fly. Am relieved early. Meeting tonight. There is talk of a transfer and tem. Cell change but with Pass I hope to overcome difficulties and be back soon.

Comments on Entry 13

No code word.

The prison they were in sent prisoners to work on repairing a railroad with stones from a quarry. The reference to a 'pass" is the means to get past the guard with a counterfeit pass.

Entry 14

I awake. Nothing happens of much interest.

*We **trmnsfer** all the wine to 1 bottle and save other for water to wash with.*

Comments on Entry 14

"trmnsfer" is the code word. The key is the third letter, "**m**."

Entries 1, 2, 4 , 5, 6, 7, 8, 9, 10, 12 & 14 spell out:

NEW AMSTERDAM

We have another mystery. Why would the MacDonald Journal have an interest in New Amsterdam? Jackson found another clue: a letter written in French dated 1657 which contained the phrase ***"la montagne Nord de Nouveau Amsterdam"*** (*"the mountain north of New Amsterdam"*). This letter is shown at the end of this chapter.

Entry 15

I awake to a normal dreary day of work. My Transfer is certain. I will be gone 5 days at the most. They will give me a knapsack with a blanket and two sheets of straw mats. Pants and gloves workmans jacket and muffs. I am grateful for a Bible, diary stays in cache. I will have soap and maybe can get some. We leave on the 23 and should be back on the 27th. I'll sneak our knife and a light for some private night work. I saw doctor for lst (t)ime Got gop for a Blister from the shoes. 3 cups of water and now I sleep and dream of Hank's friend Lintot here, he said, "I have his Pass for you to copy."

Comments on Entry 15

There is no code word. Lintot is one of the signatures on the back of the map. Was he a prison guard or was he an outside accomplice? It appears that he got the pass for their escape. A web of intrigue existed in which information was being transmitted from key people on the outside to Hank Roche. As I got into this deeper I became aware of powerful forces moving through the centuries—from the 12th to the 15th to the 17th. But who were these groups?

Entry 16

I awake and am rushed to a car (t) where a priest puts us

***in n** formation. The horses leave and I am off. A(ll) Saints Day my stay was extended until. They really tore up the Railroad. I work on one book Hank's plan of escape route with much success. Return to Defeat. My cache is found and much is missing my knife is broken. But there is victory in defeat as I have gained much in my travels. I have some sour salt, soap, a crysine stone, a compass in bad condition but it works, a metal club ball from shell gun empty, a large candle and sulfur, a great prize. I met Hank and he has made contact. Sent message "H.R. From Dorchester on the 4th January." He also got 49 nails, matches, chocolate and wood blocks. I* *aloo* have a clock, some metal strands, fresh paper, a magnet and half a cup bottom train ran over it. They found hat, water, cup, shirt, code book rope. Money and a bag of gold foiling. They missed the Pass, diary, calendar for which victory is due. Now e make rock cache in wall common and start over to meet our deadline and pray for bad weather to operate.

Comments on Entry 16

"in n" is a code word. The key is the third letter, "**n**."

"aloo" is also a code word. The key is the third letter, "**o**."

We have **NEW AMSTERDAM** and now add: **N O**.

Dorchester is the clue: *Sent message "H. R. From Dorchester on the 4th January."* Hank made contact with someone from the prison in Dorchester, which is five miles from the sea near Weymouth. Weymouth is in Dorset County on the mouth of the River Wey on the English Channel coast. Hank Roche had reached a contact on the outside and sent a message saying that they planned to escape from Dorchester on January 4. The message must have been received by someone who passed it on to Llewellyn Deloros. I was able to establish that there was a prison in Dorchester in the early 1900's and that it was near the English Channel. It confirms the route Roche and MacDonald took on their escape.

Entry 17

I awake and start to get things in order. Hank has not added to the cache yet. I do very little for I am very tired. We discuss o(u)r tr(i)p to Sesey compound and leave on the Feast of St. Barromean.

Comments on Entry 17

There is no code word. Selsey (correct spelling) is a town on the English Channel coast south of Chichester where there was an installation or "compound." It is 9 ½ miles from Nab Tower (a town on the coast). These locations conform to what I found in my research, which revealed that there was a prison near Selsey, built in 1877.

Entry 18

I awake and make some poetry to give us an idea of weather conditions during the month with the record.

Jaruary	*brings snow*
February	*brings rain*
March	*brings breezes*
April	*brings sneezes and sweet primrose*
Moi	*brings blocks of lambs on the Golden Hillsides in full bloom*
June	*brings tulips, lillies and*
July	*brings cooling showers for the lovely flowers*
August	*brings sheves of Cam*
September	*brings warm fruit and good hunting*
October	*brings the beauty of the Pheasant Dull*
November	*brings the blast and our joy, cold*
December	*brings the sleet et le jour de libre departe.*

Comments on Entry 18

"*Jaruary*" is a code word. The key is the third letter, "**r.**"

We now have ***NEW AMSTERDAM N O R.***

Entry 19

*I **atake** this morning and start to work but Hank says " he who works like a fool toils long" We work at night by candle light using the second match but keeping the charcoal for ink. We make a map of France and our route when we are free marking our compound and camp. When we leave we go to Preaux after leaving Chichester and its bay 9½ miles from Chichester Bay's Point is Nab (T)ower where we will get a regular boat awaiting we hope and new clothes. Then we will go to from Preaux, Cornex. Toyes, then down the SIENE (x) to Toyes then on to La Paractets Sens Chales, Vesely, where we meet Delores, St. Jean D"Anely, Mail (L) ezear in that order and then take another boat to Ceuta*

Afhica_by way of Spain then to Rabat and Hank's home on the south shore of Madeira Island and then to Cremona next year and plan for the trip to the Americas. We should be in Nab Tower by the Feast of St. Titus. The key to the map is as follows:

[Map key omitted. See "Key" at bottom of map image, below.]

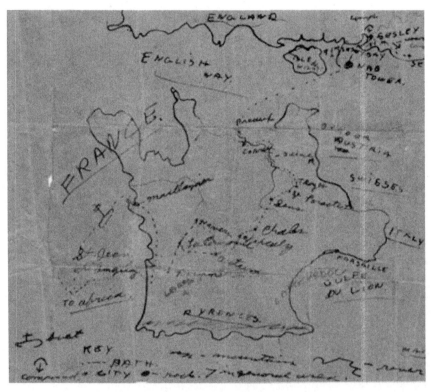

Escape Map Referenced in Entry 19

Comments on Entry 19

"I atake" is code word. The key is the third letter, "**t**.

"Afhica" is also a code word. The key is the third letter, "**h**."

To determine the validity of the reference to Chichester, I contacted the Chichester District Council and learned that in the 18th century Chichester had a prison. In the mid nineteenth century a police station and gaol was established in the same building and later relocated to Southgate. The entry about Chichester shows that it is located north of Selsey on the coast of the English Channel. Roche and MacDonald are correct when they write that Nab Tower is about 9 ½ miles from Chichester. There was a railway in West Sussex which ran from Chichester to Selsey, which existed before the First World War. This confirms the entry where the men were sent out on gangs to repair a railroad track. There was a track running from Chichester to Selsey that was damaged by a flood in 1911 which would have needed repair.

Their plan is to escape from the prison in Chichester, or Dorchester, and make their way to its bay, rowing nine and a half miles to Nab Tower. There they would meet Llewellyn Deloros, who was waiting for them, and together they would cross the English Channel to Preaux, France.

Map of Southern Coast of England

The black arrow points to Chichester/Dorchester and Selsey. The red arrow depicts their passage across the English Channel to Preux, France.

We now have **NEW AMSTERDAM NORTH**

Entry 20

I awake and do not go to compound for the roads are bad. The road team goes out and lays blocks over the muddy roads to move the caissons over.

I make a big discovery bending a piece of highly glazed paper see its inner side good for our boat Pass when Block stamp is made. Sir Vine calls a surprise inspection but finds nothing. I see Hank who found a piece of flint today.

Comments on Entry 20

"I make" is the code word. The key is the third letter, "**a**."

The reference to "Sir Vine" refers to Sir Lawrence Vine, apparently the prison warden.

We have **NEW AMSTERDAM NORTH A.**

Entry 21

We start to mark out our directions for boat on sea with our compass. I find small metal locket. Get apple.

Miles	(o)	Dir	Point to Point
9.5	240	SE	Cody to N. T.
100	0	SE	N.T. to P.
27.2	0	NE	P. & C.
189.4	0	SE	C. & T.
6.8	260	W	T. & L. P.
27	10	W	LP & S.
47.3	350	SE	S & CH
3.4	100	SE	CH & V.

27	84	SE	*Vexaly & Autum*
70	40	NW	*A & Nevers*
68	100	W	*N. & LC.*
180.2	60	SW	*LC & B.*
29.4	40	NE	*B. & St. Jean*
94.3	20	NW	*St. Jean & Mai*
350	140	SW	*M. & Ortigulas*

189.5 miles from La Chapelle Banks at 2012 depth in leagues approximate.

Comments on Entry 21

Every one of the places listed on the journal has been verified with the National Geographic Atlas of the World. The prisoners begin at *Cody* and go to *Nab Tower* in England, from where they cross the English Channel to France. At *Preaux,* they continue across France, listing miles, degrees and directions. *Cornex* to *Le paractets, Troyes, Chales, Vexely, Nevers, La Couronne, Autun, St. Jean d" angely, Maillezais,* and to Spain at *Mondeneda.* Each place is marked with a symbol. "Mai' stand for *Maillezais,* a town near the west coast of France inland in the area of La Rochelle. From *Maillezais* they sail to *Ortigulas,* on the north coast of Spain. *Ortigulas* does not appear in the journal but Jackson brought it out with chemical applications to a blank space in the journal between entries. The accuracy of their journey and the names they record show a precise knowledge of places where they will stay—all Benedictine abbeys. These stop-overs have been carefully planned out and clearly have been pre-arranged. They identify with symbols which are monasteries and which are Bishopries.

Entry 22

I awake and Hank surprises me with his mathematical knowledge for he said he has figured out the tides on data commonly known when he was out of jail and upon the fog horn blasts each morning that the tide is low on blast per foot.

TIME Table

Time	Feet Up	DAY
H. M.	Ft. I	
00:25	0.9	Childmas
01:.27	4.2	Feast of Circumiscium
03:30	4.5	Feast of St. Titus
06:05	4.7	Feast of Armada

The Feast of St. Titus would be the best as far as I happened to have set its day for our escape because of the high tide favorable to removing a boat. March 6 or Feast of Armada is better but by then we would be moved to steady work at Sesey. We make a table as best we can telling each place and its importance to us as seclusion. We have

deeided *to go to Mondonedo instead of Ceuta of straight. We got an old stick and nail and will put them together later. I started work on my pants with apple acid and water part.*

NAMES
Sesey
Preaux
Cornex
LeParactets
Toyes
Chales
Vexely
Nevers
La Couronne
Autum St. Jean d"Angely
Maillezais
Mondeneda SP

Comments on Entry 22

"TIME" is a code word. The key is the third letter, "**m**." Capital letters = 4; see entry #5.

"deeided" is another code word. The key is the third letter, "**e**."

Of note, both *Mondonedo* and *Ceuta* are on the coast of North Africa. *Ceuta* was an important city known for smuggling. Gold and other resources were brought to Ceuta from the interior of Africa for centuries. From Ceuta, ships would transport the goods to various ports on the Mediterranean. These two cities belonged to Spain.

We now have **NEW AMSTERDAM NORTH A M E**.

Entry 23

I arake and find that men have taken some things from below the straw while I slept. They took the locket, magnet and club shot but didn't find the loose block for which I am thankful. When I started to cuss them ending with you fucking son of a bitch Hank Proverbed me La Memaria del mal es por vida ladel bien presta se alvida. I stopped tonight. I widened the 5th block in the wall and the rope ladder is coming nicely. Two more will be enough. Also I must sew bag for things when we leave. Paper is bad here and printing is worse. Printing for Pass is not going well but with Vines initials we may get gain through.

Comments on Entry 23

"I arake" is a code word. The key is the third letter, "**r**."

We have *NEW AMSTERDAM NORTH AMER.*

Roughly translated, the Spanish proverb Hank speaks means, "The memory of bad stuff lasts a lifetime while the good is often forgotten."

Entry 24

I awake to an interesting day. We started real work today

Maiing a new tool, a flint head knife. First I drive a nail into a stick of wood I got with Hanks' Brass Bolt and the wall then I rub the other end level, split it with the chisel and gouge out a slot. I then took the nail in wood called a chipper and with a chisel formed an arrow head from the piece of flint with a jaw on one side and a thick point. I then placed it into the slot and bound it tight with pieces of rope formed together using fishermans knots and ending with a tight slip knot. I finished the Pants today. They are nice and white.

Comments on Entry 24

"Maiing" is a code word. The key is the third letter, "**i**."

We have **NEW AMSTERDAM NORTH AMERI.**

Entry 25

I awake to work in the rain and today Hank joins the cache with his tools" Brass Bolt, money, 12f, wick, needle, pills, wire, shirt, candel, box of metal pieces, thread and his knife.

We cork tonight on some important equipment.

Comments on Entry 25

"We cork" is a code word. The key is the third letter, "c."

We have *NEW AMSTERDAM NORTH AMERIC.*

Entry 26

I awake and work is heavy but there is a mix up in the gangs and I get off 2 ½ hours early. At night we continued to work and finish the letters of the Wardens initials for the Pass. We cut them from leather and fixed them to the wood black.

Comments on Entry 26

There is no code word. There is a space after Entry 26 which Jackson tested with chemicals.

Entry 27

I awake and Hank adds his hat emblem to cache and the badge we have made. I think it will pass muster. Hank say Pierce was a brilliant scholar and may have had a cache in my cell. I look tonight and see what results, maybe in the dismay. Hank says that H20 X C2H502=Ink-C2H703. I sleep on it.

Comments on Entry 27

The jumble of letters/numbers surrounding the word "Ink" in the final line remains a mystery.

Entry 28

I visit barber and he agrees that Pierce was a brilliant

scaolar *that may have invented some kind of gun cotton. I have found nothing of his in the cell but have used two matches searching and smoke a cigarette.*

Comments on Entry 28

"s**caolar**" is the code word. The key is the third letter, "**a**."

We now have **NEW AMSTERDAM NORTH AMERICA.**

Note: It should now be obvious that the code is spelling out the settlement of Manhattan Island ruled by the Dutch in the years 1623-1676. Why is New Amsterdam in a code? What was going on in New Amsterdam that would make it important to this mystery?

Entry 29

The weather becomes colder and I feel sorry for Hank who has endured the cold for so long. I am kept warm by the prospect of freedom and of the thought of Hank's secret.

Comments on Entry 29

There is no code word. We can imagine that prison life in winter had to be extremely harsh. Liam comments about the length of time

Hank has been in prison but he is cheered by the plans to escape and the "secret" Hank has shared with him. Was this meeting between Hank and Liam accidental? Of all the men in this prison, why did he connect with MacDonald? Nothing in this journal is accidental. We can speculate that, somehow, someone arranged for these two men to meet once they were imprisoned.

Entry 30

Weather is below zero and work is slow. Food is hard to digest as is the wine we now receive. The rope ladder is coming along o.k. from the rushes on the floor. The stone blocks are all loose and waiting to be moved. Chocolate is going fast. The pills Hank has helps to ease the pain in his stomach that we all have as the winter progresses. We took food back. I have been here

__1 mhnth__ and 23 days if I am right today is the 17th of November.

Comments on Entry 30

"1 mhnth" is the code word. The key is the third letter, **"h."**

We have **NEW AMSTERDAM NORTH AMERICA H.**

Entry 31

I have not written for some time to save paper and because not much has happened. I have used another match today, leaves 10. I have eaten half the Chocolate and Hank the other and each smoked a cigarette leaving 1 for tinder. The candle dwindles less as I have not worked on the rock pile all week due to a problem with some wall supports for which I am sorry as there I can get what I need. I am developing a cough and may have to resort to Hank's horrible pills. We have gotten by means some black cloth and some tangled horse hair which I shall unravel as it makes good thread and the horse won't miss it I am sure. For this we light both candles. I have

__deuperately__ tried to get all we need by December but time is running out. We still need a belt, gun simile, hat boots and handcuffs *providing the coat will be in Lft. Lintot locker. But hope is the light of the world.*

Comments on Entry 31

"deuperately" is the code word. The key is the third letter, "**u**."

I think it is safe to assume that this Lft. Lintot is Etienne Lintot, and that he is helping them in the escape. Recall that Lintot's signature is on the back of the map along with three others.

We now have: **NEW AMSTERDAM NORTH AMERICA H U**.

Entry 32

Today a long awaited rain has fallen for which I am thankful because I don't have to work on the pile.

Comments on Entry 32

There are no code words here.

Entry 33

Today it is still raining and we go to work in relief shifts. Due to bad weather I get an overcoat and slip another one on over it so that I only return one as the second is close to the one I need to wear for the escape. We get meat because it is the eve of the Feast of St. Catherine.

Comments on Entry 33

There are no code words here.

The reference to the Feast of St. Catherine indicates they are following a Catholic calendar.

Entry 34

We have meat today and learn all our wayside places are

Benedictne *monasteries as is well as Hank can claim an affinity with that Order. Cornex is the only one that is different and it is of* *an odd nature. It is called a Premonstrateemian. We may stop at the Isle of Wight after Nab Tower for supplies. We are using candle wax fast. There is a plan of escape we drew on chocolate wrapper.*

Comments on Entry 34

"Benedictne" is the code word. The key is the third letter, "**n**."

That Hank is connected to the Benedictine Order is an important clue. The Benedictines were affiliated with St. Bernard of Clair-vaux, an early patron of the Knights Templar.

Below is an escape map from the MacDonald Journal, which the prisoners originally drew on a chocolate wrapper. Note on the lower left, the arrow pointing "To London," which would be northeast from the prison. Also note on the lower right, the arrow pointing "To Freedom" and "To Sessy."

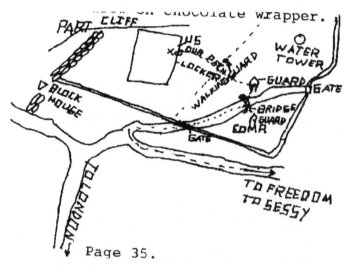

Page 35.

Map of Escape

We now have: ***NEW AMSTERDAM NORTH AMERICA H U N.***

Entry 35

I awake today and give thanks to God for the Good meal we got as the Gov. of the province is come and good impressions are necessary to keep the money that we never see coming. We had duck roasted and wild and the singing not done, corn on the cob and I stole 2 cobs and beans with corn bread oil and wine with apples on the side. I stole one and complete the pant

***kntes**. I need another match to make corn cob pipes but alas no tobacco.*

Comments on Entry 35

"kntes" is the code word. The key is the third letter, "**t**."

We now have: ***NEW AMSTERDAM NORTH AMERICA H U N T.***

Entry 36

The *Feast of St. Joseph marks the coming of winter and according to my calculations 29 more snow storms. Today ends the month and I sleep, mark the calendar and it is bitter cold.*

Comments on Entry 36

"The" is the code word. The key is the third letter, "**e**."

The Feast of St. Joseph would have taken place in December, 1913.

We now have: **NEW AMSTERDAM NORTH AMERICA H U N T E.**

Entry 37

I awake on a new month and the paper is hard to write on as it is so cold the weather freezes paper and ink. We have another outside contact on Christ's Day and look forward to it. We start clothes production starting with boots. Soap hold out ok.

Comments on Entry 37

No code. The new month may be December, 1913. Christ's Day we believe is Christmas.

Entry 38

I have not written for a long time to save paper. We are in the middle of our 3rd snow storm and the snow whirls around making visibility impossible. The bells are 16 aboard the R. N. 41 and she is sinking from clogged ice. I have finished the boots. I cut soles square and then using horsehair sewed on 2 wood buttons I have had for a long time and used a little gold paper from a candy wrapper I got at Sesley camp. Then I sewed the old socks and put ink on them to make them black and I show now a fair cuff.

Then I entered the Storage area on the east front used for holding reinforcements supplies and slipped rubber tubing spliced a strip with my knife, home made, and put it together to make a belt cross under my coat then made a loop of horsehair to make a place for grass to be stiffened to look like fun under

my roat. *I have also make our handcuffs from wire Hank had and then by cutting into small pieces and looped them into each other with my knife. Now I am all set. I have gotten all our plans together and we are in the process of making a (B)ag to hold all our things I said that I should try to get a band from RA. Bag but Hank say NO he thinks it would be too revealing. Ink is going down and paper is worse to write on. The weather was beautiful on the Feast of St. Lucia but as the blue sky turned to gray yet fleecy clouds, my heart saw nothing so beautiful and I shall remember it for the rest of my days. The grey face of evil came down from the clouds and the weather suddenly became colder. Then rain, snow and Hell. Now we are*

demp *in the month in making a suitable bag and building possessions to take along. The journey to the docks will take two days and the first day will be*

[there is a blank after "will be," the entry ending abruptly for unknown reasons]

Journal Page Showing Entries 37 and 38

Comments on Entry 38

"my roat" is a code word. The key is the third letter, "**r**."

"demp" is also a code word. The key is the third letter, "**m**."

It now spells: ***NEW AMSTERDAM NORTH AMERICA HUNTER M.***

Entry 39

Spent at the MAA'BALCADS CASTLE now LONG since abandoned by the Normans. I have been taking Hank's horrible pills of pepper for my bad cough but I have had stomach trouble and other disorders. The cold weather affects my body but freedoms thought keeps me warm and in fair health. We must devise a plan to dispose of our treasure if we find it in such a way that it will come to the ORDER and they won't have it up against us. The wood of my tool is warped and is coming open and the blade is dull. We are now low on candles and the small one is tone.

Matches *are very low.*

Comments on Entry 39

The words, "*MAA BALCADS CASTLE*" and "*LONG,*" all being in capital letters, tell us that this is part of the code. The letters signify the number 20. See the numerical table in Entry #5.

"*Matches*" is also a code word. The key is the letter, "**t.**"

The reference to the "Order" remains a mystery as to who they are and how they are involved in the plans for the escape and the mission as a whole. This is the first mention of a "treasure." What "treasure" are they talking about? What does he mean by, "they won't have it up against us" and that the treasure should come to the Order? I think it is fair to assume that they are referring to the "clay jars of knowledge hidden in North America." The statement that they may find the treasure and will have to dispose of it so that it will come to the Order implies that there there are playing with some dangerous people in this Order who could harm them.

Entry 40

I awake to find all is cold and rotten from raining weather. I make more ink tomorrow and by my calendar it is the 18th of December and we are idle except for finishing up on the rope ladder. Our Beards are growing and I must get a Mirror. Hank will try his sector. We have been separated. We are pushed to finish the blockade before Christ's Day.

Comments on Entry 40

There is no code word. The date is December 18, 1913.

Entry 41

I awake to find that the weather has cleared and we will be working Harder to my dismay as it leaves less time for our plans. Hank hurt his leg and was sent to the doctor to put a bandage on it. He has hurt the left side of the ankle on the right foot and will be laid up for about a week. The fall

of n boulder from the fortress wall should have killed him but two cross beams were above him and equalized the pressure on all but his right foot. I asked him how he felt and he answered in Spanish something that I should write, Entra la cuna y la seputura no hay cora sequra, and I said no more on the subject.

Comments on Entry 41

"of n" is the code word. The key is the third letter, "**n**."

(Those readers who know Spanish will be able to translate the passage. It refers to female anatomy.)

The entire coded sequence spells: **NEW AMSTERDAM NORTH AMERICA HUNTER MTN.**

Now that the coded message is complete, there are no more code words.

Entry 42

I awake early and see that heavy cold envelopes us. We are now in the 4th snow storm coming on the Feast of St. Thomas and lasting for the rest of the day. I did some repairs on a leather jacket. Hank sneaked a punch out of the shop and with a little work it will make a fine tool on my shoe when I descend the wall and sharpened could be a fine weapon. I work by candle light and think of Jennings "Break, break, break on the cold gray stones oh sea" and I would that my tongue could utter all the thoughts arise in me but I must save paper so I sleep.

Comments on Entry 42

A tool is prepared for the escape.

Entry 43

I awake and work hard and then finish the special shoe. Hank tells me that Hank is a nickname for

Hephaetus–God of Fire.

Comments on Entry 43

Hephaetus was an ancient Greek god connected to metallurgy.

Entry 44

T'is mad idoltry to make the service greater than the God and I pray for guidance this day of rest when the wrath is felt even by our hand in clove's by HANK and me. God Bless us and deliver us from Satan's power. Tomorrow is St. Francis Xavier's Day and we let a candle burn all night and we dispose of the wax by eating it, Hank takes the coin from the bottom of the wax and holes it and makes a necklace in penance and prayer. A. has a toothache and Hank say repeat the WARNING LINES 1000 TIMES and it will leave you. I think he was so tired he forgot the pain but some believe in it.

Peter sat on a marble stone weeping.

Christ came by and said Why weepest thou?

Oh my lord my God my tooth doth ache and sore said Peter

Arise O Peter said the Lord it aches no more.

Comments on Entry 44

The passage, **"WARNING LINES 1000 TIMES"** is in capitals and is a coded sequence totaling 21, as explained in the numerical table in Entry #5.

Entry 45

Today I awaken to a great snowfall on St. Francis Zavier's Day and after hard work we all pray as a group. I have finished the bag and the ladder has but 12 rungs to go. Hank is just as impatient as I.

Comments on Entry 45

St. Francis Xavier Day is marked in the Catholic calendar; his feast day falls on December 3.

Entry 46

It is still snowing and I volunteer for a patrol. There are not many that will go out in 14 feet of snow at 40 degrees. Many resent us for going but it is how we will get what we need to make our escape, tools, information of weather, guard placement and a good layout. This is important to us as we will be in range of fire all the time.

Comments on Entry 46

They are planning for an escape in which they will be within the range of fire from the guards at the prison.

Entry 47

Today is a day of Feasting and we get meat vegetables and some wine. I have never tasted such lousy wine before, it has turned to vinegar I'm sure. 50 New men arrive tonight and our plan will depend on the slowness of their acquaintance with the camp guards.

Comments on Entry 47

"A day of Feasting" is Christmas. The arrival of new men affects their plans for escape.

Entry 48

I have much to do and work on the pile all day. Hank makes his contact using a stone hidden up his rear and taps his message and mine. We get some wine, chocolate and matches and cigarettes some cloth and 12 coins. We are now at the Feast of the Nativity. Escape not a week away.

Comments on Entry 48

Hank has a contact in the prison and he uses a stone to tap out a coded message. Someone is working in the prison as a guard and conveys Hank's message to outside men to help with the escape only a week away.

Entry 49

The usual grind takes us past the next few days and 2 days after the Feast of John the Evangelist having past the Feast of St. Stephen and on the verge of success.

Comments on Entry 49

References to the Feast of John the Evangelist and the Feast of St. Stephen are notable. Again, the Catholic calendar is followed or used as some sort of code.

Entry 50

I am worried because I am hearing of double guards being put on because of the new year 1914 and the leaving of prisoners on the transfer to new places as is common this time of the year. We must leave tomorrow and tonight we sort out what we must and it is as follows. First our costumes and our stored fuel oil. Next our knives, soap matches and compass, we decide to leave the flint. The rest we leave for posterity. We leave also the razor after shaving with the mirror Hank stole from the doctor and taking the calendar ink and pen and my prized possession this book. We take the maps of route, the bolt and our pass and stamp. We memorize the plan and I burn it. We wait for dusk, I put on my costume. We remove the wall stones and climb down. I put on Hank the handcuffs and with the Pass in hand we walk to the gate show the pass and are let through leaving this Hell House forever we now go to the store house outside the gate and hitting the guard over the head with the bolt in a sock we kill him and escape with some food an ax and two knives. We go about 2 miles and finding a hut bed down and then snow falls heavy covering our tracks and they will never know how we did it.

I sleep soundly

Ha, Ha, Ha, Ah, Ah, Ah

Comments on Entry 50

It is now the New Year—January, 1914. Liam MacDonald and Hank Roche escape. A year of planning has gone into this clever and daring plan Liam MacDonald wears a guard costume they made and has a pass and a stamp to get past the guard. Roche plays the part of a prisoner and wears the handcuffs they made.

The term *"my prized possession this book,"* is evidence that Liam MacDonald was the writer of the journal. Years later it came into the possession of Bertie MacDonald's husband and she sold it to Jackson. Did Liam MacDonald bring back the journal to someone in his family who kept it as a family heirloom? When Dan Spartan interviewed Bertie MacDonald, she remembered the journal had a brass object with it and she mentioned at that time a "Mr. Deloros." Did Deloros get the journal? Doloros and Lintot were not prisoners and neither of them wrote the journal. We have also ascertained that Hank Roche is not the writer, as evidenced by the many second person references to him by Liam.

Entry 51

ON THE ROAD TO NAB TOWER

We are awakened by a loud noise outside which we find to be "Rabits" a common crook and his cohorts. They are being chased. We hold off the party for a while and then building a fire we escape in the smoke. We cross over streams, bogs, small huts, woods and other things. Then we climb over a hill and see open space and down to the Harbor. Morning finds us there with the bells tolling and the cannon roaring of our escape and the robbery of "Rabits" men. Rabits and Roberta are killed in a skirmish to get contact I to stop a wire to the police guards in the harbor. We cross the field and come upon 2 guards waiting for us. We surprise them and I slit ones throat while Hank stomps the other out with his boots. We took what they had and left our empty guns and continued to get a skiff. The snow is deep and the weather bites into us like a saber of a tigers fang. We row, our hands falling off and after several hours we read Nab Tower where we are greeted by my old friend, Lewellen and one other hand. We take some refuge in a cabin which they have a fire going and we sleep.

Comments on Entry 51

The *harbor* referred to is the English Channel, and it is here that guards intercept them. In graphic terms they describe how they kill the guards, get a skiff and row until they reach Nab Tower. *"Lewellen, my old friend"* is waiting for them at Nab Tower. This is Llewellyn Deloros, one of the men whose name is on the back of the map and a friend of Liam MacDonald. Deloros aka Doloros accompanied the other three men on the mission to get to the church in Cremona.

Entry 52

*I awake and find the rest of the men are up and getting a beef dinner with yams, pomme de terre, tomatoies and café **NOIR** pour nous n"ai pas de lait. I take a bath in clean water and I have a clean shave and lather with L'amphin and ruffled clothes, boots, silver and diamond pistols and on boat:*

5000 in Francs and

500 lbs of salt

500 lbs of sugar

50 Kegs of Café

1000 gallons of fresh water

100 kegs of rum

dishes, spoons, metal cups, glasses, knives

4 small 41 g. pots

2500 lbs of firewood

1 tinder box per person and sulfur matches left over

We carry all equipment and our ship is a 4 rigger with four yard arms per mast and a 35' Mainer flying Neutral colors. She stands 50 feet between the deck and the poopdeck and carried 12 feet beyond the end of the Spencer Boom. Her bow rises of the foremast shrouds by 4'3" and her starboard storm carries a lower deck support of 41" and 43" on the port and her bow deck covers 14" Guns and her sides hold seven cannons. Below the extension railing she caries an extra two cannon and carries an extra gun on the aft mast above the spencer gaff of 12" to the foot. We named her the Quetzalcoatl. Now at 03 hours 30 minutes on a 4'3" rise on the Feast of St. Titus we Leave for France and if God sees it peace for which to live until fate takes us to our eternal end.

The Last Page of Entry 52

Comments on Entry 52

The code word is "*NOIR*," with all 4 letters in capitals. Four is the key.

Referring back to Entry 44, we have "WARNING LINES 1000 TIMES," which signifies the number 21. When we add the 4 from "NOIR," as per Jackson's instructions in Entry #5, we end up with a total of 25.

They leave for France and name the ship *Quetzalcoatl.* The choice of this name—recall that it is the name written on the mysterious gold triangle "nail" found in the brass device—adds to the mystery surrounding these men.

Entry 53

At long last our journey to New Amsterdam begins in earnest. The Order has provided a sloop and provisions for our quest and the unknown awaits us as we travel into the West and North.

Comments on Entry 53

"Our journey to New Amsterdam" is code for their destination. New Amsterdam no longer existed in 1914, or course. It is likely that New Amsterdam is a code word for the place (New York) where the treasure is hidden.

A ship and provisions for the quest has been provided by the "Order." Again, we see this mysterious and evidently wealthy and powerful Order mentioned.

As for their quest, they identify their route to be west and then north. The obvious interpretation is west across the Atlantic and then north to northeastern America, to the Hunter Mountain location (in New York's Catskill Mountains) named in the coded journal entries.

Entry 54

The Summer Solstice Sunrise shall be our guide as we follow the ancient path laid down with much care and marked by chrystine stones, natural quartz blocks and constructed stone monuments until the Masters Tombstone is reached and the goal in sight then shall we give thanks to the Goddess, so says Hank.

Comments on Entry 54

This last entry in the MacDonald journal is tantalizing. I presume it is referring to their final destination, Hunter Mountain. It informs us that Hank Roche had ancient information about this area. Where did he get this from? He says they will be guided by the *"Summer Solstice Sunrise."* How would this guide him?

The obvious question is, how would Hank Roche have known that there was an ancient path on Hunter Mountain? A possible answer is that Roche, MacDonald, Lintot and Deloros reached the church in Cremona, Italy and learned of a 12th century voyage to the area made by the Knights Templar, led by Ralph de Sudeley (this voyage is described in detail, below). It is possible that the Templars surveyed the Hunter Mountain area and brought back descriptions of landmarks (along with maps), perhaps marking this "ancient path."

Regarding the summer solstice sunrise reference, it should be noted that dozens of ancient stone structures aligned to solstices and equinoxes have been found in New York and the New England states by members of the New England Antiquities Research Association (NEARA), along with other researchers. It is entirely possible, therefore, that one or more of these structures were used to mark the Hunter Mountain treasure.

Regarding the "Masters Tombstone" reference, I believe this is referring to the so-called Devil's Tombstone, an enormous upright stone standing near Hunter Mountain directly south of Plateau Mountain. This massive stone would have served as an obvious landmark for ancient travelers.

The reference to the "Goddess" is an odd one for a group with obvious strong Catholic leanings, and opens a new area of research. Was

Hank Roche part of a group that venerated the ancient Goddess? We have another mystery to deal with, and another clue to help us in our research

Roche and MacDonald escaped on January 1, 1914. World War I broke out in September of 1914. They had time to get across France before war broke out. The journal says Roche and the others stopped at Mondonego and Ceuta and then went to the island of Madeira. From Madeira they apparently went to Namibia in West Africa, based on the concealed message in the journal. Were they in search of the gold and diamonds known to be in Namibia?

In summary, Roche, MacDonald, Deloros and Lintot reached the church in Cremona and found the key to the location of the Cave of Lost Scrolls on Hunter Mountain. A ship was outfitted for them to sail to America. It may have been 1916 or 1917 when they arrived at Hunter Mountain. Once there, they were able to find the cave where the clay tubes had been hidden, led to the location by the Templar Document. Perhaps they made contact with G. Benvenuto in Italy before crossing to America, and perhaps Benvenuto some-how assisted them. Recall that the name "G. Benvenuto" was on the receipt from 1906 and that he had information about the navigation device. This device was also some kind of a direction finder. Like many aspects of this mystery, there is much we don't understand about this device. But apparently it led our prison escapees and their accomplices across the Atlantic and to Hunter Mountain.

Further Analysis of the Journal

It is worth taking a few moments to review what we have learned. For five centuries the Templar Document was kept hidden in the Church of San Sigismundo in Cremona, Italy, protected by certain families and some unknown "Order." Who was this Order that had the financial means to furnish a four-masted ship with can-nons and supplies in 1914? Did this Order have access to gold and diamonds in West Africa to fund this voyage? Obviously they were intent on retrieving whatever it was that had been hidden on Hunter Mountain. Entry #12 continued to haunt me:

*"**Hank tells me the secret knowledge is cached in 12 scrolls in clay jars hidden in a cave in North America for over a thousand years and the key to its location is in a document kept in the Church of San Sigismundo Cremona built by Francesco Sforza duke of Milan in the fifteenth century.**"*

A reader might question this as a wild, unbelievable story. But, these prisoners and their accomplices were not fools, as proven by their precisely executed and dangerous plan of escape. I felt I had no choice but to conduct a full investigation into Francesco Sforza, Duke of Milan. My research uncovered centuries of international intrigue as various powerful families and groups jockeyed to protect and/or recover the treasures hidden on Hunter Mountain.

CHAPTER 5

Coded Messages Lead to Gold in Africa

It appears from the invisible ink sections in the MacDonald Journal that Roche, MacDonald, Lintot and Deloros had more than one goal. Not only did they want to get to the Church of San Sigismundo and access the Templar Document which would lead them to Hunter Mountain and the Cave of Lost Scrolls, but they planned on going where there was gold and diamonds in West Africa.

Jackson had suspected there was more to this journal than just what could be seen by the naked eye, and so as detailed earlier, he applied heat and chemicals to the MacDonald Journal. He found sections in the journal which had invisible ink in spaces between its entries. Darker areas are burn marks where Jackson used heat and chemicals to search for hidden messages. Some of the pages are shown below.

**Journal Pages after Jackson
Applied Heat/Chemicals**

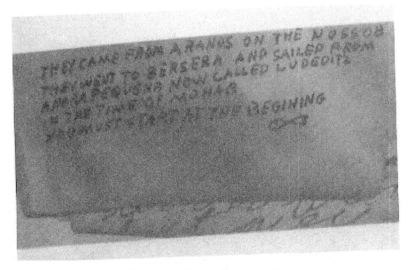

Journal Entry Enlarged

The text from the message contained in the enlarged image (immediately above) is reproduced below:

THEY CAME FROM ARANOS ON THE NOSSOB

THEY WENT TO BERSEBA AND SAILED FROM

ANGRA PEQUENA NOW CALLED LUDEDITZ [LUDERITZ]

IN THE TIME OF MOHAB

YOU MUST START AT THE BEGINNING

Aranos, Nossob, Berseba, and Angra Pequena are all places in Namibia, a country in southwest Africa. This is the diamond region of West Africa. Aranos is a town in Namibia on the Nossob River. Berseba is a town near the Atlantic coast of Namibia. Note the fish symbol on the bottom right; the fish is a symbol used by early Christians.

The Gold Triangle

Readers will recall that Angra Pequena was inscribed on the gold triangle that was found in the concealed compartment of the brass device. This was the brass device hidden in a garden planter on Bannerman Island. Here it is pictured again:

A N G R A P E Q U E N A

As a reminder, the other side of the triangle reads *Quetzalcoatl*, the Aztec deity and the name of the ship used by the escaped prisoners to cross the Atlantic.

Jackson wrote that he had the gold triangle object tested and it was 800 to 1000 years old. He also had the brass device and the copper disks tested and all were found to be from the year 1750, plus-or-minus 50 years. He does not give us the names of the people who conducted the tests, as they were connected with the Spartan agency. However we know that they were skilled in cryptography, photography and metallurgical testing.

Angra Pequena

The invisible ink message told of an unknown group in Namibia who made their way to the coast to *Angra Pequena,* which is now called Luderitz. Whoever wrote the message knew that Angra Pequena was Portuguese and that the name of the area was changed to Luderitz in 1896. I could not find any historical references to the "Time of Mohab."

The atlas I checked said in bold letters that the entire coast of Namibia was a "Restricted Diamond_Mining Area." One source I consulted indicated that the dry bed of the Nossob River was believed to have diamonds even today. The diamonds and the gold were known to the local people and had been looted for centuries by invaders. In the 19th century, Cecil Rhodes, a British general, founded the famed Kimberley diamond mines in this region. Eventually the Boer War broke out between the Dutch settlers and England prior to the First World War as both countries fought to get a foothold in this part of Africa and take advantage of its rich mineral resources.

Note that Portuguese kings had been sending explorers down the west coast of Africa as early as the 1300's. Portugal was a Knights Templar base and longtime Templar ally. It is therefore entirely possible that the Templars knew of the riches to be found along the Namibian coast.

An Azimuth Clue

Readers will recall the copper rectangle found in the brass device, pictured again below:

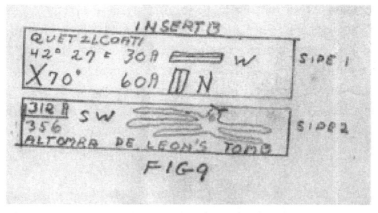

Copper Rectangle Found in Brass Device

The markings on the left of side 2 of the object—the numbers *312* and *356*, and the letters *SW*—seemed to be directional headings, but remained a mystery to me until I consulted with Ohio researcher, Richard Moats. His explanation of these markings is set forth in the Epilogue to this book.

I will discuss the Oak Island connection to this mystery in Part 4 of this book, but this is another piece of evidence linking this mystery to treasure sites on both sides of the Atlantic.

The Big Question

The four men involved in the prison escape were headed for the diamond and gold mines, perhaps to finance their trip to North America to search for the Templar document or perhaps as part of their work on behalf of the Order which they often referenced.

It must have been either Roche or Deloros who inserted the hidden messages in invisible ink pointing to the sites in West Africa. But where did they get this information from? Again, it seems entirely possible that the Templars had knowledge of the African mines and the Oak Island treasure, and likely also maps. The obvious question then becomes: Where did they get these maps? It is entirely possible these maps were inside the scrolls the Templars recovered during their search in the tunnels beneath the Temple Mount. It is also likely that the mysterious Order mentioned in the MacDonald Journal is somehow related to the Templars.

CHAPTER 6

A Sacred Mountain in Northeastern America

Modern Researchers Find an Ancient Path:
A Calendar Stone and Stone Constructions

The last entry, #54, of the MacDonald Journal contains a detailed description of features that mark the "ancient path" to Hunter Mountain:

> *The Summer Solstice Sunrise shall be our guide as we follow the ancient path laid down with much care and marked by chrystine stones. Natural quartz blocks and constructed stone monuments until the Masters Tombstone is reached and the goal is in sight then shall we give thanks to the Goddess, so says Hank.*

Let's list some of these individual features:

- Ancient path laid down
- Summer Solstice Sunrise
- Constructed stone monuments
- Masters Tombstone
- A reference to the "Goddess"

It is evident that someone had to have been on Hunter Mountain previously in order to provide such detailed information. Significantly, the descriptions given in the journal match what modern researchers have found in and around the Hunter Mountain region of New York State. The nearby Putnam County features more than fifty stone chambers which align to solstice and equinox sunrises and sunsets. Likewise, neighboring Vermont boasts its own stone chambers in complexes which also mark equinox and solstice events.

One specific find is worth mentioning. About seventy years after Roche and company journeyed to Hunter Mountain, a hiker found a "calendar stone" on Plateau Mountain, the peak facing Hunter Mountain. The hiker, Gary D. Jaycox, wrote in the NEARA Journal (Volume 16-2) in 1981:

> *The author would now like to report the existence of a single calendar stone in the Catskill Mountains. Its unique geometrical properties function to provide an observer with several important sighting alignments. Located within the central Catskill Mountain region of southeastern New York State the calendar stone is positioned at an altitude of 3,100 feet on the southwestern slope of a mountain at **Lat. 42° 09' N** and commands an extensive view of a major portion of the Catskill system to the south and west. From its location, clear unobstructed views of the setting sun along the horizon are possible for much of the calendar year.*

The latitude Jaycox recorded as Lat. 42o 09' N puts us on Plateau Mountain. Again, this is in close vicinity to Hunter Mountain—the bases of the two peaks abut, separated only by State Highway 214 running through the narrow valley between them. Recall that the Hunter Mountain latitude of 420 27' 30 N is inscribed on the copper rectangle found in the brass device, pictured again below.

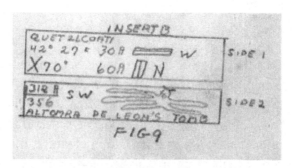

Copper Rectangle Found in Brass Device

Similarly, a large boulder sits atop Plateau Mountain. The boulder features a prominent point which aligns with the winter solstice sunrise. Former NEARA Vice President Glenn Kreisberg reports:

> *The large boulder with its top slid off has a prominent point that aligns with the winter solstice sunrise to the southeast. On the stone's surface are numerous inscriptions one of which ... appears to be a sun glyph facing the winter solstice sunrise. Nearby there is a large low moss covered triangular shaped trailside boulder on the summit trail that points the way to the ... Calendar Stone reported by Jaycox ... displaying several alignments with the southwest setting sun.*

Are these Plateau Mountain stones and glyphs the "summer solstice sunrise guide" described in the journal? More research is needed here.

The Hammonasset Line

Tom Paul, a retired engineer and NEARA member, discovered a line of unusual pre-Colonial stone structures and alignments running from Montauk Point on Long Island, across Long Island Sound, through Connecticut, and into New York State. The Hammonasset Line, as he named it, is comprised of a series of stone structures, cairns, and unusual walls. The line marks the winter solstice sunrise and the summer solstice sunset, much as do many other ancient sites including Newgrange in Ireland, Uaxactun in Guatemala, Palenque in Honduras, and the temple to Karnak in Egypt. Below is the Hammonasset Line plotted from Montauk Long Island to Stony Cove, New York, at an angle of 42.5 degrees above due west.

Importantly for our purposes, the Hammonasset Line crosses the eastern slope of Overlook Mountain and intersects the Devil's Tombstone, located in the valley below Plateau and Hunter Mountains. We remind the reader of the statement in the MacDonald Journal that the "summer solstice will be their guide until they reach

Hammonasset Line plotted from Montauk, LI to Stony Clove, NY at 318.5 degree

The Hammonasset Line

the Master's Tombstone." This indicates that Hank Roche and his associates may have found their way to Hunter Mountain from the tip of Long Island by following the Hammonasset's summer solstice sunset line—that is, the "ancient path laid down."

A Goddess Symbol on a Hunter Mountain Stone

Recall that the final Journal entry concludes that when the mission is complete, *"then shall we give thanks to the Goddess."* Why the Goddess? For a group which seemingly had strong Catholic leanings, this seems like an odd deity to give thanks to, even more so given the early 1900s time period. It turns out there are some intriguing artifacts on and around Hunter Mountain that shed some light on this Goddess reference. Journal Entry #5 contains an important clue. As Jackson writes:

> *Looking under #25 in the table we see 42 with a 9 next to it. Is it by coincidence that at 42.9 degrees N. Latitude by 74.12 deg. W. Longitude there is a stone on Hunter Mountain in New York state that has carved on it a triangle*

often associated with the Mother Goddess and sometimes referred to as a Tanit symbol.

As Jackson notes, the triangle symbol has historically been associated with the mother goddess. Below is a picture of the triangle carved on the Hunter Mountain stone:

Triangle Carving

A second clue that may shed light on the Goddess reference is the mysterious symbol of the octopus with five arms carved on the brass device and shown again here:

Copper Rectangle Found in Brass Device

The five-armed octopus may have been used as a reference to the Merovingians, a family that ruled the Franks for nearly 300 years beginning in the middle of the fifth century. According to legend, the Merovingians descended from the mythical, five-horned sea creature called a "Quinotaur." The important point for our purposes is that many researchers believe that the Merovingians were themselves Goddess worshipers. We will return to both of these clues—the triangle and the 5-armed octopus, below.

It is also worth mentioning that many researchers believe that the Templars adopted and resurrected the Goddess tradition in the 12th century after they found 1st century Gnostic texts, showing that the Goddess was venerated in early Christianity. We will return to this Goddess reference later.

Devil's Tombstone

The massive boulder known as Devil's Tombstone, measuring seven feet high by five feet wide, may be the *Master's Tombstone* described by Hank Roche. It is located just south of Hunter and Plateau Mountains. From Devil's Tombstone, there is a historic trail which leads up Plateau Mountain to the Calendar Stone. Hunter Mountain is visible in the distance in the upper left hand side of this picture of the Devil's Tombstone:

Devil's Tombstone
Hunter Mountain in Background, Upper Left

Constructed Stone Monuments

Overlook Mountain is located about twelve miles southwest of Plateau and Hunter Mountain. Researchers Glenn Kreisberg and Dave Holden have found stone walls, cairns, standing stones, astronomical alignments, star maps and the effigy of a serpent. These astonishing ancient alignments and serpent effigy (together called the "Draco Alignment") may be the "constructed stone monuments" referred to in the MacDonald Journal. In any event, they are further evidence of ancient peoples living in this area who built stone structures aligning with solstice and equinox alignments similar to those in ancient Europe.

Conclusion

Even today, almost a century later, artifacts and sites in and around the Hunter Mountain area corroborate the information contained in the MacDonald Journal. We find stone chambers, Goddess symbols, a Master's Tombstone, stone monuments and, most importantly, a summer solstice sunset "ancient path" that leads Roche and his associates straight to Hunter Mountain. The question remains, what did they find there?

CHAPTER 7

Paris: A Breakthrough!

We return to Bill Jackson's unrelenting search. The year is 1971 and he is in Paris with Dan Spartan. Dan introduces Jackson to Pierre de Valzac, a rare book dealer in Paris. Pierre de Valzac was one of Dan Spartan's associates in the Spartan Agency and was a collector of antiquities. He possessed a rare pamphlet co-authored by Gauden Roche and Galvao Benvenuto, dated 1715. Benvenuto's great, great, great grandson, Gustaveste Benvenuto, had sold the document to the Paris dealer.

Recall, we have already learned about (1) Benvenuto and Roche being on the 1906 receipt of sale of the brass device to Jackson, and (2) Hank Roche playing a starring role in the events recorded in the 1913 MacDonald Journal. We now have a third set of Roches and Benvenutos, this time dating back to 1715.

Jackson bought the pamphlet from de Valzac and immediately understood that what he held in his hands was immensely important, so much so that he immediately wrote to the Church in San Sigismundo, Cremona, Italy. Below is a quote from Jackson in which he describes what he saw in the pamphlet that was so stunning to him:

> The third was a rare pamphlet written in 1715 by Galvao Benvenuto and Gauden Roche. This I purchased from Mr. Spartan's friend, Mr. De Valzac in Paris, France. It was in this one that I found mention of the American Indian word Onteora meaning 'Land in the Sky' being reference to another document written in Italian and located in Cremona, Italy. It was in the possession of the great grandson of one of the authors, Gustaveste Benvenuto.

Analyzing the Paris Pamphlet

The title of the 1715 pamphlet was: *La Applicazione de le Francese, Gallese et Scozzese a la Lingua de Indiano Americano.* Translated into English, this reads: "The Application of French, Italian and Gaelic to the languages of the American Indians."

Jackson's attention was riveted on a footnote which read, in an odd and cryptic mixture of French and Italian (Roche being French and Benvenuto being Italian): "Vouzallex a Onteora documento a Chiesa San Sigismundo Cremona Intitolare Un Anno Che Noi Ricordia." Translated into English [with punctuation added], this reads:

"Go to the Onteora document at Church of San Sigismundo, Cremona, Entitled, *A Year We Remember.*"

Jackson obviously knew that what he had found was important. This Paris pamphlet directed someone to locate the Onteora document in the Church of San Sigismundo, the document being entitled, "A Year We Remember."

This was an exciting breakthrough. We now knew that a portion of what we later came to call the Templar Document had a name—in fact two names:

The Onteora Document, and A Year We Remember

Recall that the author of this document was the Templar, Ralph de Sudeley, and that he led a Templar expedition to the Hunter Mountain region in the 12th century. When I first learned that de Sudeley's fascinating log was known by the name, *The Onteora Document,* I was shocked. Why? Because I knew that the name *Onteora* was the Native American name for New York's Catskill Mountains. How could a 12th century Templar knight possibly have known this, unless he had indeed made the journey across the Atlantic?

Dots were beginning to connect both across centuries and across continents. I dove deeper into my research.

The 1715 pamphlet compared French, Italian and Gaelic names to American Indian names. Was this a scholarly exercise or was there some other reason to make this comparison? Was it possible that Gauden Roche and Galvao Benvenuto were looking for the cave on Hunter Mountain in the early 1700s? If so, they would need to communicate with the Indians in the area. We can only speculate.

I refer the reader again to the bombshell statement in the Mac-Donald Journal, written in 1913, where Hank Roche tells Liam MacDonald that:

> *[There is] secret knowledge cached in 12 scrolls in clay jars hidden in a cave in North America for over a thousand years and the key to its location is in a document kept in the Church of San Sigismundo, Cremona built by Francesco Sforza, duke of Milan in the fifteenth century.*

To reiterate: *The Onteora Document* (aka *A Year We Remember,* part of the larger Templar Document) was known to exist in the Church of San Sigismundo in the 15th century. It was known in 1715 by Benvenuto and Roche and, in 1913 by Hank Roche. For five hundred years this secret had been passed down by some mysterious Order.

Now it had landed in my lap.

CHAPTER 8

Jackson Obtains the Templar Document

Retracing Jackson's steps has been like being lost in a labyrinth. Periodically I would stumble upon clues that might help me find my way, but often these clues were attached to shadowy people, or written in invisible ink, or kept hidden by secret societies. Jackson, through his work in the intelligence field, was comfortable operating in the shadows. But what did I know of this kind of world?

After purchasing the pamphlet from the Paris book dealer, Jackson wrote a letter to the Church of San Sigismundo in Cremona, Italy. He and church officials exchanged many correspondences. Finally, he was able to arrange a purchase of the 12th century *Onteora Document* (aka *A Year We Remember*) from the Vatican, where it had ended up. He wrote to Dan Spartan:

> *I then approached Father Christofer as a way of getting to see this document and he helped me to get an interview with Bishop Fulton J. Sheen who interceded with the Holy Father to get me to visit the Vatican Library while I would be in Rome on your business for General K.*

Father Christofer was a liaison to the Vatican for the Spartan Agency; he arranged an interview for Jackson with Bishop Fulton J. Sheen, a popular New York religious figure and television personality, in New York City. Jackson told his story to the bishop, who contacted the pope in Rome and facilitated the sale to Jackson. Other documents were offered to Jackson along with the *Onteora Document* (aka *A Year We Remember*)—it is the collection of all these documents which I refer to here as the Templar Document.

Further correspondence with the church revealed an important, but perhaps unsurprising, fact: The Templar Document was in the process of being donated to the Vatican by Gustaveste Benvenuto, of the Benvenuto family that plays such a large role in this mystery. I have learned that Gustaveste's mother traced her family lineage back to Bianca Maria Visconti, the wife of Francesco Sforza, Duke of Milan and patron of the San Sigismundo Church. Apparently many of the San Sigismundo records had been donated to the Vatican Library by the Benvenuto family. But it is worth noting again that the Templar Document's original home was in Cremona, at San Sigismundo Church—a Knights Templar power center from the 12th to the 14th centuries.

Spartan Operatives in Rome

A 2008 letter to me from a Spartan Group associate of Jackson, Alex C., sheds light on the details of how Jackson negotiated the purchase of the Templar Document in 1971. Alex C. was a Spartan member who later helped me translate the Theban portions of the Templar Document. Alex C. wrote:

In November of that year my wife and I went for a holiday in Mallorca at Arta...With him [Spartan] was another person, Dr. William Jackson. Mr. Spartan told us that they, Mr. Jackson and he, had just come from visiting with an acquaintance of theirs in Paris, France, Mr. Pierre DeValzac was a dealer in rare books and manuscripts at the time and was living at 15 Rue de la Fontaine. Dr. Jackson showed me a small pamphlet printed in 1715 by a Henri Roche [mistake, should be Gauden Roche] ... it had something to do with linguistics. Dr. Jackson was very excited in having gotten it...

He then showed us a letter from the church stating that the document in question was to be donated to the Vatican in ten days but that it could be viewed prior to that. The person writing to Dr. Jackson he referred to as Father Benvenuto.

I had to inform Dr. Jackson that Gus Benvenuto was not a priest but was the recently retired Custodian of Records of said church. I had brokered a sale of some documents earlier that year involving Mr. Benvenuto. I offered to put Dr. Jackson in touch with Mr. Franco Franzetti who was working at the Vatican in regards to the restoration and cleaning of ancient documents. I called him from the hotel and Dr. Jackson arranged to meet him in the Vatican four days hence as he was intentioned to visit there with a certain archbishop on other business. I gave Dr. Jackson my phone number and we parted that evening.

Alex C. knew that Gustaveste Benvenuto was selling old church documents; in fact, Alex C. had brokered some of these sales. (Apparently the Italian laws prohibiting the sale of antiquities were not rigorously enforced.) Alex C. also knew a Mr. Franzetti in the Vatican Library, who was working at cleaning and restoring ancient documents for the Vatican. Alex C.'s letter continued:

Four days after my meeting with Dr. Jackson and Mr. Spartan I received a call from Dr. Jackson to find a lawyer to arrange the sale of the document in question from Gus Benvenuto to him prior to the donation of it and other letters concerning the building of the San Sigismundo church to the Vatican.

His Holiness had agreed that the document was not of interest to the church and could be sold if Dr. Jackson wanted to buy it. The asking price was 15000 Lire. I told Dr. Jackson that he needed a Notaio not a lawyer as things were done differently in Italy and referred him to Mr. Guiseppe Famiglia. He thanked me and that was the last time I heard from him. Guiseppe informed me that the sale took place in Rome after the document was reviewed in the Vatican Library for 12000 lire and that Mr. Franzetti had verified its authenticity and that of the signature of Ralp de Sedely.

The last line is of utmost importance: It tells us that the *Onteora Document* (aka *A Year We Remember*) was inspected by Mr. Franco Franzetti, a restorer of ancient documents in the Vatican Library, and that Mr. Franzetti authenticated the signature on the document of *Ralp de Sedely*. The correct spelling of this name is *Ralph de Sudeley,* and he is the author of the *Onteora Document* (aka *A Year We Remember*). After exhaustive research, I confirmed that de Sudeley was an English member of the Knights Templar. It is he who led the mission and voyage to Onteora in 1178-1180. Sudeley's log, which he entitled "A Year We Remember," was originally archived in 1180 in Castrum Sepulchri, a Cistercian abbey consecrated by Bernard of Clairvaux and located in the principality of Seborga, along the coast of northern Italy close to the border with France:

Castrum Sepulchri

This location provided direct access to the ports of the Middle East, where the Templars maintained a major and long-lasting presence:

Map Showing Seborga

More importantly, Seborga offered the Templars a safe haven—away from the curious eyes and potentially sticky fingers of European royalty and Vatican officials—to collect, store and maintain the priceless relics and treasures they obtained while in the Middle East. As one modern-day official of Seborga explains it, the Templars ran Seborga during the 12th century as "their own state," free from external rule, and likely used Seborga as a repository for important relics and artifacts:

> *The Templars managed the Principality of Seborga from 1159 by a decision of Pope Alexander II , in place and for the account of its legal Lord, the Abbey of Lérins (in today's France, in front of Cannes), until their end in 1312. Additionally the elected Prince of Seborga and the elected Grand Master of the Templars were 8 times the same persons throughout history. The Templars in practice had their own state in Seborga, while they never had one in the Holy Land.*

And this opens an unusual point of view on History. No doubt that the Templars had capacities useful for special tasks, from transportation to translation, from banking to financing etc. The discovery of the Templar Document confirms that the Principality of Seborga was used in the Middle Ages as a discrete "shrine" for delicate /embarrassing elements like pre-Christian relics, non-official religious texts etc.

Baron Jean-Philippe Arnotte

Former Consul of the Principality of Seborga

in the Great Duchy of Luxembourg (2000-2015)

In simple terms, Seborga served as an ideal location for the Templars to hide their treasures.

Things changed when the Templar Order was outlawed in 1307. It is likely then that the Templar Document (that is, de Sudeley's log, *A Year We Remember*) was transferred from Seborga to the San Sigismundo Church in Cremona, Italy, about 200 miles to the northeast:

Cremona, Italy
[Credit, Wikipedia]

I can only imagine the excitement Dr. Jackson must have felt in Rome when he first began to translate parts of this fascinating document. He had stumbled upon something that could rewrite history.

The Vatican Library, 1971

Having purchased the *Onteora Document* (aka *A Year We Remember)*, Dr. Jackson's next tasks were to translate it and attempt to ascertain its authenticity. His testing revealed that the paper was parchment and the ink of an oak gall (aka iron gall) composition, a standard medieval ink formulation. Furthermore, he had already had Ralph de Sudeley's signature verified as authentic by the Vatican Library expert. He wrote in 1994:

Originally I chose 1130 for the date based on a test of the paper but it could be anywhere between 1100 and 1200 A.D. This is based on the oak gall content of the ink.

Dr. Jackson then turned to translating de Sudeley's log. The document was written in an archaic script known as Theban. (Theban is not a language; rather, it is an alphabet whose letters translate one-to-one to letters in the old Latin alphabet. Historically, it was used as a cipher.) The Theban transliterated into Latin and Italian, with some passages in Old English. Once these transliterations were complete, Jackson—with help—translated the whole into English. It took Jackson two years to do this, from 1971 to 1973.

Looking back at the chain of events that led to Jackson's acquisition of the Templar Document, I am struck by how fortunate we are that the documents were not buried in the Vatican records and lost to history. Jackson recalls in 1994:

Gustaveste Benvenuto was going to donate it [the Templar Document] with other letters and documents to the Vatican. I was able to view it in the Vatican Library and after translating the first page from the Theban I knew it was something of value. I bought it.

With Jackson's three words, "I bought it," he acquired a price-less document from the 12th century. Jackson accomplished what few people achieve in a lifetime. He was about to change history. Scores of authors have written about the Templars, most basing their conclusions on rumors and legends. Jackson had in his possession an actual primary source document.

CHAPTER 9

The Church of San Sigismundo

The Church of San Sigismundo in Cremona is a masterpiece of Renaissance architecture and one of the finest in northwest Italy. The church is two stories, with a rose window to celebrate the Virgin Mary over the entrance.

The Church of San Sigismundo, Cremona, Italy
[courtesy Jessica Gritti, Ph.D.]

The interior follows a Latin cross path and houses artwork, relics and ancient texts, many collected by Cosimo de Medici from monasteries throughout the Holy Land. It is not surprising, therefore, that this church, in an area long associated with the Templars, was where the Templar Document was stored. As we recall from the MacDonald journal, Roche and McDonald escaped from the prison in England to find the "key," which was said to be housed in the San Sigismundo Church. One obvious possibility is that the "key" was the Templar Document itself. Or perhaps the "key" was the brass navigational device with the hidden inscribed objects, as we know Jackson had dated the brass device to the 1700's. Either way, answers to this mystery would be found by studying Cremona and the people who lived there.

Understanding the Significance of the Sforza Family

The Templar Document was in Cremona for five centuries until it was sold in 1971 to Dr. Jackson by Gustaveste Benvenuto, a descendant of Maria Bianca Visconti. Cremona was the dowry Maria Bianca Visconti brought to her 1441 marriage to Francesco Sforza, the Duke of Milan. The Church of San Sigismundo was commissioned in 1447 to celebrate the union between the Visconti and Sforza families, who had previously been ancient and fierce rivals.

Francesco Sforza was a military leader and diplomat with political connections throughout Europe, whose goal was to unite all of Italy. His military prowess was legendary. Sforza was born of common stock, but his military skills gave him stature and he had designs on acquiring more territory. When Maria Bianca Visconti married Francesco Sforza, it united the Visconti nobility and the Sforza military power. The union created a powerful court in Milan.

Relief of Francesco Sforza

Maria Bianca Visconti

Maria Bianca Visconti was a key to this unfolding story. Maria was from an ancient family with deep roots in northwest Italy, where they controlled towns surrounding Milan and built imposing castles. The city of Cremona was very special to her; she spent much time there and eventually died there. As the Duchess of Milan, she was involved in diplomatic affairs and even led a battle, commanding troops to defend an invasion of Cremona. This woman stands apart from the depiction of women of her time.

Five hundred years separated the Duchess of Milan from Gus Benvenuto, who sold Jackson the Templar Document. A branch of the Benvenuto family from the 15th century lived in Crema, a town close to Cremona, and it appears that they were collectors of old texts and documents. The Visconti/Sforza and Medici families inter-married in the 15th century, an important development in this story.

Maria's marriage to Francesco Sforza produced eight children and one important granddaughter—Caterina Sforza, who would marry into the Medici family. The Medicis were the most powerful family in 15th century northern Italy, with links to London through their banking enterprises. This Milan/London banking connection would play an intriguing part in this mystery. Raised for a time by her grandmother Maria after her father passed away, Caterina's marriage to a Medici produced descendants who became queens of France and the most noteworthy and powerful women in the six-teenth century. Descendants of the Sforza/Medici family included two queens and many others in European royalty. Catherine de Medici (1519-1589) married King Henry II and ruled as Queen of France and then Regent when her son Francis became King. Marie de' Medici (1573-1642), another Queen of France, was married to King Henry IV, who sent Samuel de Champlain (rumored to have been his illegitimate son) to explore and settle Newfoundland and Nova Scotia.

The Sforza/Medici connection, and the union's royal offspring, lead to the strong possibility that the secrets of the Templar Document were passed down through the centuries by European royalty.

Maria & People of Great Influence

Maria Bianca Visconti had relationships with famous European figures during her lifetime. One of the most important people who visited her in Cremona was Rene d'Anjou (see Cecila Ady, *The Court of Milan Under the Sforzas*). Meetings between Maria Bianca, d'Anjou and Francesco Sforza in 1453 had repercussions beyond Italy.

Rene d'Anjou is one of the most famous historical figures of his time, a man who is given credit for initiating the Renaissance. His titles included: Duke of Anjou, Count of Provence, Count of Piedmont, Duke of Bar, Duke of Lorraine, King of Naples, and titular King of Jerusalem and Aragon including Majorca, Sicily and Corsica. His daughter married King Henry VI of England.

It is interesting to note that at one point d'Anjou employed Christopher Columbus on one of his ships, the Ferrantina. Did Columbus learn of the route across the Atlantic from Rene d'Anjou, who had been told of the Templar voyage by Maria Bianca Visconti in 1453? Were copies of Templar maps passed down through d'Anjou to Columbus? Historians have referenced secret maps that Columbus is said to have had showing a route to America. Would these have been ancient maps found by the Templars and passed to Rene de Anjou, who then supplied Columbus with them?

A Possible Origin of the "Order"

Rene d'Anjou commanded a navy which often assisted Francesco Sforza in his frequent battles with Venice. Stemming from this naval relationship, d'Anjou and Francesco Sforza founded the "Order of the Ship and the Double Crescent." Did the mysterious Order Hank Roche belonged to in the 20th century have roots in 15th century Italy?

Templar Power in Northwest Italy

I wrote earlier that Northwest Italy was a Templar power base from the 12th to 14th centuries. As documented by Elena Bellomo in her book, *The Templar Order in Northwest Italy,* the Templars had a presence in almost every town and city in this region of Italy.

Cremona had been a Templar city as far back as 1165. Families throughout the area supported the Templars with money and land grants and sent their sons to fight in the Crusades. The Templars, in turn, brought religious relics, ancient texts and other precious artifacts from the Holy Land to harbors on the coast of northwest Italy via their ships. (See Bellomo, pages 46-47.)

Padua: Link to Zeno Brothers & Henry Sinclair

The Italian cities of Milan and Pavia are located close to Cremona on the Po River, which flows as a life line across northern Italy to Venice and the Adriatic Sea. Tributaries flow from the Po River south to the Mediterranean coast where Ventimiglia, a Templar port, and Castrum Sepulchri (Seborga) are located. To the northeast are the cities of Padua and Venice. The city of Padua, just inland and only 25 miles west of Venice, is our focus here because of its connection to the Zeno family (through the bishop of Padua, who was related the Zenos) and to the 14th century Scottish historical figure, Henry Sinclair, Earl of Orkney and Baron of Roslin. Sinclair is believed by some historians to have made a voyage to America in 1398 and carved the famous Westford Knight carving in Westford, Massachusetts.

My research uncovered another possible piece to this puzzle, a set of papers known as the "Benvenuto Dialogues," written by "Benvenuto Italian of London." These papers were housed at the University of Michigan and had been translated from Italian to English. They were published in 1610 but, based on information contained and current events discussed in the papers, I have ascertained they were written in the late 14th century. The "Benvenuto Dialogues" were addressed to a "Prince Henry," identified as "Admiral of the Seas." I have concluded that the Prince Henry addressed in the "Dialogues" was the Scotsman, Henry Sinclair (and not the Portuguese Prince Henry the Navigator, who rose to prominence later, in the 15th century). These letters are yet another intriguing piece of evidence possibly tying the Benvenuto family to travel to America prior to Columbus, via Sinclair. More work needs to be done on this possible connection.

A Lost Leonardo da Vinci Painting

A 2011 article in the Wall Street Journal had an intriguing tie-in to the MacDonald Journal. The article reported that Christie's auction house mistakenly sold a priceless piece of art by Leonardo da Vinci for about $21,000. According to researchers who claim to have identified the origins of the hotly debated painting, it is said to have come from a 500-year-old book of the family history of the Duke of Milan, Ludovico Sforza—the son of Francesco Sforza and Maria Bianca Visconti. The portrait is of the Duke's daughter, Bianca Sforza. As I wrote earlier, da Vinci spent sixteen years in the Sforza Court in Milan, from 1483 to 1499, and was a close friend of the family.

La Bella Principessa **(Bianca Sforza)**

I began to play connect-the-dots with the da Vinci and Sforza relationship. One of da Vinci's students, Jacopo Carucci da Pontormo, painted "Supper at Emmaus." It shows Jesus with a mysterious glowing triangle above his head. The painting raises the question of what ideas and symbolism were brought into northwest Italy from the Holy Land by the Templars. The unusual glowing triangle in the painting reminded me of a first century tomb in Jerusalem excavated in 1985. The excavation uncovered a triangle carved into the façade of the entrance to the tomb. Known as the Talpiot Tomb, some researchers believe this crypt held the bones of Jesus Christ and his family.

Supper at Emmaus   **Talpiot Tomb, Jerusalem**

The triangle symbol on the façade of the tomb frame features a circle within it. Did this triangle framing the circle represent the ancient Goddess, the symbol of an ancient fertility tradition which existed for thousands of years in the Mediterranean world? Recall the odd and mysterious reference to "the Goddess" in the MacDonald Journal. I wondered, was it possible that the Templars carried this symbol back to Italy, where it was incorporated into the Pontormo painting?

A Family Inheritance of Templar Secrets

The Benvenutos were increasingly linked to this complex story, as follows:

*1971, Gustaveste (Gus) Benvenuto sold the Templar Document to Dr. Jackson.

*1820, G. Benvenuto possessed the brass device, understood the markings on it, and had a parchment written in Latin which explained the symbols on the brass device.

*1715, Galvao Benvenuto co-authored a linguistic pamphlet with Gauden Roche which referenced an "Onteora Document," aka "A Year We Remember," located in the Church of San Sigismundo, Cremona, Italy.

It seemed to me that the obvious conclusion was that the Templar Document was known to the Benvenuto family in the 15th century and passed down through the centuries to descendants. There was a burning unanswered question that I kept coming back to: Could a Benvenuto have passed information to Hank Roche in the English prison? Was Benvenuto a member of this secret Order Roche referenced, the one I believe had its origins with the Sforza family? Most important was that Gustaveste Benvenuto's ancestor was the Duchess of Milan, Maria Bianca Visconti.

I began to research the Benvenuto family further. What I found turned up some fascinating connections and revelations.

Three Letters

Letter #1—The French Connection to Hunter Mountain in 1657

Three letters helped shed light on this mystery. The first of these letters was written in French to a "M. Courvesier" by Abraham Robert, and dated *"6 Juin 1657"* (June 6, 1657). It is reproduced below, along with a translation:

6 Juin 1657

M. Courvoisier

Cette jour les douze justiciers, avec Henri II visite le pays de Nuechatel accompagne de vingt-quatre gentilshommes et d'une bonne centaine d'hommes de sa suite du soldats, domestiques et divers. Le soldat de premiere classe M. Roche de Touraine a sur il personne la lettre de M. Van Gelder et M. Block et le document a exhibite la montagne Nord de Nouveau Amsterdam.

Notaire et secretaire du Conseil d'Etat,

Abraham Robert

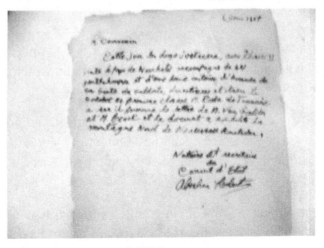

1657 Letter

June 6, 1657

On this day twelve dispensers of justice with Henry II visit the Neuchatel country accompanied by twenty four gentlemen (squires) and a good one hundred men of his escort, soldiers servants and others. The first class soldier Mr. Roche de Touraine has with him the letter from Mr. Van Gelder and from Mr. Block and the document showing the mountain north of New Amsterdam.

[Signed]
Notary and secretary
of
State Council
Abraham Robert

The last line in this letter refers to "*la montagne Nord de Nouveau Amsterdam.*" This translates to "***the mountain North of New Amsterdam.***" Apparently an unknown group was exploring Hunter Mountain in 1657. To add to the mystery, the bottom left of the letter features a sketch of Hunter Mountain written in invisible ink and uncovered by Jackson:

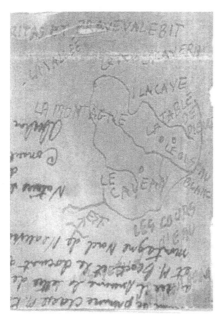

Invisible Ink Reveals Drawing

The invisible ink section identifies eight locations on Hunter Mountain:

Magna est Veritaset pravevalebit
[Great is the Truth and it Shall Prevail]

La Vallee	The valley
La Montagne	The mountain
La Cave	The Cave
La Table De Pierre	The stone table
Le oiseau blanc	The white bird
Le Cavern	The cavern
Les Cours d' Eau	The current of water (a stream)
Le Feu	The Fire
*Est (*with an arrow*)*	East

This map is an exact reflection of what exists on Hunter Mountain today. All these features exist on the mountain in present time—the stone table, the white bird carving, the stream, everything. Later in this book, we will see that every place listed here is also described, in detail, in the Templar Document. I wondered: Had the Templar Document, and de Sudeley's journey, become known to some secret group in 1657?

I had two tasks in front of me: First, could I trace the writer of this letter, and second, could I use this information to identify the people who were visiting Hunter Mountain? I examined the letter more closely. The first part of the letter tells of *twelve dispensers of justice*—does this indicate a group with a legal connection? Henry II ruled France from 1547-1559, a century before this letter is dated; he is said to be visiting *Neuchatel* (Switzerland) with 24 gentlemen/squires and has an escort of one hundred soldiers and servants. The second part of the letter contains the name *Mr Block,* who is likely the explorer Adrian Block, who mapped much of the coastal and river valley areas between present-day New Jersey and

Massachusetts in the early 1600s. Most importantly, the letter indicates there is a *document* showing Hunter Mountain—obviously, this indicates a prior visit to the area.

A clue to the origin of this letter is the name Henry II. To repeat, King Henry II was married to Catherine de Medici, a direct descendant of the 15th century Sforza/ Medici marriage—I believe this reference to "Henry II" refers to one of his descendants, likely a nobleman of his time. There were violent religious wars in France in the 16th century, leading to the dispersal of the Protestant Huguenots, who fled the religious persecution. One of the places they sought refuge was in Dutch-controlled New Amsterdam, on the island of Manhattan and in the surrounding Hudson Valley.

Another possible connection between the Sforza/Visconti/ Medici line and the New Amsterdam colony is Queen Marie d' Medici, a descendant of this line. Queen Marie d' Medici was married to King Henry IV, the king who sponsored Samuel Champlain's exploration of New England and Canada in 1603-1607. She had planned a coup which resulted in her banishment from France and her subsequent settlement in Amsterdam in the Dutch Republic.

These clues were tenuous, but they seemed to be pointing to a connection between the Sforza/Visconti/Medici line and the settlement in New Amsterdam.

Letter #2—Deloros Turns Up in 1918

The second letter I examined contained clues which were anything but tenuous. It was written on March 13, 1918 by an Alistair MacDonald to a "Mr. Le Boeuf" and was found in Dr. Jackson's papers. This bombshell piece of correspondence concerned the unapproved sale of a certain journal from the Charles Morrison Library in Edinburgh, to Mr. Deloros. This was a Freemasonic library; Charles Morrison had donated his books and documents to it in 1849. The letter is reproduced below:

Mr. Le Boeuf

13 March 1918

I am sure that you are aware of the acquired collection of Masonic works of the Late Mr. Charles Morrison on December 14, 1849 and the more recent donations of other hand written works from our Italian Brothers. These were a most valuable addition to the library of the Lodge that will be treasured over the years. However you may not be aware that amongst the hand written material collected there are unrelated documents some of which give notations upon the reverse pertaining to particulars of certain Rites. Others appear to be of no immediate consequence to the subjects of the Lodge. However they should not be discarded as what is not apparent now may come to light in the future. One such item I should call upon you to bear witness to the conditions surrounding its removal from the Library and sold to our esteemed member Mr. Deloros. The Journal of Sir Caradas of Deloros Tower is the document in question. At first glance this appears to have no reference to any Masonic Rites or purpose. It tells about two individuals incarcerated in a Military Prison in England and their plans to escape from it just prior to the World War. This is hand written in an often illegible scrawl using a bluish black ink and consists of some eighteen pages of foolscap folded to create thirty two entries. One such entry mentions the work you have commissioned me to undertake for you. I quote thus from it herein: Entry Number Twelve, "I awake for a normal day. Cache is coming along nicely. The ½ pence slip I have and the back can be used for the Pass. Moaday may get a bit of green PAIN (t) Hank tells me the secret knowledge is cached in 12 scrolls in clay jars hidden in a cave in North America for over a thousand years and the key to its location is in a document kept in the Church of San Sigismundo, Cremona built by Francesco Sforza, Duke of Milan, in the fifteenth Century. I am tired. I sleep." Besides the obvious connotation to Benvenuto's manuscript there is a glaring mistake in the word Monday and the strange arrangement with the small "t" in PAIN (t). These are not errors of negligence however as there is design in this of a more sinister nature. Each entry contains some misspelled words whose incorrect letters spell out a message concerning the location of those 12 jars of scrolls. Anything so concealed without the tender most care would deteriorate over time as parchment or animal skins will not withstand the changing temperatures of the North American climate. Unheated caves and porous clay jars will make little resistance to the elements over time. However if these jars were sealed with the glazing of alum and the scrolls wrapped tightly around a glass core and surrounded by oiled cloth then the jars sealed with clay, wax and lead poured over an anvil to spread it thin, making a pliable metal cover to seal the jars, then buried down below the frost line in a rock vault constructed with such care as to have the seams sealed with clay mixed with the shells of eggs to provide lime and having hot sand to fill the unused space within the prepared cavity then these may have so survived. Our endeavor then appears as one worthy of possible success.

There are many other such hidden messages also included in this ambiguous document. There is at the beginning misspelled words that leave no doubt that the reference to E A P refers to an Entered Masonic Apprentice. Further time is measured by Feast Days of the Roman Catholic Calendar when we know that their church condemns our existence. There is some secret purpose to this which I have thus far been unable to fathom. Also several meaningless and definitely out of context phrases in Spanish and French, one most vulgar, are displayed and are listed here.

Entry Number Twenty-three. "La Memaria del mal es por vida la del bien presta se alvida."=47
Entry Number Forty-one. "Entra la cuna y la sepultura no hay cora segura."=38
Entry Number Fifty-two. "……café NOIR pour nous n'ai pas de lait."=20,24

Considering that these may serve a hidden purpose I have counted the letters of each and the totals follow the quotes. Entry Number Fifty-two contains the French word "NOIR", black, in all capitals. This I felt was significant. Further it is capitalized after the word coffee. If just a four letter word was required then why was not "café" capitalized. I have surmised that the numerical equivalent for this sentence should have two numbers 20 and 24. The 4 letter word is capitalized to stand out as a reference for all foreign language entries I believe.

Since neither the Quran nor the book of Mormon contain sufficient numerical data to be considered I chose the Bible as the book of Psalms has 150 chapters and have recorded here the results as Chapter 20 verse 4,

Chapter 24 verse 4, Chapter 38 verse 4 and Chapter 47 verse 4.

20:4= "Grant thee according to thine own heart, and fulfill all thy council."

24:4= "He that hath clean hands and a pure heart; who hath not lifted up his soul unto vanity, nor sworn deceitfully."

38:4= "For my iniquities are gone over my head; as a heavy burden they are too heavy for me."

47:4= "He shall choose our inheritance for us, the excellency of Jacob whom he loved."

As Symphosius used metaphor in his riddle of the fish, Est domus in terris, clara quae voce resultat.
Ipsa domus resonat, tacticus sed non sonat bospes.
Ambo tamen currunt, bospes simul et domus una.
Thus does this Journal use I believe metaphorical statements to convey some secret instructions for the initiate as the above seems to indicate if the biblical verses are taken out of their original context and perhaps applied to a future quest. So it is that you see this was a valuable document containing secret coded information possibly of immeasurable value that upon the surface appeared to be of no importance. This was probably the reason that it was sold to Mr. Deloros. Perhaps also the mention of Sir Caradas of Deloros Tower refers to a member of Mr. Deloros family. Although the sum was of significant value, and that in itself portents a dire motive, it should have been retained by us. I hope you will agree to this and take steps to insure that no further manuscripts of the Collection or Library are dealt with in this deplorable fashion and those responsible are taken to task for their actions.

It was just luck that I copied the contents of this journal while doing the research you commissioned me to do thus having its content before me or it would have been lost as a result of the sale. If other hidden messages remained in the original these have now been lost to us. I also have been confidentially informed that the sale included a translation of the work of Alanus de Insulus from the Morison Collection where cryptic marginal notations therein tend to support the view that at least one of the clay jars mentioned in the Sir Caradus Journal of the twelve hidden in North America contain an original work of Al-Kuwarizimi entitled " The Compendious Book on Calculation by Completion and Balancing" written about 830 AD. and mentioned in the works of Brother William J. Hughan. Latin translations of this work did not reach Europe or our shores till the 12 century so should this prove to be true then its value is beyond calculable measure. Your attempt to reacquire this document and locate the remaining scrolls, if any, should be undertaken as soon as is within the decorum of our position to do so. This then is the riddle we must solve if success is to be ours. Who made the marginal notations is not known but were most likely done prior to 1840.

As we persue the enlightenment of spiritual knowledge through the manuscripts of the ancients we are assailed by diatribes, overcurious initiates and over lustful brothers more bent on the secular than the spiritual. As our path becomes more complicated I pray Salva me ab ore leonis.

Your humble servant,
Alistair McDonald

MacDonald-Le Boeuf Letter

The letter is clearly referring to the MacDonald Journal (identified in the letter as "The Journal of Sir Caradas of Deloros Tower"). And obviously this "Mr. Deloros" is the same "Doloros" who helped Hank Roche and Liam MacDonald escape from the prison in 1914. The letter relates that the library received donations of "hand written documents from their Italian brothers." This is likely a reference to the Benvenuto family, especially in light of the comment in the letter that, "there is an obvious connotation to "Benvenuto's manuscript"—that is, the Templar Document! This letter proves that knowledge of the Templar Document had survived through the centuries.

The letter also gives us our first clue as to what treasure might be buried on Hunter Mountain. The writer describes an original work by Al-Khwarizmi, a Persian mathematician who lived in the 9th century. The book, entitled *The Compendious Book on Calculation by Completion and Balancing*, was written in 830 AD and was believed to be buried in a clay jar on the mountain. An original 9th century book by Al-Khwarizmi would be worth millions—as the writer says, "beyond calculable measure."

This rare book comprised only a small portion of the treasure. The letter describes, in detail, how "12 jars of scrolls" had been buried, sealed and protected in such a way as to survive "hidden in a cave in North America for over a thousand years."

In addition, the letter confirms Jackson's belief that the misspelled words in the journal serve as some kind of code. The letter, in fact, takes Jackson's conclusion one step further by suggesting the references to various Christian holidays comprise a further (yet unsolved) set of clues.

The letter opens up another mystery. Who is this Mr. Le Boeuf, and why is he involved with Alistair MacDonald, who I think it is fair to say is related to the MacDonald Journal author? MacDonald writes that he copied the journal, "while doing the research you commissioned me to do." The men were clearly looking for the hidden scrolls on Hunter Mountain. Did they find them, using the copy of the journal Alistair MacDonald made before it had been sold? I think this is unlikely. Recall that Jackson uncovered writings made with invisible ink in the original journal—presumably these important clues would not have been seen and copied by Alistair MacDonald when he reproduced the journal. In any event, a further research task that might shed light on this would be to determine if a copy of the journal exists in the Morrison Library in Edinburgh today.

Finally, the letter gives us an important piece of new information: that the MacDonald Journal was sold to Mr. Deloros (aka Doloros). This man turns out to be of great importance as this story continues—he ended up working for certain Vatican officials in the 1940s. This connection to the Vatican is even more intriguing given Alistair MacDonald's warning that the journal purchasers had a "dire motive" in completing their acquisition.

Letter #3—Roche Code Page/Ancient Sailing Directions

The next item I examined (not really a letter) is a tattered single page of paper encased in plastic and sealed with staples, found in Jackson's collection. I do not know where Jackson got it. I speculate that Hank Roche found a document in the cave on Hunter Mountain after his and Liam MacDonald's escape from jail and then later encoded it using a World War I code, as shown below:

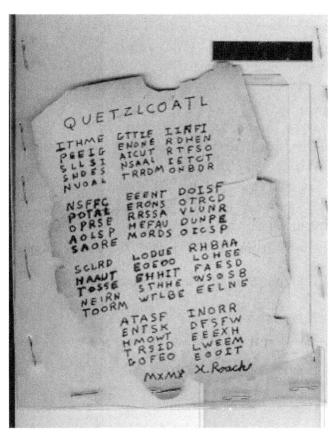

The Roche Code Page

Note that the document is signed in the lower right by "H. Roach," presumably a slight alteration to the "Roche" spelling. Note also the **M X M X** on the bottom left, perhaps a Roman numeral code signifying the date 1919. The X in this date contains an extra barb on the upper right staff and has been called a "Hooked X" by researcher Scott Wolter (see *The Hooked X: The Secret History of North America*).

Researcher Don Ruh cracked this code, using a World War I code contained in the 2012 novel, *The Titanic Secret*, by Jack Steel (see pages 142-145). The decoded message reads:

> ***Sailing directions to the Land of Timbers fur fish and fierce feathered people and of Onteora the store house of ancient knowledges three oaus from the pillars of Hercules SW six suns SSE to the Trident Islands SW here two suns E is the land of riches Apes and temples but go west one moon to a river of blood colored birds and more temples.***

The word "Quetzalcoatl," written across the top, is an important clue. Mr. Ruh, due to his intelligence training, was able to deduce that it was the key to deciphering the code. Recall, this is the third time the name Quetzalcoatl turns up. It is the name the men chose for the boat they used to sail to France after escaping prison, and it was also inscribed on the gold triangle found in the navigation device, pictured below:

Q U E T Z A L C O A T L

A few other clues jump out. First, the reference to the "pillars of Hercules" marks this as an ancient message—the Pillars of Hercules are the ancient name for the Straits of Gibraltar. Second, the name "Onteora" is not commonly known—it could only have come from someone who had access to or had read de Sudeley's log, "A Year We Remember," where he writes, "*in the Land Onteora there they hid the ancient writings, the secrets of the ages.*"

The coded message refers to "*the Land of Timbers fur and fish,*" an apt description of a New England area heavily forested and populated with fur-bearing animals. It further identifies "*fierce, feathered people,*" an obvious reference to the Native Americans.

The journey itself is a bit circuitous. First, the message directs us to sail past the Pillars of Hercules in a southwesterly direction. (The meaning of the words "*three oaus*" is unknown.) Then travel "*SW six suns*"—that is, southwest for six days. Then sail "*SSE* (south by southeast) *to the Trident Islands,*" which are the Tristan de Cunha Islands in the south Atlantic midway between Africa and South America. (It is likely this stop is to replenish stores and get water.) Then we sail "*SW two suns E*"—southwest two days—to the land of "*Riches, apes and temples.*" This is South America. From there we go west to "*a river of blood, colored birds and more temples.*" This may be the La Plata River in Brazil, the source of the valuable Brazilwood, a redwood tree from which the red dye known as "royal red" was produced. (Interestingly, red dye was in high demand in 15th century Italy to dye the gowns of royalty.) The red dye from the cut timbers stained the water in the river red. Though the message is silent, presumably from there we are to follow the coast north to the New England area.

The pieces were beginning to fit together. But still I wondered: How far back does this mystery go?

PART II

The Templar Discovery in Jerusalem

The 12th century dawned with Crusaders capturing Jerusalem. The First Crusade began in 1096 and carried thousands of Christian warriors answering the call of the pope to recover the Holy Land from the Moslems. By 1099, the Crusaders had conquered Jerusalem. The Al Aqsa Mosque—located near the Dome of the Rock on the Temple Mount—was being used by King Baldwin I and later by his brother King Baldwin II as their palace. A team of Templar Knights from Champagne, France occupied part of the Al Aqsa Mosque as their headquarters. It is from the mosque that the Templars set out on their search under the South Wall, part of the ancient wall of the city of Jerusalem.

Many historians believe that the Templars from the Champagne area in France had knowledge that there was something of great value in the tunnels under the South Wall, possibly from Hebrew texts describing measurements of the Temple Mount before it was destroyed by the Roman legions during the 1st century CE. Legendary accounts described riches that may have been hidden here, such as King Solomon's treasure and the Ark of the Covenant. Ancient Hebrew texts existed among Jewish communities in France, particularly in the yeshiva of Troyes, the capital city of Champagne. The nobility of Champagne had friendly dealings with a notable rabbi of the time, known by his acronym, *Rashi*, whose famous writings are studied even today. Secret knowledge of what was hidden in the subterranean tunnels and chambers below the city of Jerusalem may have passed down to the French nobility. It is also worth noting that many of these French nobles from the Champagne region trace their lineage back to the ruling Merovingian dynasty of the 5th-8th centuries, CE—readers may recall the five-armed octopus, believed to be a symbol of the Merovingians, which appears on maps and devices in this mystery.

The Count of Champagne and Hugh de Payens, both from the Troyes area of France, arrived in Jerusalem in 1104, where they stayed until 1116. These men were among the founders of the Knights Templar Order. There was one brief interlude when the Count of Champagne returned to Troyes. Hugh de Payens remained in Jerusalem for twelve years. Little is known of their activities during these years.

Unknown except to certain Champagne nobility was that there were hidden documents and treasure below the ancient South Wall of the Temple Mount of Jerusalem. In a blow by blow description, The Templar Document takes us into the tunnels beneath the Temple Mount, where we learn about the discovery of a chamber which held four ossuaries, a discovery that changed both European and American history.

One of the ossuaries contained scrolls and maps—one map showed a route to a land known as *Onteora,* where a cache of scrolls had been hidden during the 1st century CE when Roman legions advanced on Jerusalem. Three other ossuaries held items such as gold bars, a decoding device, and navigational aides. This discovery launched the Templar voyage to northeastern America, to *Onteora,* in the last quarter of the 12th century.

Obsession and Discovery

Eight hundred years later, Bill Jackson found the Templar Document which recounted this Templar saga. As the reader may recall, Jackson followed a series of clues and leads that took him from Bannerman Island in the Hudson River, to a historical society in Westchester County, New York, to his acquisition of a century-old journal, to a pamphlet written in 1715, and finally to a church in Italy which held the 12th century Templar Document, a portion of which was entitled, *The Onteora Document/A Year We Remember*. As we will read about later, his search also led him to an ancient cave on Hunter Mountain, to a shipwreck off the coast of Newfoundland, and to Oak Island, in Nova Scotia.

As we have learned, a large portion of the Templar Document is comprised of de Sudeley's log recounting his voyage to the Hunter Mountain region, entitled *The Onteora Document/A Year We Remember*. We will now focus on the first part of the Templar Document, which describes the Jerusalem discovery in the first quarter of the 12th century. The document is pictured below, opened to the last page. Note the loosely bound pages:

Last Page of Templar Document

The first page of the Templar Document displays three differing cross symbols, one a so-called Templar cross. The Latin phrase *"Veritas Vos Liberabit,"* translated as "The Truth Shall Set You Free," is written across the page:

The Templar cross in the lower portion of the page is unique in that it features four small circles with X marks inside. These circles are an important Templar feature, which I will return to below in my discussion of Oak Island.

What is the meaning of this phrase? I believe it refers to the "new truth" which emerged from the Templar discovery in the 12th century of a secret tradition of Gnostic beliefs, beliefs which were passed from Jesus through his brother James. These Gnostic beliefs were the "true" teachings of the early Church, unaltered by later Church leaders.

First Page of Templar Document

Flashback: Two Thousand Years Ago in Jerusalem

During the time period 63-70 CE, Jerusalem was bombarded by Roman siege engines. Fierce fighting took place as defenders attempted to save their city. As we shall read about below, during the fighting a secret event occurred: Scrolls, maps, navigational devices and gold bars—along with the bones and skull of a man—were hidden in an ancient chamber deep below a subterranean area of tunnels and cisterns under the South Wall of the Temple Mount. One chamber was carefully chosen as the repository for four ossuaries.

Extensive planning went into the choice of this underground hidden area. A trap was constructed in one of the tunnels that would cause an intruder to fall into a hole lined with protruding knives. The purpose of this trap, of course, was to protect the four ossuaries. If by chance the trap was traversed, a solid wall faced intruders. No one would have known that a chamber existed beyond the wall. This chamber remained untouched for more than a thousand years.

Meanwhile, a second action took place at the same time. Under the cover of darkness a group fled the area with a precious cargo and made it to the harbor either at Jaffa or Caesarea, where ships were waiting to transport the contents to a far off land to the west. This land was known as "Onteora." Most historians are not aware of the evidence showing that the region of, and the route to, Onteora was known before the 1st century CE by Carthage, Rome and the Hasmonean kings of Judea (ruling in the 2nd to 1st centuries BCE). The coast of Judea was an active international shipping area, as evidenced by ancient shipwrecks stretching along the east Mediterranean coast. Ships from this area sailed throughout the Mediterranean and even across the Atlantic in search of minerals such as gold, silver, tin, copper, lead and iron. Carthaginian and Roman coins have been found scattered across America, evidencing these journeys.

After the Roman destruction of Jerusalem in 70 CE, the Temple Mount platform lay desolate and in ruins until Emperor Hadrian, in 130 CE, built a temple dedicated to Jupiter on the site where the two Jewish Temples had once stood—the first built by Solomon and destroyed in 586 BCE by the Babylonians and the second built by Herod in 20-19 BCE and destroyed in 70 CE by the Romans. After the Romans, the Byzantine period followed. In 636 CE the city fell to the Arabs; they built the Dome of the Rock on the Temple platform and the Al Aqsa Mosque on the South Wall.

**The Dome of the Rock (top) and
Al Aqsa Mosque (Gray Dome, Lower Left on the South Wall)**

Prior to the construction of the Al Aqsa Mosque, a Byzantine church, St. Mary's of Justinian, stood at this location. Beneath this church there was a Roman level of ruins, and beneath those existed ancient Jewish ruins, as pictured below:

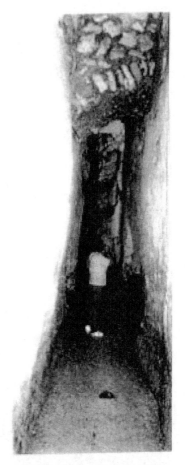

Beneath Western Wall

There are no photos of the area deep beneath the Temple Mount and no archaeological excavation is allowed below the Temple Mount platform by Moslem authorities. The photo shown above was taken by the author in the Western Wall Archaeological Tunnel excavated deep below the Temple Mount. The remains of houses from the 1st century CE are visible, including the so-called "Burnt

House" evidencing the Roman destruction of Jerusalem. The photo gives some idea of the immense stones in these tunnels, some of which weigh 100 tons or more. The Templar team made their way through ancient tunnels such as this in their exploration in the early years of the 12th century.

Summary: The Templars in Jerusalem

1096: Godfroi de Bouillon, Duke of Lower Lorraine, descendant of Charlemagne, leads Crusader army to Jerusalem. He becomes King Baldwin I in 1098.

1100: Baldwin II, brother of Godfroi de Bouillon (Baldwin I), becomes King of Jerusalem.

1104-1106: Count Hugh of Champagne from Troyes and Hugh de Payens, his relative, arrive in Jerusalem. In 1108 the Count returns to France. Payens remains in Jerusalem and takes part in the exploration under the South Wall.

1114: Count Hugh of Champagne returns to Jerusalem and remains in Jerusalem for two years, returning to France in 1116. Hugh de Payens remains in Jerusalem for twelve years from 1104 to 1116. When Count Hugh of Champagne returns to France he gives the monk Bernard land for the abbey Clairvaux. Bernard becomes famous as Bernard of Clairvaux.

1119: Hugh de Payens becomes the first Grand Master of the Templars and serves until 1136. Godfroi de St. Omer is his right hand man. Count Hugh of Champagne leaves France and becomes a Templar in 1125.

1128/1129: Council of Troyes.

1128: Hugh de Payens travels to Normandy and England and meets King Henry I, who gives him gold and land for "Temple Church" in London.

1128: Hugh de Payens goes to Scotland and meets King David I, who gives land given for Balantrodoch, a Templar site.

Templar Activity Around South Wall

In the early twelfth century, after the Crusader conquest of Jerusalem, the Templars occupied the Al Aqsa Mosque on the southern wall of the Temple Mount and found an ancient entry to the tunnels beneath the mosque. (This area was named Solomon's Stables by the Crusaders, who used underground vaults to stable their horses.) The Templars built a massive tower outside the Double Gate and blocked up the ancient gates so they could explore and work in secrecy from the interior of the mosque. The photo below shows the dome of the Al Aqsa Mosque, which is on the western side (left side of image) of the ancient South Wall. Solomon's Stables are located on the eastern (right) side of the wall.

South Wall

Though there is not widespread acceptance among historians as to what the Templars found in their excavations, there is little doubt they occurred. As historian R.W. Hamilton wrote, "Everything goes to show that certain vaults are the work of the Templar Knights who occupied the Aqsa during the 12th century." (See *The Structural History of the Aqsa Mosque: A Record of Archaeological Gleanings From the Repairs of 1938-1942*, by R.W. Hamilton, F.S.A. Director of Antiquities Palestine.) Hamilton's report is authoritative in documenting that the Templars were in an area below the Al Aqsa Mosque. He established that the masonry was of Templar origin in the vaulted areas and showed mason's marks left during Templar renovations during the twelfth century. Hamilton's conclusion is clear: "The Templars occupied the mosque and did major construction work there."

Also clear is the distinctive Templar cross found carved on a wall in a tunnel by Captain Charles Warren in his exploration in 1867-1870, pictured below:

Templar Cross Found by Captain Warren Beneath Temple Mount

Warren was the only person since the Templar exploration in the 12th century to explore the subterranean chambers beneath the Temple Mount. Warren was able to sink shafts deep below the Temple Mount and dig with permission from the Ottoman authorities.

Captain Warren Beneath Temple Mount

It should also be noted that Warren was a Freemason who founded the *Quatuor Coronati* lodge in London—did he possess ancient knowledge that sparked his search? His book, the *Recovery of Jerusalem,* stands as a testament to this exploration and is the only existing factual description of the tunnels and cisterns that lie beneath the Temple Mount.

Other, that is, than the Templar Document we are about to examine.

The Templar Document

With the above as background, I now turn to the Templar Document itself, as we explore beneath the Temple Mount along with the Templar knights in the early years of the 12th century. The opening section of the Templar Document is written in the Theban script and translated into Latin. Theban was in use in the 12th century. It was often used by Cistercian monks and therefore would have been known to the Templars. The old form of Theban (pre 17th century) does not have the letters "J" and "U" and helps us date the Templar Document as ancient. Below is a Theban alphabet chart from Wallace Budge's book, *Amulets and Talismens.*

Theban Script. Note that Letters "J" and "U" Are Not Included

Recall that the strange markings on the brass device were Theban, and that the fragments in the clay tube from the garden ornament also were written in Theban.

The Templar Document begins with the name "Aelia Capitolina," the Roman name for Jerusalem.

Passage 1

AELIA CAPITOLINA

We six have now entered beneath the South Wall. The entrance is very narrow but opens up soon into a large natural cavern of limestone. Godfroi says that we should remove our armor, you too Hugh he says to me and we all comply as it will be bulky in the confines of the crypts. Jacques leads the way with a lantern extended on a pole the ring fixed over the spike of the axe. The oil sputters in the dampness of the chamber.

We retain our weapons and maile Godfroi and Beaumont have helmets to protect them from the falling debris from the roof. Moisture penetrates from the street above the roof. One end of the cavern glows with an odd green glow. We proceed towards it cautiously and see steps going down. Bernrd calls out De Paynes you take the rear. Jacques keep the long ropes and Buford to go back for the scaling ladder. It will be slow going. I could smell the stench from the entrance. There were about a dozen steps down and we were among the dead. God Save Us.

The *South Wall* is the historic ancient city wall that surrounds the Temple Mount on the southern side. As described above, the Templars found an area beneath the South Wall that gave them entry to the tunnels below the Temple Mount.

The first name in this passage is *Godfroi*. This possibly refers to Godfrey de St. Omer, an early founder of the Knights Templar. He is giving orders to a man named *Hugh.* Godfroi orders them all to remove their armor but directs a special order to Hugh, to wit: *"you too Hugh he says to me."* The words "to me" mean that Hugh is the writer of this section. This could be Hugh, the Count of Champagne. He was in Jerusalem in 1104-06 and again in 1114-16; he eventually became a Templar Knight in 1124. Or it could be Hugh de Payens, cofounder and first Grand Master of the Templar Order.

Whoever Hugh is referring to, a later line in this passage makes it clear that Hugh de Payens was indeed part of this group: *"**Bernrd calls out de Paynes you take the rear.**"*

It is possible that *Bernrd* is Bertrand de Blanchfort, Templar Grand Master from 1156-1159. *Beaumont, Jacques,* and *Buford* are not known.

The passage mentions *limestone,* an accurate description of the type of rock in Jerusalem.

Confines of the crypts: They see crypts or burial caves under the South Wall. Hundreds of burial caves have been found around Jerusalem, some in the southern section of the Temple Mount.

Buford is sent back for a *scaling ladder.* Note that Buford is not one of the "We six" of the opening line—he is a seventh man. His retrieving a scaling ladder may mean that some of the men had been in the cave beforehand and were prepared for what equipment they might need. (Godfroi ordering the men to remove their armor in anticipation of it being bulky ahead further evidences a prior incursion.)

The words, **"stench from the entrance .... we are among the dead,"** are also instructive. They are in an area of crypts. Some of these burial caves were close to or under the ancient walls that surrounded the Temple Mount.

Passage 2

Jackson left a note saying that the remainder of page 1 was destroyed and pages 2 and 3 were missing. The record now begins on page 4. Jackson remarks that *Hugh* is not described in the first person in this section, thus the writer has changed.

What could have been on the two and a half pages missing from this first section? Whatever was on these missing pages apparently was so important it was removed. Another mystery.

> *The Ivri have taken much care in the structure. We are now down to the fourth level. The smell from decayed and rotting flesh is almost gone here. Only bones are in the holes cut into the walls. Hugh's arm brushes a corpse and the head falls into the path. I cross myself and gently place it back.*

Hugh is the only person mentioned in this passage. He is not the writer. The man who crosses himself is the writer.

The first word *Ivri* means Hebrew. They are passing through a Jewish burial tomb. Jews in the 1st century CE followed a burial custom in which they cut niches in the walls of the tomb to place the bodies of their deceased family members. After a year the bodies would decompose and the bones would be collected and placed in the ossuary specially prepared by the family. This practice existed from 30 BCE to 70 CE and sporadically until around 135 CE. What the men must have stumbled upon—what they call *bones in the holes*—are the uncollected bones that were left unburied due to the Roman destruction of Jerusalem.

The Templars passed through three levels and were now down in the fourth level. These tunnels had been untouched since the 1st century CE.

Passage 3

The walls are mostly mud here but the path is set on stone and slopes steadily down. The entrance to this level was from the end of the last but not by steps as before but by a descending ramp turning on itself so we walk below the way above. The first level was about ten chains long and the second nine chains the third and this about six chains and six rods. At the seventh rod we again descend by steps to another level turning once again to now walk North as we did on the first level. It is poorly kept but there is no bodies here.

The way is narrow Godfroi's sword scrapes the walls bringing down caked mud from above. Our feet are covered with water. There are rats and other vermin here. We have killed several. The air is close and it is hard to breathe. The candles flicker and the lamp has gone out twice.

We are several hands short of six rods when Bernrd suddenly cries out and disappears to his waist. He has fallen into a hole Only his sword and scabbard turned on the trillion and fron have saved him from going down. To this he clings. The water suddenly all drains into the hole. Beaumont and Jacques pull him up. Lionel has lit a torch and prepares to throw it into the hole but Bernrd cries Nay. There may be oil below. Godfroi states it is the smell of the dead but Bernrd say Nay.

In this passage there is one missing name out of the six Templars—Hugh. It stands to reason he must be the writer. A new man, *Lionel*, is introduced. It is possible that Lionel is Lionel de Walderne, part of the royal family of Denmark.

This dramatic passage describes a descending stone path going down several levels. Each level is measured. The first level is 10 chains long, equaling 660 feet; the second level is 9 chains, equaling 594 feet; the third level is 6 chains and 6 rods, equaling 396 feet. The total of 1,650 is more than one-quarter mile. They are deep within the tunnels below the Temple Mount. Just short of six rods, Bernrd falls into a hole. They have come to a deadly trap.

Deep within the subterranean tunnels a deadly trap had been constructed to prevent further passage. The six Templars, joined by Buford, come to a hidden "deep hole." Bernrd partially falls into the hole but is saved when parts of his armor catch on the sides.

Passage 4

We lower the lantern by a rope into the hole. It is ten hands wide and very deep. From the sides around it are protruding old rusted metal points some sword lengths long. A man would be sliced up falling through that and the lamp reveals at the bottom spikes. Why such a trap almost to the end of a blank wall? What does it guard states Bernrd. Hugh probes the wall when the scaling ladder brought forth and lain over the hole for us to walk onward to the far wall. It is mud but half his blades length he reaches something solid. We remove our daggers and dig. The solid is wood. Lionel uses the axe and we are through the timbers some two to three hands wide. We are into dirt and through it with half the length of a spear.

In this passage Bernrd, Hugh and Lionel are the main characters. But none is the writer.

Bernrd questions why there is a trap at the end of a blank wall. The lantern is lowered by a rope and they estimate the width of the void—ten hands wide is about six feet. The depth is not given but they note it is very deep with rusted metal points protruding from the sides and metal spikes at the bottom. Obviously the trap meant death for anyone entering this tunnel. They question why there is a trap at the end of a blank wall. Bernard suspects that the trap hides something beyond the wall; they dig and probe.

Passage 5

> *We open the hole to reveal a huge chamber of natural rock. The roof extends far above us but there is a small opening far above as we see light through it. It must be from the street above on the surface. We have entered this place two hours after Terce and by the candle mark it must be near Sext.*
>
> *There are metal sconces on the walls but they are very rusted and we do not use them to hold our lights. This is a curious place. It is almost a chain long and half a chain wide. There is a cross bar of metal at one end where a flat slab of rock rests. It has a groove at one end and a hollow in its center. There is a dark stain all over it. Jacques states it is an Ivri sacrifice alter. The bones of sheep and birds beneath our feet tell that he speaks the truth. Behind it the bronze bar forms a short rail from which seven small cups hang. The Ivri symbol states Bernrd.*

They cut through the wall with their daggers and opened a hole. Tunnels, ramps and passages deep underground lead to an ancient, concealed, huge chamber of natural rock (limestone). There is a small opening which brings in a shaft of light. They surmise there may be a street above and archaeological investigations confirm that there were streets and markets running in front of the South Wall. Terce and Sext are times of the day, three and six o'clock.

Metal sconces on the walls indicate past use. A chain long and half a chain wide means the chamber would be almost 66 feet long and 33 feet wide.

The altar with a dark stain on it of dried blood and the bones of sheep and birds all point to a sacrificial ritual. Jacques knows about this ritual and says it is an "Ivri sacrifice alter." Bernrd knows about Jewish symbols and he recognizes the *Ivri* symbol as a menorah (a Jewish candelabra) based on the "seven small cups." From what is recorded here Bernrd knew a little Hebrew and also knew about the ancient rite of Jewish sacrifice and about the menorah. Where did Jacques and Bernrd acquire this knowledge? One possibility is that Jacques and Bernrd, knights from the Champagne area in northern France, had contact with the Jewish community that lived in Troyes, the capital city of Champagne. These unknown connections open up the possibility that they had learned much more about the ancient Temple Mount. Had they also been told where to dig?

Passage 6

> *There are no seats except around the walls there are flat stone pieces set upon other stones so as to provide a seating place but no evidence that was the use. There is a trough and water within, a ritual bath perhaps. It runs through a hole in the wall. This is where the water under foot came from. One day it will undermine and collapse this level.*
>
> *At the four corners of a squared floor defined by marble stones set in the floor forming an oblong square rests four limestone boxes. They are called bone boxes and the Ivri bury the bones of their dead in them. There is a loculi behind each one but no bodies are within.*

The unknown writer describes the "trough" as a possible ritual bath, thus they are familiar with the "mikvah" bath, a Jewish ritual of purification—a mikvah requires running water, which explains the water running through a hole in the wall. Was this mikvah once used by priests in attendance at the Temple who had to purify themselves so as not to contaminate the sacred Temple area?

The writer uses the term "bone boxes," which are ossuaries. The use of the word "loculi" is important and this is the correct description. As previously discussed, in the 1st century CE the Jews of Jerusalem buried their dead in tombs cut into the bedrock slopes surrounding the city of Jerusalem. These burial chambers were lined by single rows of burial niches called "kokim" ("loculi" in Latin) cut into the walls. The deceased were placed in the niches until the bodies decomposed.

Ossuaries, or "Bone Boxes," from the First Century

The ossuaries were only in use for a short period and help us date the tomb to the 1st century CE.

Passage 7

To the right of the Alter stone we open that one first it has a rosette of six petals interlaced with small dots and the flat lid is very pitted and worn as would be due to the damp. Writing on the long side indicates one dinar two obol and the writing may be a name but it is very worn and there is the bones of a man within. We count the ribs.

Hugh notes it is strange the head is separated not on the spine but cleanly severed. This man died when his head was cut off with a very sharp axe. The bones show little splintering where the axe slid over them. There is a name and I read a little Ivri so it is to me that falls the making out of what is written. It is Yon. To us this would be John.

Bernrd bags the bones.

Hugh sees the ossuary with the bones of a man whose head is separated. He describes how this was done. The description is chilling—this ossuary contains the bones of a man with his head cut cleanly off. Bernrd bags the bones from this ossuary. The name on the ossuary is "Yon," or "John" to the Templars (there is no J in Hebrew). The name on the ossuary contained a rosette of six petals; the rosette was a standard decoration on ossuaries in the 1st century CE.

Writing on one side of the ossuary read "one dinar" and "two obol." This is a known tradition, a practice known as "Charon's obol" that is followed in the Hellenic world. The dinar and obol were coins placed with the deceased to pay the ferry man, Charon, to carry the deceased across the river separating the living from the dead.

The bones in the ossuary are bagged by Bernrd. I believe, based on comments in Passage 8, that they were taken with the other contents to Castrum Sepulchri in Italy, pictured here:

Castrum Sepulchri; Modern Name is Seborga

The contents of this ossuary potentially have far reaching implications. Could these have been the bones of John the Baptist, whom the Templars were known to revere? And could the head be related to legends about the Templars revering a skull, often identified as Baphomet?

Passage 8

> *In the box to the left are twelve long clay tubes with writings in one that we break the wax seal on. It is all in the Ivri text and I see that it is of the book of God but in scriptuo continua making it most difficult to read. There are others in a strange script too. We take them all of them. Bernrd states we will bring them to Castrum Sepulchri with us. There is a man called Jakobus there of the Germanic tribes who may be able to read them.*

Twelve long clay tubes with writings in Ivri (Hebrew) text are found in this ossuary. The writer recognizes that the text is the "book of God" and that it is written in *Scriptuo continua*. This is an ancient method of writing the Torah, in which the Hebrew letters run together continuously and there are no spaces between words. This indicated that the writings in the clay tubes are ancient texts. Other writings are described as being "in a strange script." This is not likely to be Greek, as Greek would be recognizable. It may be Theban, which would be the first evidence we have that the Theban alphabet dates back before the 1st century CE.

My research has revealed more about the contents of these clay tubes. Each tube held three to four scrolls totaling approximately thirty-six to forty-eight scrolls. Ancient maps were with the scrolls. One map showed the route to the "Land of Onteora" in northeastern America. Another map showed the sea route to Loango in West Africa. Later we will learn that Sudeley sailed there but offers no reason as to why. I can't help but wonder what other lost maps and knowledge these scrolls held.

Bernrd gives us a most important clue by telling us the location where they will bring the clay tubes (and presumably the other items they find)—*Castrum Sepulchri*, in Seborga, Italy. In the 12th century, Castrum Sepulchri was the repository and library for the relics, artifacts and writings found in Jerusalem. It was known as the *Shrine of Relics.*

Jakobus of the Germanic Tribes (meaning Jewish) is likely a man named Jacob, a Jewish scholar who was working at Castrum Sepulchri. Bernrd knows of him which means that he has been to Castrum Sepulchri. It was not unusual for Jewish scholars to work as translators in the medieval world. Translation was an important occupation of Jewish scholars in the medieval period as they knew Arabic. The Rhineland held large Jewish communities in the early middle ages. The Crusades were a dangerous time for Jews in the Rhineland and in parts of France where they faced baptism or death. Bernard of Clairvaux was a staunch opponent of violence against the Jews, perhaps because he needed them to translate texts brought back to France by the Templars.

Passage 9

> *The box at the back now on my right is sealed with lead seals over a lip on the edge of the box and its cover. This is unusual. There is a design of pillars on one long side. This could be a doorway to an Ivri temple. We cut the seals off and Bernrd takes one to go with us. Within is some rotten sheep hides. Even after a long time the smell of the sheep remains in them.*
>
> *Below them and stacked in a pyramid shape are small elongated blocks of Gold each stamped with a seal that Beaumont recognizes as that of the Ivri King Solomon.*
>
> *This is a treasure beyond our dreams. This will help the money moving plans.*

The box at the back—they tell us this ossuary is sealed with "lead seals" on the upper part of the ossuary, which is designed with "pillars on one long side." The pillars remind them of the doorway to an Ivri temple—this could be the Temple of Solomon. Again we see how knowledgeable they are of Jewish traditions.

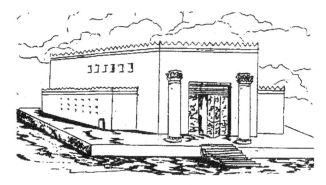

Jewish Temple with doorway and pillars

They cut the lead seals off the ossuary and see "rotten sheep hides" inside, which still smell despite their age. Below the sheep hides are "elongated blocks of gold each stamped with a seal," stacked in a pyramid shape. Bernrd recognizes the seal of King Solomon, likely a six-pointed star.

Their comment that this is a "treasure beyond their dreams" needs no explanation. Were they searching for this from legendary accounts of treasure hidden below the Temple Mount? I believe the reference to their "money moving plans" is a reference to the banking empire the Templars built soon after this discovery.

Passage 10

> *The last box is now opened quickly expecting more Gold but below the sheep hides we find none. Instead there are five devices of metal and of curious type. Bernrd states we will bring them to Hildagard of Bingen who works on the Liber Subtilitatum Diversarum Naturarum Creaturarum in the Shara Mountains and may be able to discern their use. I will describe each as best I can.*

Bernrd's statement about Hildegard of Bingen anchors this document in history. Hildegard of Bingen was born in 1098 and died 1179. She was a political advisor and correspondent to kings and popes, a twelfth century abbess who founded two abbeys and wrote extensively on scientific subjects, natural healing and mysticism. She was basically unknown until recent times; there has been a revival of interest in her in modern times. Bernrd must have known her, and also that she was writing *Liber Subtilitatum Diversarum Naturarum Creaturarum* ("The Book of the Secrets of the Different Nature of Creatures"), describing the healing power of plants and animals. Letters exist showing extensive correspondence between Hildegard of Bingen and Bernard of Clairvaux, the founder of the Cistercian Order and an early supporter/ally of the Templars. Archives from Seborga attest to Bernard of Clairvaux's visits to Castrum Sepulchri. He referred a "Great Secret" in 1113—was he referring to this Templar find in Jerusalem? Was it Bernard of Clairvaux who sent the Templars to Jerusalem, and also to consult with Hildegard?

Five devices of metal and of curious type. This is one of the most extraordinary discoveries. As we shall see, these were ancient navigational devices. They are described in detail in the following passages.

Passage 11

> *Now a shaft of light passes from the hole above and illuminates a spot on the marble floor. We stare as it reveals a big eye. When we place torches to it we see it is laid out with tiles once of many colors in the shape of a big fish. Beaumont thinks by the candle mark it is the noon mark we see. Since it is Midsummer's Eve Bernrd believes it sets a mark on the eye on purpose and this was an early Christian meeting place.*

Light shines on something on a spot on the marble floor which looks like a "big eye." It is a mosaic in the shape of a large fish. The light comes from a hole far above the chamber. This may have been a vent (called a "nefesh hole") built in the burial chamber to adhere to Jewish religious law which allowed the forces of impurity to exit a burial chamber.

Midsummer's Eve is the summer solstice. The menorah, the altar for sacrifices, the ossuaries and the ritual bath with running water (mikvah) all mark the tomb as a Jewish one. Possibly the first group using the tomb were Jews, and then later users were followers of Jesus. The fish was the symbol of early followers of Jesus.

Passage 12

The five metal devices found in the ossuary as described in Passage 10—four navigation devices and one decoder—are all part of Passage 12. I subdivide the passage into five sections below:

DEVICE I

It is a bronze cup about a hand wide lined with fired clay of a brown color. At the center bottom of the cup embedded in the clay rises a glass spike about two finger high coming to a point. A small conical shaped piece with a thin iron needle protruding from two sides of it is balanced on the tip of the spike. No matter which way we face the needle still points the same but it we bring a sword by it it spins around settling back to it original position when the sword is removed.

The writer here describes a compass with a magnetized needle. The Templars experiment with their sword and see that the needle reverts to its original position when the sword is removed. The invention of the compass is attributed to the Chinese circa 200 BCE. Apparently, knowledge of the technology had made its way to Jerusalem in the first century CE. It is curious to note that the use of the compass did not reach Europe until the early 13th century. Did the idea of a compass with a magnetized needle come to Italy from the Templar discovery?

DEVICE II

It is about a hand by a link and is made of brass. There is a basket of wire formed in a round shape upon its flat surface. The flat surface is cut so as to resemble the shape of an animal with four small feet a wide head at which is a hole and through it a metal brass rod about the size of a small finger about one link long and fitted at its top a square piece of metal like a shield boss slightly conical in shape with two flat handles. The handles have horizon way slots in them and across each is a fine thread of silver so fixed that it can be moved along the length of the slot. At the center of the boss is a hole square in shape and two silver threads are in this also the sky way fixed the horizon way movable as the other two. A round piece of bronze weighted on its under side with lead rests in the basket so as to be turnable in it and inscribed with odd characters I recognize as those on the scrolls. A five pointed star surrounds them and the numbers I, III, V, VII, IX and some numbers that look as the Arab script but I am not sure that is what it is.

The writer mentions a five-pointed star surrounded by Roman numerals I, III, V, VII and IX. He says other numbers may be Arab script but he is not sure. And he mentions "odd characters" that he saw on the scroll—could they be Theban letters? The reference to the "sky" and "horizon" indicate this is some kind of navigational device.

In an effort to learn more about this and the other devices, Jackson engaged in a longtime correspondence with Fr. Michelle Piccirillo (an esteemed biblical scholar and archaeologist, known for his work on the Madaba Mosiac Map in Jordan; he taught at the Studium Biblicum Franciscanum in Jerusalem). Fr. Piccirillo, who also assisted Jackson in other areas of his research, referred to this device as a "Star Finder," elaborating that, *"The numbers seem to indicate that these are the months of the year. If that is so then a number of voyages were required to complete these observations and that alone indicates a regular trade route."* In other words, the device had been used regularly in the past as a navigational aid using the stars.

DEVICE III

A tube of metal could be armor but thinner shaped square the length of two mans' feet and smaller at one end but a hand square at the other. Again silver threads are placed equal spaces apart both horizon way and sky way along the sides of the square at the large end. The small end has a little lip on it and makes a small hole. Above the large end on one side is a triangle of metal from whose point hangs a cord with a small pointed weight. Along the bottom of the triangle forming the top of the tube are lines in equal spaces and markings that appear to be numbers as appear upon an Astrolabe.

It may be to measure inclines.

The writer appears to be describing an astrolabe, pictured below:

Astrolabe

An astrolabe was used to calculate the altitude of celestial bodies, to help determine latitude. This is consistent with the description, "It may be to measure inclines."

DEVICE IV

This is best described as sailors hooks. It consists of metal rods small and bendable in size formed into a square with one vertical side bent like a long bow. Above the center of the bow is a horizontal rod to the opposite side with one curved above and

---

below forming a fowl wishbone. Towards the bottom end is another horizontal rod to the edge. Diagonally across these are four other rods not evenly spaced running from top to bottom. Across the top in the first and second squares formed by the rods are two small wire loops centered on each square. On the second horizontal rod is a third and fourth wire loop. On the lower wishbone line two more and one each near the bottom on the diagonal rods.

There is a small flat plate fixed with wires to the bottom edge on which an arrow is depicted by hammered indents pointing to a star shape and the word KOLCHABE. Below this are the following words,

LUPUS, CORINA, ARA, AQUARIUS, ROM, GEMINI. Opposite each are the following also MOON FULL, LYRA, SYGNUS, MOON FULL, MOON PERIH.

This device, described as "sailors hooks," is another navigational device. Note the similarity between the constellations and moon phases listed at the bottom of this passage and those marked on the mysterious brass device discussed earlier in Chapter 1, again connecting these groups over the centuries. Fr. Piccirillo, the scholar who helped Jackson understand Device II, wrote of this device:

[Device IV] appears similar to a drawing from a museum on Easter Island—The Marshall Island Chart. The people used this type of device to populate all of the Pacific Islands and also reached South America. The key to its use is the length of the "hook" or little rings placed at intervals on the horizontal rods. Through these are viewed a star, most often the Pole Star with one horizontal bar on the horizon. If the star fell in the loop then you were on your starting latitude. If you were above the loop you had to go south to reach your latitude and below you would go north. The device found in the ossuary worked in a similar fashion but used two stars as a guide—one placed at

a junction to the right of the hook and to the left with the Pole Star in the Hook.

A picture of such a device is displayed below; note the "hook" or "ring" or "loop" in the upper right quadrant, through which a navigator viewed the pole star to determine his location:

Marshall Island Stick Chart

The word *Kolchabe* is an important clue that confirms the device's use as described by Fr. Piccirillo. Kochab is a star in the bowl of the constellation Ursa Minor (the Little Bear.) This star was used as the pole star from circa 1200 BCE to 500 CE by the Phoenicians for night sailing. Professor of Astronomy Louis Winkler (State College, Pennsylvania, retired) writes:

There was no bright star near the pole during the 1st millennium BC. However, there was a bright star in the constellation of Ursa Minor 12 degrees distant from the north celestial pole in 1000 BCE and it served as the pole star.

This star was Kochab. Its minimum and maximum elevations could be used to determine geographic latitude and true north. Professor Winkler continues:

> *A voyage from the Mediterranean taking the northern route via the Greenland and Labrador Currents could have employed Kochab readily. Circumstances for navigation from the Mediterranean Sea across the Atlantic were favorable...*

Device IV, therefore, would have been of essential use to a navigator crossing the Atlantic in ancient times. In fact, I believe it was used by de Sudeley and the Templars in their 12th century voyage to Hunter Mountain.

DEVICE V

This is a large brass circle with a small hole in the center and a triangle shape at the top and bottom. These triangles are not on the same radii. At the sides on these on a smaller radii are a square hole and an oblong. One smaller than the other.

There are two smaller holes equal distance either side of the central one. Through these are two pins that are fixed to a second disk below of the same size and of bronze. A pin passes from this second plate into the center hole of the upper one. The two smaller pins pass through this plate also and are joined by a piece of flat strip at the back. Between the two pins at the back is a cross piece much like a shield strap but rigid.

When the flat piece is pulled the two pins retract from the top plate and it can be turned on the center pin its end flattened out. The flat strip between the pins at the back acts as a spring to push the pins back in when the next set of holes is reached. There are twenty four sets of holes around the center of the top plate. Between the two plates is a piece of dried leather fixed to the back disk by four small tabs bent over from the back disk.

> *The twenty four sets of holes are through this piece as is the two small rods and the center pin.*
>
> *Burnt into the leather on three circles of various diameters are three series of letters. When the Arabic letter is in the upper triangle then the other letter is in the lower and Ivri letter in the right square and a series of dots in the oblong but an Arabic A does not repeat and Ivri A but of the other symbol and the dots I don't know. It is some sort of coding device. Purpose unknown. When we emerge from the caverns we are just in time for None.*

Device V is a decoder. It has Arabic and Ivri (Hebrew) letters and a series of dots. They leave the caverns at the time of "None" prayers, which is the evening. This is the last entry in the Templar Document, but far from the last step in this adventure.

The Jerusalem Discovery, 1104-1116

To sum up, the navigation devices, the decoder, the maps, gold, and the bones and skull of a man named John were taken from the Jerusalem tomb by the Templars. The Templar Document states, and my research confirms, that these items were brought to Castrum Sepulchri in Seborga, Italy where the scrolls were translated by Cistercian monks with help from Jewish scholars. The scrolls told of a hidden cache of treasure in a land called Onteora and a map (or maps) showed the route.

Bernard of Clairvaux was instrumental in formulating plans to recover the scrolls. He was related to Hugh de Payens, the first Templar Grand Master and one of the six Templars who explored the Jerusalem tomb as described in the Templar Document. (Later, de Payens met with King Henry I in England and received land for Temple Church in London, the first Templar headquarters in England. He also traveled to Scotland and met with King David I, receiving the land for Balantrodoch and Kilwinning. I believe de Payens told both kings of the Templar discovery in Jerusalem.)

The Council of Troyes was convened in 1128, at which Pope Honorious II gave the Templars extraordinary powers and autonomy. Planning began for the mission to northeast America, known as Onteora. The mission was sanctioned by Bernard of Clairvaux. A Templar team brought the navigation devices to Hildegard of Bingen, who trained the men in their use. It should be mentioned that, based on the opinions of experts, these devices had been used in the Atlantic as early as the 1st century BCE.

A journey across the Atlantic was not without its challenges, however. The Templars turned to Scandinavian allies who had experience navigating in the north Atlantic—in particular, King Valdemar I of Denmark. Eskil, the Danish Archbishop of Lund and an appointee of King Valdemar I, was a close friend of Bernard of Clairvaux, which resulted in the spread of Cistercian monasteries in Denmark and along the Baltic shores and an alliance between the Templars and the Danish king. Recall that one of the Templars in the Jerusalem tomb, *Lionel*, may have been Lionel de Walderne, a member of the royal family of Denmark.

With this as background, we now turn to Ralph de Sudeley's journey to Onteora.

PART III

Templar Voyage and Mission to Land of Onteora

We now come to the meat of this story: Ralph de Sudeley's account of the years from 1178 to 1180. His mission was to recover scrolls hidden in the 1st century CE, transported from Jerusalem to Onteora, where (we will learn) a community of Norse and Welsh stood guard over them.

It is worth reviewing de Sudeley's deposition again, recorded in 1180 in Castrum Sepulchri:

> *I Ralf de Sedely shall undertake this quest by the Grace of God and the order of the Grand Master Amand. I state that all of the above is as I remember it and to so place my sign and name below to so attest this by the Grace of God in the Year of our Lord 1180. (MCLXXX).*
>
> *Place My Sign*
> *Ralp de Sedely*

As I wrote earlier, when Dr. Jackson purchased the document in 1971, the signature of *Ralp de Sedely* was verified as authentic by Franco Franzetti, a restorer of ancient documents working in the Vatican Library.

The de Sudeley family crest, reproduced below, also appears on this deposition next to the signature. The crest matches crests on the Sudeley Castle in Winchcombe, Gloucestershire, England and also crests appearing on the genealogical chart of the castle today.

De Sudeley Family Crest

This account was recorded by a monk in the abbey as *Le Voyage de MCLCXXVIII A Onteora A Moine de Dominicnus Il Revevoit La Deposition Avec M Svedley.* This is translated as "The Voyage of 1178 to Onteora a Monk of Dominicans Received the Deposition of M Svedley."

As readers may recall, de Sudeley entitled his account, "A Year We Remember," which comprises a significant portion of the various writings I refer to as the Templar Document.

Table des Matiers

The first page in the document is the *Table des Matiers,* or Table of Subjects, written in Theban. There are 11 lines of Theban text. The first two lines translate to the words, *Table des Matiers.* Lines 3-6 each list a name of one of the Gospels. The remaining lines reference items relevant to contents of the Jerusalem tunnels and tombs. We examine each line in more detail below.

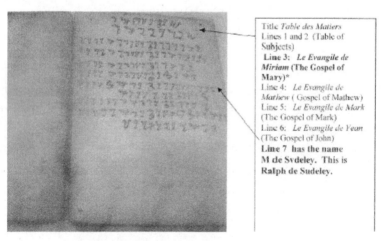

Title *Table des Matiers*
Lines 1 and 2 (Table of Subjects)
Line 3: *Le Evangile de Miriam* (The Gospel of Mary)*
Line 4: *Le Evangile de Mathew* (Gospel of Mathew)
Line 5: *Le Evangile de Mark* (The Gospel of Mark)
Line 6: *Le Evangile de Yean* (The Gospel of John)
Line 7 has the name M de Svdeley. This is Ralph de Sudeley.

Table des Matiers, **or Table of Subjects**

The listing of four gospels on the Table of Subjects page is a curious inclusion. Line 3, reading *Le Evangile de Miriam*, The Gospel of Mary, is the most curious of all as this gospel had been lost to history for fifteen hundred years until it was rediscovered in 1896 in Egypt. The three other gospels listed in lines 4-6 are *Le Evangile de Mathew, Le Evangile de Mark,* and *Le Evangile de Yean*, the Gospels of Mathew, Mark and John.

Line 7 is very important, as it makes a direct reference to Ralph de Sudeley's voyage to America and the date 1180. Line 7 is pictured here:

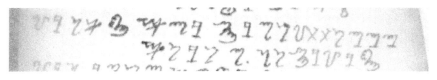

Line 7

The line reads, *Le voyage de MCLXXVIII Avec M Svdeley*, or "The Voyage of 1178 Master of Svdeley." The name 'Svdeley' is obviously intended to refer to de Sudeley.

There exists another important clue in Line 7. The date 1178 in Roman numerals contains two so-called 'Hooked X' characters, first identified and written about by researcher Scott Wolter. See circled characters below:

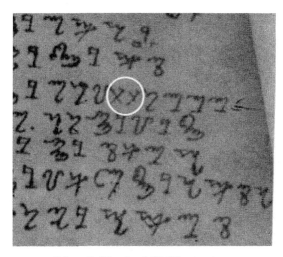

Line 7, Hooked X Characters

Wolter believes the Hooked X was used by the Cistercians and/ or Templars as a sort of calling card, a secret code conveying that the document containing the Hooked X was written by them. Here, the Hooked X characters are embedded and hidden within the Theban script.

Line 8 reads, *Les Enchante de Noir*, "The black chant/enchantment." This entry remains a mystery.

Line 9 reads, *Les Images de L'Objye dans le Soutrain*, "The pictures of the objects in the tunnel." (Note that *soutrain* is the Old French word for tunnels; in modern French the word is *Souterrain*.)

Lines 10 and 11 refer to images of some unknown object in a tunnel. These images remain a mystery to us.

Ralph de Sudeley

Before we examine the Templar Document further, it is worth examining the life of Ralph de Sudeley. Records of the de Sudeley family are extensive, documented in English genealogical records as early as the time of William the Conqueror and the Norman Conquest in 1066.

Ralph de Sudeley and his brother William de Tracy were great grandsons of King Henry 1 of England, 1100-1134. King Henry I had many mistresses and illegitimate children. One of his mistresses was Gleva Tracy, who bore a son William de Tracy, whose daughter Grace de Tracy married John de Sudeley. They had two children, Ralph de Sudeley in 1133 and William de Tracy, who was born earlier. In 1165, Ralph's father died and he became the heir of his estates and lands (his brother had inherited their mother's lands, which is why he took the Tracy name). Ralph in 1159 had married Emma Beauchamp; the Beauchamp family was a powerful one in Templar England. After his marriage, de Sudeley became an active member of the Knights Templar (many men of the day took their monastic vows after siring children).

A magnificent castle still stands on historic lands once owned by Ralph de Sudeley and his ancestors in Gloucestershire, in southwest England on the eastern border of Wales.

Sudeley Castle, Gloucestershire, England (today)

Sudeley Castle, Gloucestershire, England (1876)

Originally built as a manor house built in 1139, by 1165 it had been enlarged and was known as Sudeley Castle. The present castle was built in the 15th century. Famous people associated with the 15th century castle include Queen Catherine Parr, the sixth wife of Henry the VIII, who is buried there. Queen Anne Boleyn and Henry VIII visited the castle. It is privately owned in modern times by Lord and Lady Ashcombe (Lord Ashcombe died in 2013); Lord Ashcombe was the uncle of the Duchess of Cornwall, wife of Prince Charles.

King Henry II ruled during the time the castle was enlarged, reigning from 1154-1189. The Lords of Sudeley were powerful and de Sudeley's brother William de Tracy, a knight, was in the court of King Henry II. England during the 12th century had a strong Templar presence with powerful families supporting them.

In 1170, a major event in English history occurred which had a profound effect on our story: Archbishop Thomas Becket of England was assassinated in Canterbury Cathedral. Four assassins committed the crime; de Sudeley's brother William de Tracy was one of them. King Henry II had become angered with the activities of Archbishop Becket, who was excommunicating and seizing lands of nobility. As punishment, the Pope sentenced de Tracy and the other assassins to exile in Jerusalem, where they were to fight in the Crusades for 14 years.

The record is sparse, but it appears that this scandal set in motion a series of events which eventually led to de Sudeley's mission. Whether acting out of guilt or remorse or loyalty or some other motivation, de Sudeley (who was by all accounts close to his brother) stepped forward to become a central player in the planned Templar journey to Onteora. It is possible that de Sudeley's brother, now in Jerusalem, assisted in the planning of this mission.

Historical records reveal 'missing years' for de Sudeley during the 1175-1185 time period. We are about to fill in those blanks.

Mission to America, 1178-1180

The de Sudeley mission of 1178 had its roots in the turbulent years of the 1st century CE when Roman legions were advancing on Jerusalem and secret scrolls, maps and artifacts were hidden in the tunnels below the subterranean area of the Temple Mount. As I have recounted, in the early years of the 12th century, these items were found by early members of the Knights Templar.

More than fifty years later, after much planning, de Sudeley completed a mission likely first envisioned by his Templar predecessors in Jerusalem. He left a detailed log compiled during the voyage, describing the year he spent in Onteora with the community that guarded the scrolls. He recorded geographic sites he had been to, Native Americans he met, and the community of Welsh and Norse he lived with in the Hunter Mountain area. His account was added to the existing record kept by the Templars at Castrum Sepulchri. Latin was the common language at this time, and the monk who recorded de Sudeley's deposition used it to write the record entitled, "A Year We Remember." This account was then added to the writings from the earlier 12th century Templar excavations in Jerusalem to comprise parts of the Templar Document.

I expect that some will question the authenticity of "A Year We Remember" and the Templar Document in its entirety. To them I will just say that the information contained is of such complexity that it would require experts in various fields of ancient and medieval history, linguistics, cryptography, astronomy, cartography, navigation and geography to compile. The journals include little-known details of the turbulent years of 1st century Jerusalem, the First Crusade, the rise of the Knights Templar, and Templar history in Italy, England, France and Portugal. "A Year We Remember" also offers specific details of Native American peoples and their history which are not widely known.

It has taken me almost a decade to analyze, research and compile the hundreds of names, places and connections that have been found in the Templar Document. In this section I have taken Jackson's translation (Jackson translated from Theban into Latin and then into English) and divided it into passages thirteen through seventy-eight (passages one through twelve having been analyzed in previous chapters). I do this in order to best align each piece of information with information for the reader. I then flesh out Jackson's translation with material I have researched and conclusions I have reached.

Men on the Mission

The men who accompanied de Sudeley comprised an international team of Templar Knights, coming from seven different countries around Europe, as shown on the map below:

Home Countries of the Templar Knights

In addition to the Englishman, de Sudeley, we have:

- Eldric of Clan MacDonald, from Scotland
- Lionel de Waldern, from Denmark
- Beaumont de Wurttemberg, from a German state in Holy Roman Empire
- Hubert le Montier, from France
- The Spaniard of Leon, from Galicia, Spain (northwest Spain)
- Ishma'il al-Mutamid, from Cordoba (southern Spain)

The first name on this list plays an especially important part in this saga. The MacDonald Clan fought at the Battle of Bannockburn in 1314 (in which the Templars were said to have arrived to carry the day for the Scots in their battle against the English). Eldric appears to be an ancestor of Liam MacDonald, the prisoner who wrote the 1913 MacDonald Journal and who apparently carried this family history down through the generations.

The plans to recover the scrolls in Onteora took many years to unfold after the Jerusalem tunnel and tomb finds of the early 1100s. Bernard of Clairvaux died in 1153, but his plans were carried out by his close friend, the Archbishop of Lund in Denmark, assisted by King Valdemar I of Denmark, Bernard de Blanchfort, and Odo de St. Amand (before he became Templar Grand Master). The Danes and the Cistercians were key to this mission as they possessed the expertise to help the Templars read and interpret the Onteora map and to make the Atlantic crossing. This was the reason de Sudeley sought out King Valdemar for help. The Norse had voyaged in the 9th and 10th centuries to Iceland, Greenland and Vinland (continental North America). There were people in his court who had journeyed to Onteora and knew the route—as we learn below, one of those people was the enchanting priestess, Altomara.

"A Year We Remember"
Passage by Passage

Passage 13

We have followed the writing found to be in the Theban alphabet translated to Greek and Ivri from scrolls that were found below the stables of Solomon to Palmyra and have the devices with us.

The ancient maps show a land of Onteora far to the west but the route is far from certain. The North Finder and the Star Finder will help plot the way laid out in the sailors loop but to read it we must seek the help of the King of the North.

With the round disks we can read some of the ancient scrolls that reveal how the unclean fled to Tigwa and set sail for the kingdoms of Woton far to the North.

To the place in the past where the Goddess commanded the outcasts of Solomon to erect a temple in her honor in the Land of Onteora. There they hid the ancient writings, the secrets of the ages, the facts about our (L)ord. The disk is the key to unlock these.

> **The Spaniard of Leon and Hubert de Montier and Beaumont
> de Wurtemberg and Lionel de Walderne, the Celt, Eldric of
> Clan Macdonald, Isha'il al-Mutamid and I Ralf de Sedly shall
> undertake this quest by the Grace of God and the order of the
> Grand Master Amand.**

This passage begins with Ralph de Sudeley confirming that the group has "followed the writings" (the scrolls) found below the Stables of Solomon by the first group of Templars over fifty years earlier. Readers may recall that the Templars used the huge underground area on the southeast corner of the South Wall of the Temple Mount to stable their horses. The reference to "devices" is to the four navigation devices and the decoder.

The next reference is to "ancient maps." That is, more than one map. We know de Sudeley possessed a map of the Onteora region, but what other maps did he have? It is safe to conclude that some of these ancient maps came down from unknown sources, perhaps found in and around Jerusalem. The clear inference is that ancient peoples were navigating the Atlantic in ancient times.

The North Finder and Star Finder are the navigation devices II and III. The sailors loop is device IV, which will help them find the pole star and follow the sailing route west across the north Atlantic to *Onteora.* They are able to use these navigational devices with *the help of the King of the North,* Danish King Valdemar I.

Using the decoder (similar to a modern cipher machine) "round disks," the men can read the scrolls. The scrolls speak of "how the unclean fled to Tigwa." From Tigwa they sailed to the "kingdoms of Woton far to the North." This is a mystery. "Tigwa" may be "Tikvah" in Hebrew, which means village. The "kingdoms of Woton far to the north" likely are Scandinavian lands. This passage may be referring to the seventh century BCE, when Josiah, King of Judah, began his reforms to abolish worship of the Goddess, Asherah. "Woton" may refer to "Odin," the chief god in the Scandinavian/ Norse pantheon; in the Anglo Saxon language "Odin" is called "Wodon," and in Old High German he is called "Wotan." It may be that the "unclean"—that is, the Goddess worshipers—fled "far to the north" to Scandinavia, following ancient trade routes.

We now come to the most incredible reference, one that is almost unbelievable: a reference to a temple built in the Land of Onteora, ordered by the Goddess and erected in her honor. We need to examine this passage carefully:

> **To the place in the past where the Goddess commanded the outcasts of Solomon to erect a temple in her honor in the Land of Onteora.**

What place in the past? This is one of the most difficult and complex passages in the de Sudeley account. If we take this literally, it means a group of outcasts of Solomon were commanded by the Goddess to build a temple in the Land of Onteora. For this even to be possible, we must establish two things to be true:

1. There must be existence of Goddess worship in ancient Israel.
2. There must be evidence of temples built by Jews outside of Jerusalem.

We will look at both of these factors individually.

Regarding the question of Goddess worship in ancient Israel, as mentioned above the Goddess Asherah was worshiped for almost 400 years in ancient Israel and Judah, from approximately the 10th century BCE to the 6th century BCE. Asherah was the sacred female divinity, creatrix of the gods, symbolizing nurturing and regeneration. She was widespread throughout the land and the archaeological evidence comes from the thousands of small terra cotta female figurines found in the homes of worshippers. Some kings vehemently opposed Asherah and the practices associated with her worship. The eminent scholar, Raphael Patai, in his book *The Hebrew Goddess*, writes:

> *Ancient Israel was polytheistic and the worship of Asherah as the consort of Yahwah was an integral element of*

religious life in ancient Israel prior to the reforms intro-
duced by King Josiah in 621 BCE. Starkly illustrated in
the biblical text is the harsh repression of King Josiah
(639-609 BCE) who attempted to eradicate all traces of
the goddess Asherah.

It is clear, therefore, that Goddess worship thrived in ancient Israel. This gives further context to the statements regarding the "unclean" being forced to flee far to the north; while there, these "outcasts" were ordered by the Goddess to build a temple to her in Onteora. It is reasonable to conclude that the terms "unclean" and "outcasts" refer to Goddess worshipers shunned by mainstream Jewish leaders like King Josiah in the 7th century BCE time period.

[While somewhat beyond the scope of this saga, it is interesting to note that of the thousands of terra cotta Goddess figurines dating from the 8th and 7th centuries, many feature a triangle incised on them. This shape is a symbol of the Goddess. Goddess worship existed as far back as the Paleolithic era and is a reflection of the psychic human need to recognize the cycle of birth, rebirth and regeneration symbolized by the Goddess. Goddess worship was suppressed, but never disappeared; it went underground and reemerged in the 12th century in the personage of the Virgin Mary, championed by the Templars and the Cistercians (in particular Bernard of Clairvaux). My personal belief is that this reemergence was sparked by the discovery in Jerusalem by the Templars of scrolls in the ossuary. Interestingly, a tomb rediscovered in 1985, called Talpiot Tomb, features a triangle with a circle in the center above its entrance, as pictured here. As I wrote,

Talpiot Tomb, Jerusalem

the triangle is the age-old representation of the Goddess, while the circle represents the womb, the life-giving source. Similar examples can be found in hundreds of depictions in the iconography of the Near East. The Talpiot Tomb held ten ossuaries. The names inscribed on the ossuaries bear an uncanny similarity to the names of Jesus' family, and some scholars believe it is the Jesus family tomb. In particular, one ossuary featured the inscription, "Yeshua bar Joseph" (Jesus the son of Joseph), while another ossuary read, "Mariamne Mara," a known name for Mary Magdalene. Controversy has swirled over the significance of this tomb, but I believe that the Templars, in finding the tomb in the 12th century and the scrolls found in the ossuary about the teachings of Jesus and James, began to question orthodox Church teachings as result of this tomb. In particular, they began to appreciate the importance of the female and the Goddess. This, I think, helps explain the frequent references to and veneration of the Goddess in the Templar Document.]

What, then, of the question of temples being built outside Jerusalem? Two examples establish a precedent for this practice. First, in the 7th century BCE a Jewish community was established on Elephantine Island (southern Egypt), and a temple built there for its citizens. Second, a Jewish temple was built in the 2nd century BCE in the time of the High Priest Onias IV at Heliopolis in Egypt.

Having now satisfied ourselves that the necessary conditions existed in Jewish history for a group of Goddess-worshiping Israelites (admittedly outside the mainstream of their faith) to choose to build a temple outside of Jerusalem, we continue our examination of this passage.

The passage specifically states that the Goddess commanded "the outcasts of Solomon" to build her temple. What was Solomon's relationship with Goddess worship? It was, in fact, a close one. Solomon's reign in the 10th century BCE was replete with goddess worship. Solomon himself worshipped *Ashtoreth*, the goddess of the Sidonians. Solomon's religious practices strengthen the conclusion that the term "outcasts" as used here refers to Goddess worshipers.

Lastly, we must ask whether the ancient Israelites had the capability to make a cross-Atlantic voyage. We can speculate that their long partnership/alliance with the Phoenicians, dating back to the time of King Solomon, served them well. By this time in history Phoenician mariners had sailed west across the Mediterranean. Their search for minerals had led them to Iberia for silver, to Cornwall in England for tin, further north into the Baltic and Scandinavia for amber, and perhaps even across the Atlantic to America for copper. Indeed, the Israelites of the 9th century BCE were themselves skilled sailors and navigators. Ephraim Stem, in *Dor: Ruler of the Seas*, writes:

> *There were experienced sailors in the kingdom of Israel at this period... Dor [a port 20 miles south of Haifa] was the principal port in the time of Solomon; it was through Dor that all the commercial ties with Tyre and other Phoenician cities were maintained.*

Likewise, the ships of the time were capable of making a trans-Atlantic crossing. A 5th century BCE ship with most of the hull intact was found off the coast of Israel in 1985 and preserved. Dr. Elisha Linder, one of the founding fathers of maritime archaeology in Israel and a senior lecturer at the University of Haifa, communicated his opinion to me that this ship was capable of sailing across the Atlantic.

We are now told that the ossuary in which the scrolls were found held a collection of lost writings. "There they hid the ancient writings, the secrets of the ages, the facts about our (L)ord." The word *(L)ord* refers to Jesus, the implication being that there are facts about him which are unknown. The statement de Sudeley made about *secrets of the ages* is tantalizing. It could refer to ancient secrets relating to astronomy and navigation, allowing ancient seafarers to voyage across the Atlantic. The disk, de Sudeley reports, is the *key to unlock these secrets.*

Finally, the last name in this passage, *Grand Master Amand,* anchors this event in the historical timeline. Grand Master Odo de St. Amand was deeply involved with the Templars as far back as 1128 when his brother and Hugh de Payens inducted him into the Order. He became the Grand Master in 1171; prior to that he had been involved with Bernard of Clairvaux (before he died in 1153) in planning the Onteora Mission. Not only was de St. Amand a powerful Templar Grand Master, he was also a diplomat and military leader who fought the Moslem armies of Saladin; he was imprisoned in one of these battles and died in a dungeon in 1180.

Passage 14

> *We sail in the spring from Luongo. We make landfall at Dunwich Engeolnde to receive funds and the Bishop's blessing and stay in the Templar Hostelry near the church of St. Peter's but the Celt and the Spaniard seek rooms in the local tavern because of the nearness of the Blackfriars. There is but one horse at the Hostelry and it has a bruised leg but the Spaniard makes a poultice of Fenugreek and by the morrow it is well enough for me to ride to my kinfolk.*
>
> *I stop at Shopshire for the hammersmith to make a copy of the disks. It is crude work but it will be good for use. We will stay a fortnight awaiting the storms to abate. The Celt has found an Anan Cara whom he shares with the Spaniard and are quite content. So much for the vow of celibacy.*

This brief reference to Luongo (Loango is the proper modern spelling) opens up a startling question: Did the ossuary with the scrolls have a map or information about Loango? Could the reason have been gold? Loango, on the coast of West Africa, was an ancient kingdom within the Congo River Basin. Loango was known as an ancient gold-bearing kingdom. Yet Europeans had not voyaged to West Africa by the 12th century. It was not until the 15th century that Portugal reached the Angolan coast and the area became a key location for trade in copper, gold and ivory; it was not until the mid-1500s that the name Loango first appeared in Western writings. It is a mystery as to how and why the Templars would have known about Loango; we can speculate that the reason they detour there is related to gold. From Loango the Templars sail to Dunwich, along the east coast of England on the North Sea between England and Denmark. (I believe the journey began in Majorca, one of the Balearic Islands which lie off the coast of Spain. Majorca was a Templar stronghold in the 12th century. The Templar fleet often used a harbor in the city of Palma.)

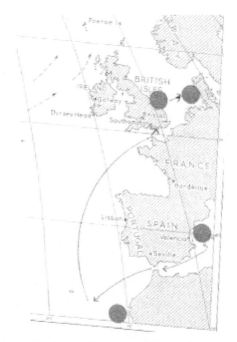

Spain to Loango to Dunwich

Today Dunwich is underwater, but it was an important harbor during the medieval period. While in Dunwich, they stay at the Templar Hostelry near St. Peter's Church. The reference to St. Peter's Church is verifiable; the church still exists today in Shropshire (in Gloucestershire), which is where de Sudeley reports that he makes a copy of the disks. Apparently he is taking no chances with the disks, knowing how important they are to the mission. We also learn that de Sudeley is near his "kinfolk," which is also verifiable as we know

Sudeley Castle is nearby. One last important point: Shropshire was a town with a large Templar presence. In fact, on March 7, 2017, the internet buzzed with news of a hidden Templar cave found buried beneath farmland in Shropshire, further evidence of the heavy Templar activity in the area.

Templar Cave, Shropshire [credit Richard Law]

The term *Blackfriars* refers to Dominican monks; apparently there was some bad blood between the two monastic Orders.

Anan Cara means prostitute. The comment, "So much for the vow of celibacy," is de Sudeley's sarcastic observation regarding his comrades' failure to abide by their Templar vows.

Passage 15

> *...at the Court of the King of the North and are well received. We are here introduced to a priestess of the Goddess named Altomara and the Spaniard is besotted with her much to our shame but the King is not offended. She leads us to the quay and*

> *states, "Fater Kat Bot." Lionel translates as he is a cousin of the queen and speaks some of their talk. "Father gives a boat." It is a long craft of the North with two decks one below and the other, a high prow adorned with a symbol of the goddess and one strong mast.*
>
> *Altomara states she has been to the temple before and will guide us but she says we must leave soon as the North waters will ice up. We must also ask permission of the local people to pass through their Land and we stock up with some odd items for them. There is beads of colors, axes. Kettles and wool blankets. There is an ongoing mistrust with some of the Local people as the Temple is within a place Sacred to them but so far no open hostility.*

Much of this passage is self-explanatory, though why the passage begins mid-sentence is a mystery.

The *King of the North* is King Valdemar I the Great, who ruled Denmark from 1146-1182.

The boat is adorned with the *symbol of the goddess.* This would be the sacred triangle or the image of Tanit. Sailors preserved the ancient belief in the efficacy of the maritime goddess Tanit. Her ancient symbol, the sacred triangle, was a protective talisman. The origin of the maritime goddess is from Ugarit, the great seaport on the northern Mediterranean coast which had its heyday in the 2nd century BCE. In Ugaritic texts the goddess was referred to as the "Lady of the Sea," the protectress of seamen. We will return to this Tanit figure much later in this section, but for now it is worth noting that the below Tanit carving was found on Hunter Mountain in 2009:

Altomara states she has been to the temple before in Onteora. This confirms there were ongoing voyages and relationships between the people in Onteora and Denmark. Historians agree that Norse voyages to America date back to 1000 CE, as evidenced by the L'Anse aux Meadows site in northern Newfoundland. (Satellite

Tanit Figure

imagery has also identified a Norse settlement at Point Rosee, the southernmost point in Newfoundland on the Cabot Strait.) Altomara knows about the ice along the route, which passes south of Iceland and Greenland and leads to Newfoundland; she suggests they leave soon, before the waters ice up.

Regarding Altomara's position in the royal court, Denmark retained many of its pre-Christian traditions. The ancient Goddess religion still existed and was accepted in the court; Altomara held a high position as a priestess of the Goddess. Altomara says they must take certain items to avoid problems of mistrust from the people who live in the sacred area. To avoid problems with the inhabitants she is smoothing the way for the Templars.

Previously I discussed a mysterious connection between the name *Altomara* and a name inscribed on the 1st century CE ossuary from Talpiot Tomb in Jerusalem: *Mariamne Mara*. Some scholars interpret *mara* as meaning master. The name "Alto-mara" would therefore mean "high master." She was a member of the royal family of King Valdemar I of Denmark and was a master of star navigation. There is much more to be discovered about the power of the priestesses to read the heavens.

Passage 16

> *The wind will take us most of the way and we will make landfall once at a place they have a settlement to take on fresh water and food. So our year begins with Beltane. To follow the Loops exactly requires that we start at a place unknown to us so we will make for Gwynedd and await favorable winds and then head West by Altomara's course.*
>
> *To appease the priest the Spaniard takes the priestess to wife. We are all in her hands and she revels in this but the Spaniard puts her in place. We have provisioned now with six ships and one hundred and forty men and women. The women fight with the men and are held equal by them. A strange practice to us.*

Altomara has given de Sudeley valuable knowledge from other voyages. She knows the westerly winds will be favorable at this time of the year, which she identifies as *Beltane,* also known as May Day on the Celtic calendar. Beltane marks the midpoint between the spring equinox and the summer solstice. Ships sailed in a tight time period across the north Atlantic, from May to August.

The reference to following *the Loops* is a reference to one of the navigational devices, which requires them to start from a site they do not know. They will sail from Denmark to *Gwynedd*, which is in northwest Wales, an area with an ancient Celtic heritage of Goddess worship dating back to pre-Christian times. Six ships and 140 men and woman set sail.

We learn that the love affair between Altomara and the Spaniard has resulted in a marriage. We also learn that Altomara's people practice an unusual custom for the time: Woman are considered equal to men and fight alongside them.

Passage 17

They Make Landfall on Oak Island

> *AEQUINOCTIUM has passed long since. The Spaniard suffers greatly from the cold but she keeps him warm as we await one moon past Midsummers Eve. We set sail North by Northwest till below the north star then west as the wind takes us we make landfall in a fortnight. There is about a dozen mud huts here but the hospitality is warm and we are well cared for.*
>
> *Here we take on a man called Clyphus who is said to have knowledge of the waters ahead. Two ships remain here. Four now set sail again and <u>we make landfall on an island of Oak trees</u>* [emphasis added] *where one ship is to be laden with wode and will return.*
>
> *We have seen no natives of this place. Hubert will return with the copy of the disks and maps of the way thus far. It is insurance.*

Aequinoctium is the vernal equinox; this is an odd reference as it has long passed (they set sail in May). But it remains cold in the North Atlantic and de Leon, being from a warm climate, suffers. Altomara warms him. They wait one month past midsummer's eve, which is the June solstice, so we are now in the latter part of July.

The route they sail is north by northwest until they are below the North Star, which they tracked with the Sailors Hooks. Do they have the compass which was found in the ossuary? The needle would point to magnetic north, rather than due north (magnetic north varies, and is not always true north)—they seem to realize this and adjust their course to a westerly one. They take on a local guide, Clyphus—this sounds like a European name and if so confirms prior journeys across the Atlantic. They make landfall on an island of oak trees. I believe this is the famous Oak Island, of lost treasure fame. Oak Island is one of the many islands in Mahone Bay, Nova Scotia but is distinctive in that it is the only one in the area with oak trees. Obviously this is an important revelation: The de Sudeley group is dealing with treasure, and they make landfall on the very island where one is believed to have been buried. I will return to Oak Island later in this book in Part IV.

Based on the description of this journey, I believe the group sailed south of Iceland and Greenland, then made landfall in New-foundland before sailing to Nova Scotia. See map below:

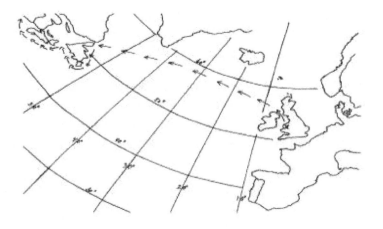

Sailing Route

One ship is loaded with wood to return with Hubert. Readers who have traveled to Scandinavia can attest to the paucity of forests. Even in medieval times, timber was a valued commodity, especially to seafaring communities. I believe this explains why our Templars, ever practical, send a ship back with wood. And, again being practical, they send disks and maps back as well, as insurance—they want to make sure future groups can retrace their steps. It also tells us that they believe they are in some danger. They do not see any natives yet, but we know from previous passages that there is some "mistrust" between the Templars and the native population.

Passage 18

Again we set sail but now three days out the wind fails us and no prayers can set it to blow again. We must take to the oars and pull in the drogue. This is a slow and tedious process but we move after several hours with a northerly current. Fog very

> *heavy settles around us and the Celt and Beaumont set to send-ing fire arrows aloft as the top of the mast one man sits to see by but it is in vain we strike solid on rock or ice and have torn a hole in the bottom and are sinking.*

Three days out and their ship hits ice or a rock and are sinking. Ice and heavy fog gives us a clue to their approximate location: I believe they are in the waters around Nova Scotia. Prior to using the oars, they pull in the drogue (an underwater drag device to improve stability) to make it easier to row.

Passage 19

> *Both Eldric and I see land and sing out. The other ship takes us in tow and then comes about and pushes us so that we land on a rocky hillside. We take off enough provisions to sustain us and part of the decking from which we will make smaller craft to row to the main land. Night is coming and the other ships fearing a similar fate head out to sea and South. One makes landfall South and West and sets about a fire so that we may take heart from its sight.*

This passage is self-explanatory. They are on Oak Island, in Nova Scotia's Mahone Bay. Nova Scotia is an ovular-shaped island running essentially east-west across the map; Mahone Bay is on the southern side, a bit toward the east of the midpoint of the island. The map below depicts the area and their journey around it:

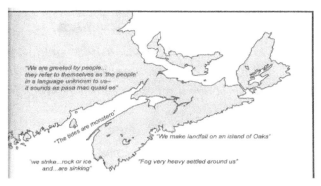

Journey Around Nova Scotia

Passage 20

> *Altomara takes sky bearings and in the morning we begin to build rafts. Wood is scarce here. Four days have passed and three rafts have gone to the other place but one has not made it and all were lost Beaumont among them. Eldric, the Celt, The Spaniard, Altomara and the one called Clyphus who so far has been of no good help to us and I set sail in a larger made boat with part of our masts top cut for a mast and sail and reach the other place where we set up to an anchor ashore. Rocks have been laid into the water to form a quay and we leave the ship in water without fear of her running to ground held fast to the shore by the great round anchor there.*

They are on a rocky hillside and Altomara takes "sky bearings." One of the rafts is lost with all perishing, including Beaumont of Wurtemburg. Clyphus has been of no help so far. It appears that someone has been here before them and laid rocks to form a quay and also left a *great round anchor* (see below).

Passage 21

> *We decide to proceed with the one ship as of the other we have seen nothing since we parted at the sinking of our vessel as it towed it out to deeper water. No sign of our passage must remain. These are not friendly waters. Many fish here and they do not respect strangers to their fishing grounds. We will take the smaller ship we have constructed with its sail and flat bottom behind the other and will reach the mainland in two days sail with the new wind. First we round the point and again set ashore so that Altomara can take sky bearings. There rests an anchor rock here not of our making and we leave below it a record of our passing. The tides are monstero.*

A clue to their location is the last sentence: *The tides are monstero.* De Sudeley is referring to the Bay of Fundy between New Brunswick and the north coast of Nova Scotia (see map above), an area known as rich fishing grounds. It may be that *Clyphus* knows these waters. They continue with one ship. They know that they can reach the *mainland in two days*. How would they know it would take two days unless Clyphus or Altomara told them? The point where they go ashore so Altomara can take sky bearings may be Cape Sable on the southern coast of Nova Scotia. Across the body of water is New Brunswick. Today a ferry connects both areas.

An anchor stone was left by another party. They say it is not theirs and they leave a record of their passing below the anchor stone. What record did they leave? They could have been on Prince Edward Island, where a huge anchor stone, as pictured below, sits on the coast today and is known to the locals.

Prince Edward Island Anchor Stone
[courtesy Isaac Stewart and Danny Henniger]

Passage 22

ch... and are greeted well by strange inhabitants of the main land. They are of a bronze color tinged reddish are dressed in furs and have various feathers of birds upon their heads. Those with many feathers have higher rank among their peoples. They

> *refer to themselves as "The People" in a language unknown to us. It sounds as Pasa mac quaid ee.*
>
> *They live in houses some thirty feet long of sticks bark and mud. There are no windows and a fire in the center makes it very smoke laden. The land is heavily wooded and is teeming with game and birds of many kinds unknown to us.*
>
> *The deer here are much larger than at home and Eldric brings one down with his long bow. The head of these people is much impressed with Eldric's skill with his bow as theirs is shorter but they are excellent with them and with a weapon of three stones at the ends of three ropes hurled about their heads and thrown. With these they bring down birds of large size.*
>
> *They are much afeared when we bring off the horses from the ship but it turns to amazement as no such animal resides here. They will provide us with one hundred dogs to pull our gear but the wheel is not known to them either and a drag of poles is all that the dogs will pull.*

The party is now in New Brunswick and the native people are the Passamaquoddy (as de Sudeley sounds out), which translates as "The People." The Passamaquoddy historically have occupied the lands of northern Maine and southern New Brunswick.

De Sudeley is a keen observer and excellent reporter. His statements that the natives do not have the wheel and are unfamiliar with horses, plus his description of their long houses, are historically accurate.

Here again Jackson's notes/translation are incomplete and we begin with a fragmented sentence.

Passage 23

> *We will spend a time with them and when Midsummers Eve has come again Altomara will make her sky measurements for the location of the Temple of the Goddess and it is decided that*

> *Hubert will return with the ship and twenty and six of us with Eldric, Ishma'il, Lionel, The Spaniard, Clyphus, Altomara and I will travel first by water, then by land over the mountains, beyond the mountains to other mountains South by West three points less than half the lesser. This is a year we may surely not forget by the Grace of God the blessing of the goddess if we survive.*

Here is the origin of de Sudeley's title for his narrative, "A Year We Remember."

The reference to Midsummer's Eve tells us that they have spent a year since they left Wales at the time of Beltane. It is now 1179.

Altomara will make her sky measurements for the location of the Temple of the Goddess. This is their ultimate destination: This is where the scrolls from Jerusalem were kept on Hunter Mountain. Hubert is to return with one ship to Castrum Sepulchri with maps of the route thus far. *A party of twenty six will continue on,* inland to the Temple of the Goddess. They travel first by water, then by land over mountains and beyond the mountains to other mountains. Their journey is over three mountain ranges. They pass through the White Mountains of New Hampshire, the Green Mountains of Vermont and into the northern range of the Catskill Mountains. I believe the directional reference to *South by West three points less than half the lesser* tells us they are seeking a destination at latitude 42 degrees (halfway between south and west being a 45 degree line, and three points less than that being 42 degrees). Hunter Mountain is located at latitude 42.18 degrees north.

Again we have a reference to the Goddess, whom the Templars clearly revere.

Passage 24

> *Hubert has taken the ship into a large river and set ashore upon an isle to the left. Upon the right bank we encounter several hundred of the inhabitants dressed colorfully with bodies painted red and white and black. Altomara states that they are ready for war but when these men in full armor sword*

> *unsheathed facing the rising sun so that it reflects me they run away in fear.*
>
> *We cross over in the smaller boat and sound for depth to bring the ship to bear. Then we unload the dogs and the twelve horses, our supplies and we say goode speed to our brethren. Hubert sets off straight way with the tide and we are alone. Altomara has spoken with the head man of these people and they have word of us.*
>
> *It comes to pass that word travels fast among the different groups here. We are made welcome and learn that it is not us they were expecting to make war on but an enemy to the south. They call themselves the Mikee-Macks and the daughter of the headman finds Lionel most pleasing. Her name is Woe-a-tweez mita-mu we call her Wasabee. Altomara is spoken to by her mother and some arrangement is come to that she spends time with him but not alone. He is able to provide some communication with her as some of the words of Gwynedd are most similar. I find this most amazing.*

They are welcomed by the Mi'kmaq—the word *Mikee-Macks* is what de Sudeley writes out phonetically. The Mi'kmaq inhabited a large area in the Canadian Maritimes and in Maine. *Woe-a-tweez-mita-mu* is a name in the Algonquin language. The Mi'kmaq are preparing for war against an enemy from the south.

It appears that Lionel is able to communicate with Wasabee, using "words of Gwynedd," which is an important clue. Gwynedd is in Wales, which indicates that Wasabee is able to speak some Welsh.

Passage 25

> *We agree to aid these peoples in their fight against the enemy. Lionel and Eldric take charge of the Battle plans. Eldric charges Wasabee's people to build a wall in a big circle nine chains round with an opening to the East. The wall is of stone three hands but at the east only one course on the ground some one hand high. A rod inside the circle he instructs them to dig*

three trenches a rod or two deep and one wide the length of the opening and several mans' feet apart. The woman weave from a water plant with wide flat leaves and long slender stalks with a brown seed atop which is goode tinder long mats that will cover the trenches on sticks below and with dirt and leaves over them.

Eldric of Clan MacDonald takes charge of the battle plans as the Templars agree to help the Mi'kmaq in their battle. He instructs them to build a wall in a circle *nine chains* round with an opening to the East—a chain is 66 feet, so this circle is about 594 feet in circumference, approximately the size of two ice hockey rinks placed side-to-side. They dig trenches inside the wall and cover the trenches with long mats made from wide leaves. A trap is being set.

Passage 26

Behind the West wall on the outside several less deep trenches are constructed but these are not covered with mats only branches and some hides and leaves. In the wode to the North Gurtrude the spear maiden sets about some twenty men with spears. Eldric has some two dozen points he sets upon the poles. These are to lay upon the ground with the men.

Clyphus, Adric, Galen and I will take some twenty of Wasabee's people and form a phalanx inside the wall behind the trenches. The rest of them are to the South in the wode. The head man sends some of his best to wait in the water and to scout ahead to the south over the river to spy on the advancing enemy. Some four hundred of them come over in boats made of bark and wode with a short oar having a thin flat blade on them some thirty men to a boat all painted up and screaming they charge us through the opening lightly jumping over the low rocks and thus pay no heed till they fall into the trenches the next wave jumps this to find themselves into another and so on.

Women are part of the battle, as evidenced by *Gurtrude the spear maiden* instructing twenty men with spears. This was unheard of in medieval Europe, except in rare instances. Note that the Templar men not only make plans for the battle, they actively take part in it.

Passage 27

Altomara blows a horn of the goat. It makes a long low deep sound and at this Eldric's archers raise up from the outer covered trench to the West and fire volleys into the enemy within. They quickly see that it is a trap and attempt to come around to the West behind Eldric. Then does Gertrude send the spear men at them and our people mounted as cavalry charge them also. At the same time the head man's people set about the guards on the boats and burn them. Then the rest of the people charge as I command our group to move forward.

The enemy takes to the water some swimming others in partly burnt boats or those they have put aright. Now a surprise. Eldric blows a horn and from the Island comes twenty bark craft pushing a raft ablaze into the retreating boats. Those swimming are clubbed in the water. These people show no quarter.

We are victorious. Alantha Rolf's woman Galan and Cedric of Londonary have been lost and some dozen of Wasabee's people. More than one hundred of the enemy are dead and many are wounded. They are dispatched but the women are taken as prize.

Altomara begins the battle with the sound of a goat horn. Ralph de Sudelely is the commander of his group and his (and his men's) military experience proves extremely useful. De Sudeley remarks that the Mi'kmaq leave none of the captured enemy alive. Two of the de Sudeley party—one man and one woman—die in battle, along with a dozen Mi'kmaq and over a hundred of the enemy.

Passage 28

> *The circle of stones that was the battle ground rests upon a hill and the village behind it still higher up both overlooking a fertile plain. This would be a good place to reside. I have mentioned this in my letters to the Temple and hope that Hubert will not mention it to the Holy Father.*
>
> *Rolf, Adric and Sven decide to remain with these people and are accepted into the group. Lionel has eaten the twelve cakes and thus Wasabee travels wither he goes. For his plans and valor in battle there is nothing else I can give him so I have him kneel and with my sword unsheathed he rises Sir Eldric. The King may not approve but he is far away and we all recognize him as such. It is the right thing to do.*

De Sudeley is impressed by the land and remarks that it would make a good place to live. Is this part of his mission—to evaluate the possibility of future settlement in Onteora? It is not clear why he does not want Hubert to mention this to the pope, who was aware of the mission to Onteora. One possibility is that the Templar leaders were looking to settle in the lands de Sudeley discovered but did not want the Church to know of these plans.

Three of de Sudeley's men decide to remain with the Mi'kmaq and are accepted into the tribe.

Lionel has *eaten the twelve cakes*—this may be a reference to an ancient marriage ritual where women baked cakes (probably in the shape of a triangle) for the Goddess as part of a fertility celebration, the precursor to the ritual of the wedding cake.

In a dramatic event, de Sudeley confers knighthood on Eldric of Clan MacDonald for his bravery in battle and his skilled leadership. Clan MacDonald was one of the clans that later fought at Scotland's Battle of Bannockburn in 1314. Readers may recall that the MacDonald Clan traditions were passed down in modern times to Francis Bannerman VI.

Passage 29

> *In a moon we take our leave and with the boat head down the coast stopping each night so that the party ashore with the dogs and horses can regroup. The Al-no-boks enemies of The People try to steal our horses but we strike a deal with their head man and Lionel leaves his Breast Plate, Shin guards and Gauntlets with him. They also provides a man called Tamo who will guide us through the many passes as the forest is thick with growth. The wode are so close together in some places a man can not pass between. Tamo takes us over a mountainous route but we see few other of the inhabitants of this land. We come to another large river with a swamp at its mouth and pushing through this bring the horses and dogs over to the south side. Here we will abandon the boat taking the sails and some tools with us.*

After a month they leave the Mi'kmaq and head down the coast of Maine. The group is divided with one party in a boat and the other on land with dogs and horses.

Al-no-boks are enemies of the Mi'kmaq. I have been unable to identify the Al-no-boks. Lionel deals with them, leaving some of his armor in trade; they provide a guide named Tamo. Tamo leads them through thick forests and over a mountainous route with few inhabitants. They come to another large river with a swamp at its mouth and push through the swampy area to the south side. I believe that the route they traveled was along the coast of Maine and then inland through New Hampshire. They may have taken the Merrimack River which flows into the Atlantic on the border of New Hampshire and Maine.

[Note that Passages 30 through 33 appear to be out of order in "A Year We Remember." The dictation of de Sudeley's narrative to the monk evidently caused this mishap. De Sudeley reported the events from his memory and also in reliance on his and others' notes (recording names, locations, etc.). Apparently some confusion or mistake caused the narrative to be transcribed out of order. I am leaving the numbering of the passages in the order they appear in "A Year We Remember," but am reordering them in

this book in the sequence I believe is consistent with the narrative timeline.]

Passage 34

leaves are turned so we change course and at the sign of the Bear we head East. We now enter the land of the Pena Cookie peoples. Altomara, Tamo and Wasabee with the Spaniard who is learning their talk go to see their headman. These people are very hungry. The game has fled and there has been no rain for a while, two moons. Our provisions are now less thus I order twenty dogs and one horse slaughtered for them. They hold a great feast in our honor. This is a strange place.

Altomara states she must prepare to give her offering of blood to the Moon Goddess. The moon is full. She enters a long structure of stone covered with earth some half a chain long and several rods wide.

A channel brings water from a spring up hill to the rear. The Spaniard states he will stay with her but she kicks him out. There are many woman here all for this purpose. They will stay seven suns. There are several more of these places and we take refuge in them.

We again begin midsentence due to some unexplained gap in the manuscript. The *sign of the Bear* could be the Big Dipper, or they could be following the pole star in the Little Bear constellation (Ursa Minor). The comment that the *leaves are turned* indicates autumn is approaching. They are in the land of the *Pena Cookie*—the Penacook tribe resided in the present-day Merrimack Valley region of New Hampshire and northern Massachusetts, an indication that the group may have been traveling along the Merrimack River.

The women are observing an ancient menstrual custom of isolation from the men, observed for seven days. Readers of Anita Diamant's novel, *The Red Tent,* will recognize that this custom has its roots among the Goddess worshipers of the ancient Israelites.

Passage 35

The horses are restless. The storm is fast approaching. These people have a person of age who dances around with the necklace of bear teeth and claws around his neck and many feathers in bands about the legs and arms. He also has Silver bracelets on and rings in his nose and ears and one through his lip. He has something about his person that rattles as he moves and he blows on a whistle of willow wode. He also has a grotesque mask on a stick and much as a yester and puts it into the faces of others.

Tamo states he is chasing away bad spirits which is what the yester would do. The practices are not that different. He is called a Shay-Man or Shaw-Man and is considered a healer and religious leader among his people. He tells the children a story. As I understand it once there were no people on the earth and the animals had to decide if they wanted light or dark all the time. The bear wanted dark. A small ground animal wanted light and so did the deer. Others wanted both. Those that wanted light did a dance and it started to get light. At this the bear ran after the little animal, the leader of the group and it ran down a hole but not before the bears claw raked its back.

In the meantime the animals that wanted both did a dance and the Great Spirit, This I suppose is GOD, chose half light and half dark but the little animal to this day has a dark stripe down its back. The children are pleased with this story. Lionel states its just a story for children but Wasabee looks at him and states. "Is it?" He looks mollified.

I am a second son but his place is a third son and is worse off than I.

As I see him now I realize that Wasabee has tamed the animal within and I am pleased for him. I ask Wasabee if she will go with Altomara but she states that she has no gift for the Moon Goddess. The storm rages without. Trees are uprooted. A horse is killed. It will be consumed as well. Nothing goes to waste here.

The word *yester* is not misspelled; there is no "j" letter in archaic Theban. The word is jester.

De Sudeley makes an interesting comment comparing his status to Lionel's. *I am a second son but his place is a third son and is worse off than I.* My research has confirmed de Sudeley's statement to be true. His brother, William de Tracy, was born first and inherited the lands from his mother, while de Sudeley inherited from his father.

Wasabee's comment that she has *no gift for the moon goddess* means she is not menstruating and is pregnant. This is what has changed, or *tamed the animal within,* Lionel, the father-to-be of her child.

Passage 36

> *After the storm and the next morning I have a chance to look around this place. There are about five hundred persons here some are with men of the North who live here also and have families here. These people have a custom strange to us. All things have a separate spirit to them and must be kept in balance with all the rest. They tell this story to explain.*
>
> *Once the ground shook and a spring came up. The underworld spirit gave freedom to the water spirit. It ran from North to West and then East till it dropped into another hole but soon emerged again from a split in the rocks at the base of the hill. The people went into this split in the rocks following the course of the water and found a silvery rock. The North people made of wode and hide a device to make fire hotter from below as does the hammersmith. There is a black rock here and it is hard to light but burns very hot when put on a stone pile with the device of the hammersmith below.*

De Sudeley describes a large multi-ethnic community of some five hundred people, including *Men of the North.* These people are Norse and/or Welsh, and some have families with them.

De Sudeley describes a custom they believe in, that all things have a separate spirit which must be kept in balance. They tell him a story from their oral history to explain this belief. The story is about finding a vein of silver. *The ground shook* (an earthquake), which released a stream in the *split in the rocks at the base of the hill.* A tunnel was found and led them to a *silvery rock*—this would be to a vein of silver. Some type of furnace is described, and they describe a device of wood and hide to make fire hotter—probably bellows. The *black rock* is a reference to coal.

Silver has been found in the northeast; there were ancient gold and silver mines in the area. The Panther Mountain crater is located about fifteen miles south of Hunter Mountain; geologists have determined that a meteorite plunged into the earth millions of years ago and buried itself forming over the eons a mountain with streams around the rim. Interestingly the Lenape named the meteorite impact area around Panther Mountain "The Wellspring of Creation." This is all consistent with the details of the Native American story.

Passage 37

> *A large caldron with this silvery rock broken up and water in it is cooked and what rises is removed. A place in hard clay is cut or in rock in a snake or round pattern and the residue of the caldron is run in it. When it is cold it is worked with cold and bone. The Silver ornaments are made thus and these people would give us half a hundred weight for the ASS. We took it and divided it up among us. The Spaniard gave all his to Altomara and for this they are held in higher regard by the People.*

Silver was extracted and made into ornaments. There were silver mines in several states in New England. A vein of silver was found in this area of New York.

The donkey (*ASS*) is so valued that the Native Americans pay generously for it. De Leon gives his share of the silver to Altomara, and the Native Americans admire his generosity.

Passage 38

> *Where the spring came from the earth the People made a stone hut covered with earth as the Sun Spirit was angry with the Water Spirit for showing the People the Silver Metal and was strong and held back the rain and the water dried up. To protect it the stone hut was built over it and the stream that ran a chain to the hole of the silver cave was covered in stone and a wall half my height built over it to protect the water from the wrath of the Sun Spirit.*
>
> *This wall serves no other purpose. This is not of goode and sound mind.*

The Native Americans erected a stone hut to protect the stream that led to the silver cave from an angry spirit. De Sudeley makes a caustic comment, implying that whoever built it was being superstitious.

Passage 39

> *The children use sticks to annoy the ass and it bellows and kicks and this they find most amusing. We are glad to be rid of it.*
>
> *When the seven days are over the women come out and with them they bring their blood and it is given in a ceremony to the Moon Goddess.*
>
> *There is on the hill top a small circle three rods across and in it two uprights and a cross piece all of stone. This resembles the Greek letter pi. When the moon is not seen the blood is poured into the circle by the Priestess. This has to my knowledge no affect on anything except the area smells bad always. Not much grows here but one plant that it is stated the roots in a strong drink made of honey will win a woman for the man.*
>
> *This sounds to me as the tale concerning the Mandrake root back home but I am silent. It does no good to argue with our guests and it is much safer too. The Spaniard states he will try it on Altomara that causes Lionel to ask why. She is already yours he says and that ends that idea.*

The menstrual cycle has ended and the women perform a ceremony honoring the Moon Goddess, in which they pour their menstrual blood into a sacred circle. This custom was unknown in medieval Europe but is an ancient practice observed among certain cultures in the Near East and Africa.

The description of a plant with roots which will win a woman may be, as de Sudeley suggests, the Mandrake Root. This plant contains hallucinogens/alkaloids. It was a known aphrodisiac and it was called the "love plant."

Passage 40

We have been a fortnight and are given a strip of hide with tortoise claws and shells long and shiny and said to come from far to the south in the waters of the great sea sewn onto it. It will be a mark of the protection of these people on us and we will pass through the land of others called the Pea-coot. They will honor the passage and we again return on course.

They are passing through *the land of others called the Pea-coot.* These are the Pequot people of Rhode Island and Connecticut. They are given a *mark of protection,* described as *a strip of hide with tortoise claws and shells.* This is a kind of passport system, to give them safe passage. These shells have come from *far to the south in the waters of the great sea.* The great sea to the south is likely the Gulf of Mexico, indicating wide spread trade and contacts. Dr. Jackson believed these shells were Dentallium shells (which you can lift to your ear and hear the sea).

[We jump now from Passage 40 to Passage 30.]

Passage 30

Then we arrive on the bank of a river with a tall mountain on our right Altomara states we have come too far. We must go back ten leagues North by Nine East but Tamo will go no farther with us. We give him a knife and a horse. He is overwhelmed that we should give him the beast but it is the only one that remains. We

> *have eaten the rest. The next day we realize that Malcoms cross-*
> *bow and a quiver of twenty arrows with steel points is missing.*
> *We search for them but they cannot be found. We believe Tamo*
> *may have taken them.*

The description of arriving at the *bank of a river with a tall mountain on our right* may point to the West Branch of the Neversink River. The tall mountain on the right would be Slide Mountain, the tallest mountain in the Catskill range, over 4,000 feet. A large petroglyph once sat in the middle of the West Branch of the Neversink River near Slide Mountain. It was a map of rivers showing the way west. The petroglyph was moved by locals in the area and now sits about a mile down river.

Altomara leads them and says they have come too far south and they have to go back ten leagues north by nine east. They are in the Neversink River Valley, between the east and west branches of the river. Retracing ten leagues to the north and nine east will bring them to Hunter Mountain.

Passage 31

> *At the top of this tall mountain is water. This is unusual and*
> *Altomara states it is the mountain of a great God of the inhab-*
> *itants of this land and is sacred to them. There is a large pile*
> *of stones here with a clear crystal one at the top with a point*
> *worked in its top.*
>
> *South from here we see a rock with a design of the Goddess on*
> *it and the name of the people that live here. The three spirals*
> *mark a passage of time at eostre. I marveled that they have writ-*
> *ing. It is the first I have seen but Altomara and Wasabee tell us*
> *these people are not native to the Land but live here as guard-*
> *ians of the mountain.*
>
> *We see none of them but feel we are watched. They are called*
> *The Cone or the Elohim.*

To repeat, if they are in the Neversink River West Branch, the tall mountain is probably Slide Mountain, where the Neversink River originates. Altomara says that it is a *mountain of a great God* and says that the inhabitants of this land consider it sacred.

The *large pile of stones* is a cairn, many of which have been found throughout Massachusetts, Vermont and Connecticut in addition to the Catskills. A clear crystal stone has been worked to a point at the top of the cairn, which we infer is significant to the local people.

Who are the people who are the guardians of the sacred mountain? They are literate and not native to this area, but apparently they are watching the de Sudeley group. The answer comes in two words: *Cone* and *Elohim*. This is astonishing, as *Elohim* is one of the names of the Hebrew God. I believe *Cone* may refer to the *Cohen*, a Jewish surname given to the priests in the Temple of Jerusalem (the word *Cohen* meaning 'priest' in Hebrew). Could these guardians of the sacred mountain be refugees from Judea who fled from the destruction of Jerusalem by the Roman legions in the 1st century CE? Alternatively, recall that in one of the previous passages we learn that the *outcasts of Solomon* were told to build a temple in the *Land of Onteora.* I will note here that the Bat Creek Stone, found in an ancient Cherokee burial mound in Tennessee, is inscribed with Paleo-Hebrew script dating back to the 1st century CE, perhaps providing further evidence in support of the first of these possibilities (see image below, at Passage 67). Other intriguing evidence along the Neversink River West Branch supports the possibility of ancient visitation. Six stones with ancient script and symbols were found in 2001, 2004 and 2007. A photograph of the 2001 stone was shown to an expert in ancient scripts in Israel and he said it was Phoenician script. The stone found in 2004 is inscribed in Paleo-Hebrew, similar to the Bat Creek Stone. These stones are discussed below.

The group continues south where they see a rock carved with a design of the goddess and *three spirals* with the *name of the people that live here.* Unfortunately de Sudeley he does not record the name of the people. But we do learn they are Goddess worshippers. The reference to *eostre* is yet another reference to the Goddess, as this is a Germanic word for the Goddess who is the namesake for the holiday, Easter.

Passage 32

> *When we have gone North and East we begin to see large stone piles about a rod or two high and all topped with the clear or white shining stone. We follow these as they border a wide road free of brush and trees. We approach a wide river and Lionel goes to cut trees to bridge it but I cry NAY for upon the far bank stands some several hundred of the reddish people and they have many bows and they suddenly raise a cry of war. I stand forth in armor but several arrows hit me before they all become silent.*
>
> *Then as one they turn and face an opposing force of tall men in leather vest with a copper colored plates front and back with many spears with green tips of metal and they all stamp their feet and beat upon drums and cry out. Then a horn as Altomara has is sounded and the spears are lowered to breast height and they advance to the beat of a drum. These people are fair to look upon with many having blonde hair and blue eyes. The native group break and flee as the phalanx reaches the bank opposite us and one hails Altomara. We are taken aback the language is of that of Gwynedd. We are made welcome.*
>
> *These are the people of the Temple of the Goddess. They are stately and tall. The shortest is two heads over me. They are fair of skin with large heads and dress much as we do but have a cloth type robe about their girth that extends over the shoulder.*

The de Sudeley party has traveled north and east from the Neversink River to an area with *large stone piles* and they see numerous cairns a rod or two (rod equals one foot) high with white quartz stones on top. A war party on the opposite bank of the river is described as *reddish people*. A large force of tall men suddenly appear. Their clothing, weapons, and appearance are unquestionably not Native

American. They wear leather vests with copper-colored plates front and back and carry spears with copper tips and drums. They recognize Altomara. They are fair, with blonde hair and blue eyes. They speak the language of Gwynedd. They are clearly from Wales.

De Sudeley compares their size to his—*the shortest is two heads over me.* Assuming de Sudeley is at least 5 feet, 6 inches tall, they would have been well over six feet. They wear a *cloth type robe* around their body and it continues over their shoulders, in Welsh and Scottish fashion.

Lest there be any doubt, de Sudeley identifies these stately, fair-skinned people as the *people of the Temple of the Goddess.* This confirms that the Welsh carried the ancient Goddess religion to Onteora, where they built a *Temple of the Goddess.*

It therefore appears that we have two groups who inhabited Onteora: the Welsh/Norse Goddess worshipers, and the Ivri (Hebrew) of the sacred mountain, who may also be worshiping the Goddess.

Passage 33

> *In the confrontation with the natives one was struck in the chest with an arrow but the metal plates caused it to not adhere as did they with my armor. He then used a short spear thrown from a straight stick with a hook at the back and flung much as a catapult. It pierced the throat of the warrior and he went down.*
>
> *We were taken to the mountain top and shown a structure with a sharp pointed roof made of stone and banked with mud. A wattle wall surrounded it.*

The weapon described here could be an *atlatl.* The atlatl is an ancient weapon, a spear thrower developed in Europe 30,000 years ago. It is the precursor of the bow and arrow.

Taken to the mountain top. I believe they were taken to Hunter Mountain and that the structure is a temple built to revere the Goddess. A *wattle wall* is a palisade enclosure.

[Beginning with Passage 41, our narrative is now back in proper order.]

Passage 41

A wattle wall surrounds it and around this a high palisade of wode some half a chain in height and pointed at the top. A heavy gate laden with flat stones was bared from within and there were sentry posts upon raised mud and stone platforms within. There were windowed rooms with fireplaces some ten in all with a central chimney to all and a central hall with a banquet table of oak and wode benches about it.

As we entered the smell of cooking meat assailed us. A woman called Gianna plays an instrument making a tinkling sound and a clapping sound alternately. It is an elongated piece of wood tear shaped with two metal thin plates across the width on swivel rods. A drum and horn also accompany her. It is not unpleasing to the ear. I am told it is called a Sistrum.

To the back was a doorway and a way down to a large chamber but if constructed or natural I could not tell. Many candles provided light while only ruslits did so above.

They see an impressive structure and de Sudeley describes it in detail. A *high palisade half a chain in height* (half a chain is 33 feet) surrounds it. There are sentry posts, rooms with windows, ten fireplaces with a central chimney, and a central hall. This building was apparently well heated, an important feature for the preservations of any documents.

A *Sistrum* is a musical instrument which originated in ancient Egypt.

Passage 42

To the rear of the wall was an effigy of the Goddess with much flowers about her and Pine sprigs over her and a well of water before her and lamps of oil about her. To the left was the sign of Blodeuwedd and Cymidei Cymeinfoll with her Cauldron of Regeneration the three spiral circling the dot ever present. Also was the sign of Gwyn ap Greidiawl Creiddlad Gwyn ap Nudd about the sacred triangle and to the right the sign of Arianhrod.

Surrounding the Goddess with flowers is a Welsh tradition. Water symbolizes the life-giving force of the Goddess. *Blodeuwedd* is the Welsh mother goddess of spring, associated with flowers.

Cymidei Cymeinfoll is a mythical giantess and keeper of the Cauldron of Regeneration, which restores to life warriors killed in battle. *Three Spirals circling the dot* is a common symbol of the Goddess found at archaeological sites throughout Europe dating back to the period of Goddess worship. The spiral symbolizes the regenerative power of the Goddess and is found at ancient megalithic sites such as Newgrange and Malta. The dot represents the womb. The *sacred triangle* is an ancient Goddess symbol which appears across Europe, the Near East and America and depicts a female anatomical feature and also symbolizes the three stages of a woman's life—the maiden, the mother and the crone. All these symbols and beliefs were adopted by the Welsh from ancient Goddess traditions.

The name *Gwyn ap Greidiawl* means son of Greidiawl. *Gwyn ap Nudd* is, in Welsh mythology, the first lord of the underworld and a great warrior. Some authors link him to Glastonbury Tor. *Arianhrod* is the Celtic goddess of the silver wheel; *Arian* means silver and *rhod* means wheel or disk.

Much of Europe retained the ancient goddess religion despite the Indo-European onslaught which brought in the patriarchal era. The record from archaeological sites of tombs and graves reveals many symbols of the Goddess such as concentric circles and the sacred triangle.

Passage 43

There are about forty soldiers here under the command of Darius but some one hundred and fifty are stationed in the valley below though we saw no sign of them upon our advance.

In the temple area the women rule but within the enclosure of the valley it is a mutual rule with Ishtar the Governor and Gwyn his partner. There is no king or ruling class and all agree on what should be done by equal votes both men and women. I find this strange.

> *I am told this is a spiritual place and the body of the community resides to the west many days journey upon a great lake where they dig and process the copper metal. Some is traded with the local people but most is traded with the North men. This has been the way of things for hundreds of years I am told.*

[Note: In the original document the remainder of this page was obscure and/or missing. The Theban letters were unreadable. The ink was smeared or otherwise distorted from water or some acidic liquid. This was a key passage but someone had access to it and removed information about the copper trade.]

They are in the Hunter Mountain area, in the valley between Hunter and Plateau Mountains. Today a road cuts through the narrow valley. It is a protected valley at both ends, with the two mountains making natural barriers on the west and east. Readers may recall the Devil's Tombstone standing stone referenced earlier; it is located in the valley about 300 feet from Plateau Mountain.

Darius is the commander of forty soldiers in the temple area. Stationed in the valley below are 150 soldiers, evidently well hidden as de Sudeley did not see them when they first arrived. *Ishtar* is the governor and *Gwyn* is his partner; they rule equally, though women rule in the temple area. This is an egalitarian community, with all people—men and women, having a vote. This equality of the sexes is a remnant of the ancient Celtic society, where woman held their prominent positions and fought alongside their husbands in battle.

The reference to copper mining and trading is a major revelation. A minority of historians believe a well-established, trans-Atlantic copper trade existed in ancient times. The copper was transported from the Upper Peninsula in Michigan, where copper has been mined for thousands of years. The copper would have been traded to the *North men*, transported back to Europe and/or the Middle East, and combined with tin to make bronze. The *great lake* that is referenced *to the west, many days journey,* is probably Lake Superior, where extensive evidence exists of ancient copper mining and trade in the Upper Peninsula of Michigan and on Lake Superior's Isle Royale.

(For more details see Fred Rydholm's book, *Ancient Copper Mining*). De Sudeley is told that this mining and trading of copper has been going on for hundreds of years.

Passage 44

> *Upon the floor of the cavern of the Goddess was a circle of holes around the alter which from five of these holes lines extended to seven more holes in a semi circle before a square stone upon which sat a clay cauldron with the spirals upon it. The seven holes formed a small semi circle much in the shape of a smile.*
>
> *A woman with a circle of entwined vines about her head and in a white garment of some kind of leather spoke to Altomara: Are you a virgin of the Goddess? Altomara went upon her knees and with outstretched arms spoke in a language I could not follow ending with GA-STO. The woman then addressed me stating she was called Gwyn Mother Goddess of the Temple.*
>
> *Lionel translates. She explained that the holes on the floor represented days of the year. Where the five lines were was the letter "N" for the Nones of the month and it was of this part of the year that as the five lines showed they came together at the third hole which was of the bright star of the Borialis symbol of Arianrhod. When a wooden peg with a carving of a phallus on it was in that hole there would be a great festival.*

There is a circle of holes on the floor around an altar. Five of the holes extended to a semi circle which had seven holes. The rest is not clear. What can be determined is that the seven holes were arranged in a semi circle resembling a smile. This could be the oval, the ancient fertility symbol representing the female anatomy and a tribute to the power of birth. (An oval with a line through it represents the vulva and has been found as far back as the Paleolithic caves in France. It is also found in ancient cult sites in the Negev Desert, where rocks were split to depict the female anatomy.)

Altomara is asked if she is a "virgin of the goddess?" Virgin here means a *priestess*, not virgin in the literal sense. Altomara replies, *Ga–Sto,* Gaelic words meaning, *I Am.*

Gwyn, the mother goddess of the temple, explains that the holes on the ground are a kind of calendar marking sacred festivals.

Passage 45

The Spaniard did say unto Altomara that she lied for she was not a Virgin but she stated that she was for virginity is rather a state of mind than physical condition brought about by a lack of sexual contact. She was a free woman complete unto herself and without any ties to a man that she did not wish to have. This is in fact the basic form of the worship of the Goddess and though it is foreign to me as is the belief of the prophet of Islam I can understand both from having read now one of the scrolls.

I expressed a fervent desire to know more and stated this unto Gwyn. Thus I was told that I must prepare. I was taken from the Temple structure and led by a winding path down the side of the mountain opposite that from which we arrived to an overhang of rock blocked up on all sides to its top with a small opening at one end.

I was told to spend the night here after bathing in the stream to its left and to which a fall of water proceeded from above. On the morrow she would come and get me. I was to eat nothing and to drink no wine. This I thought a yoke as we had no wine since we left Braich Y Pwill in Gwynedd.

Altomara explains to the Spaniard that her state of mind was a form of goddess worship; it was not the physical state of virginity or sexual contact that determined her purity.

De Sudeley wants to learn more of the worship of the Goddess. Gwyn tells him that his learning is to begin by spending the night in a cave and she leads him to a stream and a small opening via a route down the side of the mountain opposite that from which we arrived.

(This is an accurate description of the mountain opposite Hunter, Plateau Mountain.) De Sudeley is on Hunter Mountain, where there exists still today a small waterfall and stream.

De Sudeley's joke (*yoke*) gives us the location of the harbor they sailed from in Wales: *Braich Y Pwill*. This medieval harbor exists today on the Lyn Peninsula in western Wales.

Passage 46

> *Upon the rising of the moon however she came to me and with a light of an oil lamp the oil of the rendered fat of the goose she stated as the lady of the Silver Wheel descends to Earth to watch over the tides of the sea and the tides of human fertility so does her maiden come to me.*
>
> *I told her I had taken a vow of celibacy that I could not break as it was before my God and of this she seemed pleased. I have tested you and have not found you wanting. She speaks in the language of my Land, of Engelnde much to my surprise. She states she knows many languages and is gone.*

De Sudeley is tested by Gwyn, the Mother Goddess of the *Temple*. He had bathed and fasted, in a kind of cleansing ritual. Gwyn comes to him as the *Lady of the Silver Wheel,* the moon goddess. These people know of the moon's effects on the tides and that the lunar cycle is connected to the menstrual cycle. De Sudeley's vow of celibacy is tested and he does not break it. (He was married before he became a Templar.)

De Sudeley is surprised that Gwyn speaks English. This woman is intriguing but all we know about her is that she represents the Goddess and is multilingual.

Passage 47

> *On the morrow she returns clothed again in her garments and shows me a winding path to the right that leads through a small opening in the rock as one would enter a vagina through a long passage that represents the womb into a large chamber and via a small opening*

> *at the back into the light of day in an alcove surrounded by rock.*
> *Following a narrow path down to a small cave we enter here and*
> *she states I must leave within the sand here an offering. She leaves a*
> *likeness of the Goddess Blodeuwedd and I leave some trinkets I have*
> *carried with me from home. She lights two lamps and by them I see*
> *that others have left things here also.*
>
> *At the very rear she states I am to reach into a hole and remove what*
> *I feel. It is an uneasy feeling to place your hand into a hole that you*
> *can not know what is inside but I do so and remove four rolled scrolls.*
> *I will return them to the Grand Master as I was so instructed and for*
> *which I was to be rewarded. It is the purpose of my venture here. We*
> *leave the way we have come.*

Gwyn takes de Sudeley through a rock opening shaped to represent the entrance to the vagina. They continue along a long passage, representing the womb. Clearly this is symbolic of the Goddess.

They entered a small cave where there is sand and Gwyn leaves an offering, a likeness (perhaps a figurine) of the goddess *Blodeuwedd,* the Celtic goddess of spring in Welsh mythology. De Sudeley leaves some trinkets and sees that others have left offerings in the cave as well.

At the rear of the cave Gwyn tells de Sudeley to reach into a hole and remove what he can grasp. He removes four rolled scrolls, which he calls the purpose of his mission. How did these scrolls first get here, to be protected by these people? We can only conjecture from the little information we have that there was a voyage to Hunter Mountain (aka Onteora) in the first century CE during which documents were transported out of Jerusalem to be held in safety within this community. (These would have been different documents/scrolls than the ones found in the early 12th century by the Templars.)

The reference to a reward to be given to de Sudeley gives us an insight into a possible motivation for leading the expedition. Recall also that de Sudeley was, at this time, likely still embroiled in the scandal involving the 1170 assassination of Thomas Becket, the Archbishop of Canterbury, by de Sudeley's brother—the opportunity to get out of Europe may have appealed to de Sudeley.

Passage 48

> *She states to me that as I have received knowledge from my parents at birth as have I received knowledge now. But as to the birth knowledge it must be learned how to unlock it and this is acquired knowledge. So now I exit from the vaginal opening symbolic of rebirth so I must wash in a pool as a baby is washed at birth and then climb a set of stone steps to the top of a great rock set in the stream of the pool and sit at its top in a depression there with the carving of the goose at my feet to let noon sun bath me with its warmth.*
>
> *She also states that of the four tubes I may choose one as my own. Looking at them I see that each has cut into the clay a letter of the Greeks and I see Alpha, Beta, Eta, Onicron and being anew I choose Alpha. She states I have chosen wisely.*

De Sudeley has gone through a profound spiritual experience. Gwyn explains to him that he has had a spiritual rebirth and acquired a kind of spiritual knowledge. At her instruction he climbs a set of stone steps to re-emerge from the opening and the womb to experience the birth of a new beginning. He then washes in a pool, the practice of cleansing by ritual bathing. This ritual takes us back to the Temple Mount of Jerusalem, where archeologists have found hundreds of Jewish ritual baths called *mikvahs*. Recall that John the Baptist and Jesus both practiced immersion in water as a purification ritual in the first century CE.

Gwyn tells him he can choose one of the four tubes as his reward. Each clay tube is marked with a Greek letter. Believing he has experienced a rebirth or a new beginning, de Sudeley chooses the Alpha tube, alpha being the first letter in the Greek alphabet and meaning beginning.

The reference to a goose carving atop a great rock set in the stream is an important clue. In the 1970s, Dr. Jackson climbed Hunter Mountain and found such a goose carving (which may be a dove or other bird), pictured here:

Goose Carving, Hunter Mountain

Obviously, this kind of corroborating evidence is important in validating our story.

Passage 49

Now I must pass through a long dark corridor between two rocks that has been covered with stone and earth to signify my passage from birth into knowledge. She states that now I must spend a night in a different cave opposite the one I spent last night in.

On its roof are strange symbols and lines. She states they are rivers showing the way to their brethren far to the South. These are called the Man-Den, Cone, Navasak.

She also states that Altomara shall not return with us. The Goddess has called her name. She has seen the owl. But of this I do not understand till later.

De Sudeley's passage through *a long dark corridor* symbolizes his entrance into an enlightened state, a new beginning. He then spends a night in another cave. *On its roof are strange symbols and lines.* Gwyn tells him that the lines and symbols are rivers which show the way to their *brethren far to the south,* whom she identifies as *the Man-den, Cone* and *Navasak* tribes.

Before I discuss these tribes, let us first focus on the river map on the ceiling. Jackson searched for, and found, the cave on Hunter Mountain sometime during the early 1970s. Remarkably, the lines on the ceiling were still visible. His 1974 sketch of the lines on the ceiling is here:

Hunter Mountain Cave—Ceiling Map

The rivers carved on the ceiling are the rivers that exist today—the Neversink and the Delaware. The two "branches" in the upper left are the East and West Branches of the Delaware; they combine to form the single Delaware River. The two "branches" in the upper right are the East and West Branches of the Neversink; they combine and flow into the Delaware. (For some unknown reason Jackson entitled his drawing, "Copy of Diorama Stone.") Jackson noted that the lines and symbols were not cut into the cave ceiling but were composed of an aggregate of crushed shells and stalks of a plant that over the centuries had hardened to be like concrete. He scratched off parts of this material and had it tested; according to his notes, the results showed the material dated back to at least 1,000 years ago.

Using this map as a guide, in the first decade of this century fellow researchers and I searched for the symbols depicted along the rivers. We found three of the symbols carved on rocks, as pictured below (in order: the dove symbol; the menorah or Tree of Life symbol; and the vulva or entrance to the womb symbol, surrounded by letters of an ancient script:

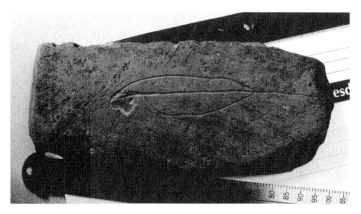

Dove Carving (Symbol of the Goddess)

Tree of Life Carving Depicting Tanit

Carving Symbolizing Entrance to the Womb

These carvings are yet more evidence corroborating the validity of both this map in particular and our entire story in general.

What, then, is the purpose of this map? Gwyn tells us they show the way to their three brethren tribes to the south. We have previously discussed the *Cone*, the "Ivri" (Israelites) who lived in the Neversink River Valley who sheltered Lionel and Wasabee. The *Man-den* is a clear reference to the Mandan tribe, the so-called "White Indians" of the Ohio River Valley (later they relocated to North Dakota) whom President Jefferson, along with many historians, believed were of Welsh descent due to their fair features and Welsh-like language. Note that the Neversink River flows into the Delaware, which in turns leads via other waterways to the Ohio River Valley. *Navasak* is unknown to us at the present time.

The map on the ceiling is remarkably similar to a large petroglyph resting on the bank of the West Branch Neversink River. This petroglyph shows a five-ringed spiral, with three "legs" protruding off its south side:

Frost Valley/Three Rivers Petroglypy

The petroglyph was studied by Jay S. Wakefield and Dr. Reinaud de Jonge in their book, *How the Sun God Reached America.* They named the carving the Three Rivers Petroglyph (others call it the Frost Valley Petroglyph) and concluded that the spirals depicted a region extending from a center and that the legs were rivers—the Delaware, the Susquehanna and the Ohio. They believed the carving was a travel guide made by a megalithic community two thousand years ago. I believe that the spiral, a symbol of the Goddess, represents the larger community and the center of the spiral marks the Temple to the Goddess on Hunter Mountain.

As we turn back to Jackson's ceiling cave map drawing, we see that he scribbled a note at the bottom, asking what the symbols represented. Some of these symbols, including the five-armed octopus, have appeared on other maps/document/artifacts in this mystery—I will return to this and other symbols later.

Not far from the Three Rivers Petroglyph, researchers also found a stone carved with six Paleo-Hebrew letters, an ancient form of Hebrew used from the 10th century BCE to the 2nd century CE:

Paleo-Hebrew Carving

Geologist Scott Wolter tested the rock at a university laboratory and concluded, based on the weathering, that this carving was at least "many centuries old."

Collectively, these are important artifacts which appear to evidence an ancient Jewish presence in the area and corroborate the events described in "A Year We Remember."

Finally, in this passage Gwynn makes a strange and disquieting remark about Altomara. She tells de Sudeley that Altomara will not return with them, because she has *seen the owl*. The owl, as some readers may know, is a portent of death in some cultures. We shall see how this prediction turns out ahead.

Passage 50

When I sat alone in the small cave I set about making a light and by it examined the tube I had chosen. The others were held by Gwyn. In it were four documents. A map on parchment and Signed Tantino d Mandrakis.

> *The second document was in Theban and said nothing til I used the disks and then it told of a vast treasure in gold and gems and precious relics including parts of the tablets given to Moses from GOD and held in a golden chest feared taken by the Romans when they overran Jerusalem and it was hidden below in the tunnels cut for water in the ruined city of Petra in the Valley of Edom and in a cavern with the mark of the crescent moon upon the mountain of Jebel Madhbah.*

De Sudeley is alone in the small cave on Hunter Mountain. He has one clay tube and he examines it, finding four documents. (Note that the clay tubes and scrolls within would likely only have survived if stored in the heated structure on the mountain. The comment in entry #12 of the MacDonald Journal is remarkable in foreseeing this.) One of the documents is a *map on parchment* signed with the name, *Tantino d Mandrakis*. The town of *Mandrakis* is on a Greek island in the Sporades. It has a small harbor and today is a tourist area for visitors coming by ferry from Athens. It was a custom in Europe for people to take the name of the place where they were born, telling us that Tantino was probably from Mandrakis. The Mandrakis map is on parchment, which is consistent with its presumed 1st century CE or earlier origin. The Greeks have a long history of seafaring dating back to the Mycenaeans. Greek sailors could have been involved in early Atlantic crossings joining up with other seamen from the Levant, such as the Phoenicians.

De Sudeley examines the second document and sees that it is in Theban. He uses the disks (described in passage #12) to decode the scrolls. What he learns is some of the most important information in the entire Templar Document.

The *second document* from the clay tube tells an incredible story of a vast treasure of *gold, gems and precious relics* as well as parts of *the tablets given to Moses from God* which were *held in a golden chest* feared taken by the Romans when they overran Jerusalem. We know from recorded history that the Romans captured treasures from the Temple in 70 CE; many of these they paraded through the streets of Jerusalem. But apparently many of the Temple treasures were saved. This account provides some specificity as to what was saved, identifying not only gold, gems and precious relics, but *tablets given to Moses by God held in a golden chest.* Clearly this is a reference to the Ten Commandments, and also likely to the Ark of the Covenant. Apparently these treasures were hidden in the ancient city of Petra, in modern-day Jordan.

Recall that de Sudeley is reading from a scroll on Hunter Mountain in the year 1178. The scroll describes features of the ancient city of Petra, including the historically-accurate references to *tunnels cut for water* and *a cavern with the mark of the crescent moon upon the mountain of Jebel Madhbah.*

Ancient Petra Water Tunnels Carved into Cliff Face
(courtesy Betsy Brewster)

Petra's history goes back thousands of years. It was the center of a vast trading network which accumulated great wealth from the transport of precious materials such as spices carried to the

Mediterranean. The rose-colored Treasury of Petra, carved into the sandstone rock face just as the water tunnels were, is a popular tourist attraction even today.

The Treasury of Petra (courtesy Betsy Brewster)

After the 4th century CE, Petra declined from its former greatness and was a lost, legendary city until the beginning of the 19th century when the Swiss explorer Johann Ludwig Burkhardt rediscovered it. Importantly, whoever authored the scroll possessed accurate knowledge of ancient Petra, even though the city had been lost to history for 1,500 years.

Passage 51

The third document also encoded was of a journey of the Spirit and told of the True Teachings of our Lord. Also of a Seal of Herod to an agreement of union between one Hasmonian princess, Myriam of Migdal and Yeshua ben Yosef of the royal House of David at Cana.

The names recited in this scroll are as explosive as they are extraordinary. Decoded by de Sudely, the document contains two stunning passages: 1) a reference to the *True Teachings* of Jesus, and 2) a reference to a sealed marriage contract.

We begin with the marriage contract. The names, of course, are what make it explosive: Jesus son of Joseph, and Mary of Migdal. Clearly this is referring to Jesus and Mary Magdalene (The lineage of Jesus can be traced through the House of King David through Jesus' adoption by Joseph). The reference to the *Seal of Herod* is likely to *Herod Antipas,* who ruled Jerusalem 4 BCE to 39 CE, after his father King Herod died. The possibility of a marriage between Jesus and Mary Magdalene is obviously a controversial subject, and is beyond the scope of this book.

We are not given any details regarding the *True Teachings* of Jesus. But it is worth noting that the Templars were eventually outlawed in 1307 based largely on accusations of heresy. Many historians believe they were practicing an alternative form of Christianity, contrary to the teachings of the Church, based on certain early Church "secrets" they discovered during their time in and around Jerusalem. A document disclosing *True Teachings* strongly implies that prevailing teachings were questioned.

Passage 52

> *When I emerged from the cave the next morning Cedric who had taken the Benedictine cowl at Shewsbury admonished me for my actions reminding me of my vows to Our Lady and the Holy Father. I in turn felt the need to respond in kind and did thus remind him of the vow he took with us at the Temple so stating that what I do now is by order of the Temple and for the Glory of God. If he came upon this quest with other intentions then his venture has been in vain and he was silent. However I know that his tongue will be well oiled.*

Cedric criticized de Sudeley for "his actions"—perhaps he thought de Sudeley had broken his vow of celibacy.

Taking the *Benedictine cowl at Shewsbury* is a reference to pledging oneself to the Benedictine Abbey in the medieval town near Shropshire; this is in the West Midland region in England, known for being Templar territory. A cowl is a hooded robe worn by Benedictine monks.

Sudeley reminds Cedric that their mission is by order of the *Temple*, an indication that the orders for this mission came from Templar leaders. Sudeley uses the phrase, a *well oiled tongue,* which describes a gossiper.

Passage 53

> *Gwyn has stated that on the morrow is a meeting with the local group at a great rock set on the banks of a river at the base of the mountain by a bald. Both she and Altomara went to meet a man called the Sac Man or Quicksa-Piet. A great healer among the Local people called the Le Nee Lan-ap-pee which I am told means First People. This mountain we are on is sacred to them as they believe their Great God lives on it but upon the opposite mountain lives the Pan-si-kee a trick player and I think a form of devilish demon. This may prove to be informative.*

These geographical descriptions match the area that exists today in the valley below Hunter and Plateau Mountains, *Pan-si-kee* being Plateau Mountain. The *great rock set on the banks of a river at the base of the mountain* likely refers to the standing stone described earlier known as the Devils' Tombstone, which sits just south of Plateau Mountain. Today a road passes through the valley between the two mountains. It may be that in the 12th century a river flowed there.

By using the term *trick player*, they may be referring to the unusual and extreme weather patterns on both Hunter and Plateau Mountains. Further, and consistent with the name Devil's Tombstone, there are legends about Plateau Mountain being the home of a demon.

Le Nee Lan-ap-pee is de Sudeley's phonetic pronunciation of the Lenape, a Native American tribe of the area which today identifies itself as the *First People.*

Passage 54

> *Clyphus, The Spaniard, Altomara, Lionel, Sir Eldric and I went with Gwyn down the steep slope of the mountain on the side where the caves were the next morning. As we approached the bottom of the ravine through which a river ran we could see to our right a bald and a large rock set beside the stream. It had a peculiar shape and reminded me of a grave stone.*
>
> *To its left was a spire of rock, grey in color spersed with white and the top rounded by man to resemble a phallus. To the right was a rounded large rock that was split through the center.*
>
> *Gwyn stated that on the first day of the third month the sun's rays cast a shadow at mid day upon the phallus which then entered the split in the rock to the right towards eventide symbolizing impregnation and marking the next day of festival to the Goddess.*

De Sudeley describes two stones, one that is shaped into a phallus and other split through the center. On a certain day, the shadow from the phallus stone enters the split in the rock, representing fertility. A discovery in 2014 revealed one hundred ancient cult sites with phallic stone structures and artifacts with vulva shapes cut into them in the Negev Desert in Israel. Phallus stones have also been found in South Woodstock, Vermont, at a site known as Calendar II.

Passage 55

> *Within the left side of the great stone and about the Phallus stone at the edge of the bald were several striking persons one of which was dressed in the hide of a bear with the head and skull of it over his own. He carried a short stick with two shells of tortoise joined together at the top which he periodically shook making a rattle noise. He had a metal ring through his nose and through his right ear which looked like silver. He appeared very old and Gwyn identified him as the Quicksa-Piet we were*

> *there to meet. The others were dressed in skins and furs with the*
> *feathers in their heads and painted up in red and white one in*
> *red and black. They were the escort.*

I have searched for this phallus stone, but it was likely destroyed when the modern road and railroad were built in the valley.

Passage 56

> *We approached over a tree set across the stream which had the*
> *top flattened to make walking easier. Thunder rolled in the dis-*
> *tance and it was a cool morning. Clyphus was looking to his left*
> *and staring into the forest beyond when I, taking up the rear*
> *and in full armor came to him asking what he was looking at.*
> *Something is astir in the forest me thinks he replied. An animal*
> *no doubt I stated but he said NAY and just at that point Alto-*
> *mara was seen making hand signs to the Quicksa-Piet with her*
> *back to the wode.*
>
> *She pitched forward and the Spaniard cried in a loud voice.*
> *Lionel, Gwyn and Sir Eldric covered the Quicksa-Piet and*
> *his people with their shields and drew weapons. I saw that*
> *there were feathers sticking out of Altomara's back. Instantly*
> *the Spaniard dove into the wode screaming and flailing his*
> *great axe.*

This dramatic account of an attack by a hostile force ends in Alto-mara's tragic death. Both entrances to the valley had been protected by the soldiers but apparently the meeting with the shaman had left them vulnerable to attack. Altomara's hand signs to Quicksa-Piet may indicate she suspected something and was warning the shaman with hand signs.

Recall that Gwyn had foreseen the death when she said that Altomara had *seen the owl*. The owl was believed to be an omen of death.

Passage 57

> *I was hit with several arrows but only one penetrated the armor and struck flesh in my left shoulder. It was the bolt of a crossbow and I felt the steel point hit bone. Still I stood but going to one knee rested a moment before charging after Clyphus and The Spaniard. He had no armor but his maile over a gambeson and some furs yet all of the arrows hitting him in the chest didn't strike home. He was among the attackers in a short time rushing up hill and the first three went down one his head rolling down hill and the other an arm missing the third was cleaved from skull to waist and the axe stuck. Then drawing blade and dagger he charged on. Clyphus dropped two as a third jumped from a rock upon his back but Gianna of Gwyn's people hit him with an arrow and Clyphus threw him over head finishing him with his dagger. Sir Eldric now entered the scene and he to was struck with an arrow in the side between the breast plate and the waiste guarde but it was a stone point and turned on his maile. The attacker was sliced both bow and man across the middle and left with his guts spilling out over the earth.*

This vividly-described battle scene is self-explanatory; this may be the battle depicted on the L-shaped device. The crossbow was an early medieval weapon widely used in Europe; apparently the weapon was taken in a raid and used by the attackers.

Passage 58

> *Another attacker jumped on Lionel's back but Wasabee defended her man and cut him across the throat burying her dagger of flint in it. The Spaniard had reached a man pulling something and bending over to do so and he was relieved of his head. Thus Ponce recovered the missing cross bow. The head of this one was presented to the Quicksa-Piet by The Spaniard on his knees. I had dispatched several and taken one as a prisoner. The attack was over. The Spaniard having presented the head*

> *which was taken and thrown to the warriors and they began to*
> *kick it around among themselves then went to Altomara.*
>
> *She spoke to him in a whisper and kissing him she passed to the*
> *Goddess. He turned to me and said, "She stated she had seen*
> *the owl. The Goddess has called her home. I will honor her as*
> *she wished."*

The graphic description of the battle continues. Here De Leon, the Spaniard, is referred to as *Ponce.*

If it were not for Altomara, the mission would not have succeeded. It was her knowledge of celestial navigation which enabled de Sudeley and his team to cross the Atlantic and find their way inland to Hunter Mountain. Her relationships with the community on Hunter Mountain and the Native Americans were also essential.

Passage 59

> *The attackers were enemies of the Quicksa-Piet and his people*
> *and of the people of the Goddess. They are known as the Cat-*
> *Skins and the Sac-Man stated that because of their actions in*
> *making war in a sacred place all other groups will not befriend*
> *them.*
>
> *Only the five groups of the many fingered rivers to the West*
> *would be friends to them.*
>
> *For our actions on his peoples behalf there would be peace*
> *between his people and those on the mountain for as long as the*
> *trees grow, the four winds blow and the sun shines.*

Quicksa-Piet and his people are the Lenape, friends of the people of the Goddess. It would be interesting to see if there was some reference to this in their tribal history. Another road to travel in this unending story.

Cat –Skins are unknown but we learn that they will be ostracized for making war in a sacred place. Apparently the entire area including the valley and the mountain was considered sacred ground, as evidenced by the Lenape calling nearby Panther Mountain "The Wellspring of Creation," perhaps because Panther Mountain is the site of an ancient meteor impact.

The reference to *the many fingered rivers* gives us a geographical location for where the attackers live—the Finger Lakes region of New York State. The Esopus River circles the rim of the buried impact crater.

The word *Sac-Man* is similar to sachem, a spiritual leader.

Passage 60

> *Altomara was taken and wrapped in a mat and placed upon the top of the stone tunnel upon a great pile of wode of the pine tree and a fire was set below and she was consumed. The bones were gathered and placed in a special box of oak wode and Ponce took her ash and placed it in the jar he had carried Myrrh that he had used to wash her body with.*
>
> *Gwyn had her placed in the cave with the carving atop its roof both ash and bone box and each of us left a grave good.*
>
> *Gwyn left the three scrolls and I the disks but the Alpha I took with me and later secreted the Eta one also. Talismans were set upon the cave and Clyphus and Sir Eldric pushed a great rock from above to block the entrance and then we made upon the hide of a deer a chart with the sky tool to mark the place where she was and to mark the place of the disks for I knew that Hubert held the others. If the Goddess Priestess thought we could not read the scrolls she may let us have more. It was a good thought as Gwyn had Sir Eldric and Lionel also chose scrolls.*

Altomara's ashes are placed in the *cave with the carving on the roof*. This carving shows the rivers to the other communities in the south. (See passage #49.) Gwyn leaves three scrolls (in clay tubes) in the cave with the disks (the decoders). De Sudeley had sent one decoder back with a ship for insurance. We assume that the decoder sent back would ensure the decipherment of the scrolls. (See ahead for a reference to this.) Talismans are also left in the cave. A huge rock is pushed there to block the entrance. The *Sky Tool* is used to mark the location of the cave on the hide of a deer skin.

Gwyn apparently is the keeper of the scrolls and she allows Sir Eldric and Lionel to choose their own scrolls, apparently (in de Sudeley's opinion) because she believes they could not decipher them without the disks (though it is unclear why she would not want them to be deciphered). De Sudeley takes the Alpha clay tube which Gwyn had already given him; he also takes the Eta scroll.

Note: Jackson searched for the cave on Hunter Mountain in the mid 1970s. He found it, with a huge rock blocking its entrance. After moving the rock, Jackson entered the cave and found a metal container with an ancient silver necklace, a small urn, and semi-precious stones (perhaps the funerary gifts left to Altomara as described above). They have never been tested. The container and necklace are pictured below:

Hunter Mountain Cave Items

Passage 61

We laid out marks on the rocks so that the chart would be better followed in the future. Clyphus had a chart of the stars for Beltane at Cypress and he felt he could track a course home by marking one of the stars here.

A large natural stone formation on the side of the mountain of the Goddess suggests a human face in its shape and at the right

> *of this a ledge that allows one to stand with a complete view of*
> *the South, East and North. So did Clyphus prove of some worth*
> *after all.*

We laid out marks on the rocks so that the chart would be better followed in the future. De Sudeley anticipates there will be a return voyage to Hunter Mountain and is taking steps to ensure the path is well-marked. There are Theban letters cut into certain rocks on Hunter Mountain that still remain there today; Jackson used these to find the cave.

As the passage states, there is a rock profile on the side of Hunter Mountain which resembles a face:

Hunter Mountain Face

By standing on a ledge, Clyphus believes he can chart a way home using the stars; recall that with Altomara dead, they have lost their guide.

Passage 62

> *Clyphus did however choose to check his measurements upon the morrow at eventide and as he was at work did a rain begin and he cried Oh Astroth and upon this utterance did a lightening bolt strike his metal and he was killed as the rain turned to snow. Gwyn claims it is an Omen but I believe it an accident of timely proportions.*
>
> *Now only those of the Templars know the disks are within with Altomara's ash.*
>
> *He is also laid to rest in a cave upon the top of the mountain near the living structure of the Goddess.*

Hunter Mountain is known for its extremes of weather; snow falls above a certain altitude while rain and lightning fall below.

Sudeley says Clyphus' death *an accident of timely proportions.* With Clyphus dead, no one outside the Templars knows the location of the cave with the disks and Altomara's ashes. This Templar secret was apparently passed down over the centuries. I remind readers of the statement made by Hank Roche in the MacDonald Journal. Five hundred years after de Sudeley left Hunter Mountain, Roche was referencing scrolls in clay jars hidden in a cave in North America for over a thousand years. He also knew that the key to finding the cave was a document kept in the Church of San Sigismundo.

Clyphus is buried in a cave on the top of the mountain near the ***living structure of the Goddess.*** What is this structure? The words "living structure" imply something that is a living, spiritual force. This remains a mystery.

Passage 63

> *I have been laid out in a hut of sticks bent over round and covered with hides. A fire is within and some evil smelling dried plant is placed in it. The smoke is overpowering and I become dizzy as though drunk with too much wine. Then I remember*

> *nothing. When I awake the arrow is removed and a poultice of the sap of a wide leaf plant covered with the inside bark of a tree and then a leather cuff strapped with lacing about my arm and shoulder has been applied. It is changed four times a day and heals well. The Quicksa-Piet tends my wound himself with a woman called Gerillius of the temple who is learning this method of healing from him.*

De Sudeley's wounds are cared for by Quicksa–Piet, the shaman whose life was saved by the Templars. He is treated with various medicinal herbs.

Passage 64

> *With a course set we prepared to depart. Gwyn gave us the bless-ing of the Goddess and of Arianrhod, Mother of Dylan and Lleu Llaw Gyffes, sister of Gwydion, Niece of Math ap Mathonwy daughter of Beli wife of Nwyvre ruler of Caer Sidi and Caer Arianrhod.*
>
> *More substantial she provided us with a guide as did the Quicksa-Piet of the Len-ap-pee who would guide us to the val-ley of the Cone for it was in the mind of Lionel that he and Wasabee should reside with them if they would grant them suc-cor as it was now evident that Wasabee was with child.*

The list of blessings given to the Templars as they prepare to leave is from the Celtic pantheon of gods and goddesses. We now understand that some members of the community on Hunter Moun-tain were Celts. As mentioned earlier, Arianrhod is the Goddess of the Silver Wheel. The wheel represents the circumpolar stars in the northern sky, believed to be a mill in the heavens that turns.

Quicksa-Piet provides a guide as does Gwyn to lead them to the *Valley of the Cone*, which we know is the Neversink River Valley. Lionel has decided not to return with Sudeley and instead he and a pregnant Wasabee decide to live with the Cone.

Passage 65

> *Lionel did put in my care the scrolls given him and stated that he now had all he ever wanted and with the birth if all went well he would seek the people of the Goddess to the south that Gwyn called the Man-Den so that Wasabee could be with people she could speak with in her native tongue. It would be his gift to her for the child. I have agreed to release him from his vow and we set out thus.*

Lionel gives de Sudeley his scrolls. Sudeley now has these along with the Alpha and the Eta clay tubes. A clay tube could hold three or four rolled scrolls. (Note that de Sudeley uses the plural, "scrolls.")

Lionel de Walderne was one of the first to join the mission. He may have been a cousin of Queen Sophia, wife of King Valdemar I of Denmark and is listed in the genealogy of the king of Denmark. Recall that he and Wasabee declared their love for each other with the ritual of the "twelve cakes," a Biblical reference which can be found in the Book of Jeremiah. This may explain why Lionel chooses to live with the Cone, who (like him) may have a Jewish background. Recall that I believe the word "Cone" is a reference to the "Cohen" family of Jewish priests. This may explain the discovery of another stone inscribed with Paleo-Hebrew letters (different than the one discussed above), also found in the Neversink River Valley in 2004, pictured here:

Paleo-Hebrew Tetragrammaton Stone

Reading from right to left, we have "Y-H-V-H" (there is also a small "x" between the V and the H), known as the Tetragrammaton. These letters spell out the ineffable name of God, whom Jews refer to as Yahweh. This is an intriguing and important artifact, providing additional evidence of ancient Jews in the Hunter Mountain area.

We also learn that the *Man-Den* people to the south (that is, the Mandan Native Americans living at that time in the Ohio River Valley whom many refer to as the "White Indians" and who are believed to be of Welsh origin), are also Goddess worshipers, as Lionel describes them as *the people of the Goddess to the south.* Having allies in the Ohio River Valley, on the route to the Great Lakes, would be useful to the Hunter Mountain residents in their copper trade ventures, as described in Passage 43.

Passage 66

> *It is very cold and snow has fallen but the guides called Sif and Dane of the Goddess know the way well. From a mountain top we can see far to the west the land of the many rivers as the disconnected fingers of a hand where live the enemies of the Len-ap-pee.*

De Sudeley and his party, with their guides (we learn later that Sif is a female), start in late autumn on their journey of return. The Finger Lakes are identified: *From a mountain top* they can see *far to the west the land of the many rivers as the disconnected fingers of a hand.* The Finger Lakes can be seen from one of the 4000-foot mountains in this area, Plateau Mountain.

Passage 67

> *We arrive in two days at a sheltered cave near a waterfall on the bank of a large river to the West of the Tall Mountain with water at the top and for the first time meet one of the Co-Han.*
>
> *They look to me as the Ivri. They wear a small hat of woven grasses upon the top of their heads and unlike the natives of this place all have much facial hair and long beards.*

> *They are of a darker color than those of the Goddess but lighter than those of the native peoples. They have heard of our exploits with the Len-ap-pee and of the death of Altomara. We are made welcome. Lionel is to be made a member of their group and will be given a place of honor in the Circle. I am happy for him.*

De Sudeley's direct observations (hat of woven grasses, facial hair and long beards) of a people he calls the "Co-han" confirms our suspicion that they are the *Ivri* (Hebrew people), or Jews. They could be Judeans who fled from the Roman onslaught in the years before 70 CE and carried the precious scrolls to Hunter Mountain. Recall the Bat Creek Stone (discussed in comments to Passage 31), inscribed in Paleo-Hebrew with the words, "A Comet for the Jews," found in Tennessee in the late 1800s by a Smithsonian Institute archeologist. This stone has been studied by Professor Cyrus Gordon, a linguist who concluded the script was first or second century CE after matching letters on the stone to Hebrew coins of the that same period. This conclusion is confirmed by numismatic evidence compiled by Y. Meshorer in *Ancient Jewish Coinage*.

Bat Creek Stone

Passage 68

> *Sif tells us we must leave when the snow melts a little and before the river ices up. We will go by water most of the way but must take the boats around a great cataract four days travel South*

and then we will reach a greater river. We will wait there till it freezes over and walk to the other side.

Then we will travel overland half North to East following the ridges descending all the while till we make a sharp change and go South.

Geography confirms the *great cataract* described in this passage. It is the "Neversink Gorge," a landmark site in Denton Falls and High Falls, New York approximately 65 miles south of Hunter Mountain (consistent with a four-day winter journey) along the Neversink River.

The *greater river* may be the Delaware. The Neversink flows southwest joining the Delaware River at Port Jervis, where New York, New Jersey and Pennsylvania meet. They will wait until the Delaware freezes over and walk to the other side. They will make a turn *half north to east* (that is, northeast) and *follow the ridges descending all the while.* This is the hilly area east of the Neversink River and west of the Hudson River. At some point they will make a sharp change and go south.

Below is a map of the Hudson Valley area drawn by Ralph de Sudeley:

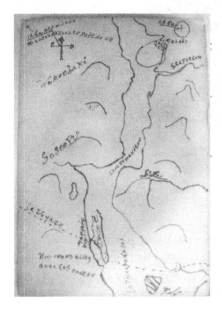

Map of Hudson Valley Area Drawn by de Sudeley

Note the signature on this map on the bottom right—*Ralp,* for Ralph. Next to his signature is the coat of arms of the Sudeley family. This map conforms to a modern map of the Hudson River Valley.

Passage 69

We reach a high bluff overlooking another greater river with a small island upon its far shore. Here the river narrows and it is here we will cross. We begin to fell trees for rafts and are soon upon the far shore. This river is of salt.

We pass in three days several stone and earth covered structures but don't stay in them. They are for the woman.

We cross another river with the help of the local people and to this to an island of great size and travel in a sheltered water way by great bark boats along this to where we can await the thaw to build a boat and sail East to our homeland across the great ocean.

Here we have an important clue: *This river is of salt.* This describes the Hudson River, which is a salt water tidal estuary as far north as Albany as a result of tides from the Atlantic Ocean. The *small island on the far shore*: They come to the Hudson River and see what is today called Bannerman Island (readers may recall the importance this island plays in our story), which can be seen from the high bluff on the west side of the river. It is the only island in the Hudson River close to the eastern shore.

The *river narrows.* The narrowest place on the Hudson River is between West Point (on the west side of the river) and Cold Spring. This is where the group crosses. We can confirm the accuracy of de Sudeley's description by comparing it to a modern map (note arrow marking Bannerman's Island):

Hudson River Map, Modern Day

They are now on the east side of the Hudson River in Putnam County, where they see *several stone and earth covered structures.* Putnam County is the home to over one hundred stone chambers; they have been investigated by members of the New England Antiquities Association (NEARA) and have been found to be oriented to astronomical events such as equinoxes and solstices, similar to stone chambers of the British Isles.

Putnam County Stone Chamber

We cross another river with the help of the local people and to this to an island of great size. As we shall learn below, this is the East River, leading to Manhattan Island.

From there, they will *sail east to our homeland across the great ocean.*

Passage 70

> *It is strange these people set great importance upon such little things as beads of color which we give them many. As Sif has said it has been accomplished and our year is completed upon the banks of the Great Salt River at the Island of the Man-ap-ti-en peoples.*
>
> *Our escort has left us two days ago at a stone shelter covered with earth and have returned with Dane but Sif has found it good to stay with us. Ship building will commence soon.*

Island of the Man-ap-ti-en peoples is Sudeley's phonetic pronunciation of Manhattan Island, a Lenape word meaning "island of many hills." The Hudson River is on the west side of Manhattan and the East River on its eastern side. The identification of Manhattan in the 12th century is nothing short of remarkable.

Their Lenape escort has left them, but their guide Sif remains.

Passage 71

> *I have asked the Spaniard about when he charged up the hill the day Altomara died. He wore no armor but maile yet the arrows did not stick into his flesh. He can not explain this except to say that Altomara had given him a copper disk some hand and a half round with the symbol of the Goddess on it and he wore it on a cord under his coat. It was swinging back and forth so it may have stopped the arrows but he is not sure. He shows it to me and it has several dents where points may have struck. I think however it occurred it was a miracle and a result of the Grace of God and he agrees.*

This passage is self-explanatory. Their belief in the talisman Altomara gave the Spaniard is not much different than people today wearing good luck amulets or religious symbols on their bodies.

Passage 72

> *The ship is in the style of the North men but with the sail lateen as has been constructed by Ishma il al-Mutamid who has accepted the Cross of Christ and taken the vows of the Order and is related to Hugh de Payens by the union of his ancestors Abddullah al-Kamal and Zohra. It is of one mast and spar and of only one deck with a portion for some shelter of the stores.*

In Passage 70 there was a short statement that ship building was to commence soon. Based on later passages, I believe they are now in the northeast section of Long Island and have sheltered in an area where they can begin building a ship.

The ship is in the style of the North men. It is a Norse ship which would be in keeping with the six ships in the de Sudeley party which sailed from Wales. The style of the ship is Norse but has something different, *a lateen sail.*

Lateen sails were used on Arabian ships and were triangular-shaped sails which had an advantage in catching and holding head winds. Thus they provided greater mobility than ships which only carried a single square sail. The lateen sail added to the Norse ship was an innovation by Ishma il al-Mutid, a Templar related to Templar first Grand Master Hugh de Payens.

Passage 73

> *We take on skins of water and a plant called mace dried and ground. It is a filling food with a little water. Some dried meats and fruits also are provided and when Sif tells us the winds are favorable we will set her to sail and will make land in two moons and half another by the Grace of God and the Goddess Arianrhod of whom Sif is a Priestess.*

> *She will go to the King of the North to tell him of the passing of Altomara and so will The Spaniard go with her as does Ishma'il and Gretchen.*

Mace is maize—they are given corn dried and ground. Corn was grown only in America.

American corn was found sculpted on the walls of Rosslyn Chapel, built in Scotland in the latter half of the 15th century.

Sif is returning with them to Denmark; apparently she has taken on the role of Altomara in guiding them on their return. She knows about the winds and the time it will take to sail across the Atlantic (two and a half months). Apparently priestesses of the Goddess had special training in celestial navigation.

Passage 74

> *We have finished the oars and they are in place. The ship rides high in the water and we add ballast of stone. We take it into the sheltered bay with six small islands but stay in the deep channel as there are shoals here. We must practice much with a small crew till we are satisfied that it handles well for us.*
>
> *This island forms two fingers with a bay between and upon the leftmost point we land and Sif marks a stone by the stars as to where the Temple lies. Eldric makes a chart and calls this place a lining place as it points both west to the Temple and East towards home.*
>
> *Now we set sail and with the Grace of God the company will be divided and I go with the scrolls to the Temple at Castrum Sepulchri*

Four geographical clues tell us they are in Long Island Sound, in the waters around the north fork of Long Island:

Sheltered bay is Gardiner's Bay, which is between the North and South forks of eastern Long Island.

With six small islands—there are six islands in Gardiner's Bay.

An island with two fingers describes the two eastern forks of Long Island, the North Fork and the South Fork.

A bay between is Gardiner's Bay which separates the North Fork and the South Fork.

Below is a modern map of Gardiner's Bay on the eastern part of Long Island:

Eastern Long Island [credit Google]

They land on the *leftmost point* of land. This is amazingly accurate and matches Orient Point on the North Fork projecting into the Atlantic Ocean. De Sudeley's description is accurate—the North Fork is on the left when one travels east.

Our conclusion regarding their location is confirmed by a map (apparently drawn in 1179 by de Sudeley or a member of his team), found and photographed by Dr. Jackson:

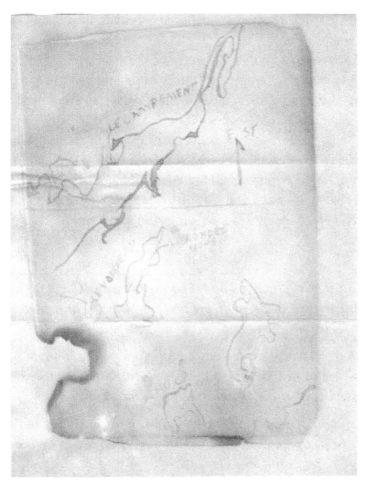

North Fork of Eastern Long Island

Orient Point is shown in the upper right of the map. The span on land running from Orient Point to the southwest in the Northern Fork. Below the North Fork is Gardiner's Bay, with islands. (Note the burnt section where Dr. Jackson applied heat to see if there was invisible ink on the map.)

There are four French words on the map:

Le Compement: the cove, or camping place

Le vasseau: the vessel

Le rendezvous: the meeting

Le feu: the fire

It appears the vessel was anchored at Shelter Island and tested in the waters of Peconic Bay.

Eldric makes a chart and names the area the "lining place," as it pointed west to the Temple on Hunter Mountain and East across the Atlantic Ocean towards home, England. Note that the eastern tip of Long Island is where researcher Tom Paul found the beginning of the Hammonasset Line, a series of stone cairns stretching from Connecticut into New York State and ending at Devil's Tombstone near Plateau Mountain. Readers may recall that the Hammonasset Line marks the summer solstice sunset, and was the path Roche and group may have followed to lead them to Hunter Mountain in the early 1900s.

Passage 75

---

and the mast is damaged and the lower spar cracked but the sail is not damaged. We are all wet and for Cedric who was aloft all are safe. He has gone to God. May he be received well.

God has certainly protected the location of the Temple of the Goddess and the disks as now the Holy Father can hear of it only from one of the Order of the Knights Templar.

We are now XII without the Spaniard and Sif. He may return with her to the Temple as his love for Altomara warrants it. I have released him from his vow.

We again begin midsentence. Jackson wrote that part of the original page was missing, plus another page. He believed that the word *storm* also may have been legible here.

A storm damages the mast and lower spar is cracked but the sail is safe. They survive, except Cedric is swept into the sea.

Sudeley refers to the pope and makes the interesting comment that the location of the Temple and the disks can be reported to the pope only by a Templar. The meaning is clear here: The Templars are in a powerful position, with leverage over Pope Alexander III.

The remaining group is now twelve, Sif and de Leon (the Spaniard) having apparently returned to Hunter Mountain (so de Leon could be near Altomara's tomb).

Passage 76

> *Sir Eldric sights land and we are soon on a rocky shore but the hull is undamaged. It is an Island on the XL course. We make landfall at Eris Head in two days and three days hence we are at Gwynedd and make for Merthyr Tydfil.*

The reference to the *XL course* is an indication they are sailing along the 40th parallel (XL being the Roman number for 40). By way of reference, Orient Point, Long Island sits near the 41st parallel.

They *make landfall on Eris Head,* on the northwest coast of Ireland. *Three days hence we are at Gwynedd,* in northern Wales. From there they make for Merthyr Tydfil, in south Wales. Below is a map showing their voyage across the Atlantic:

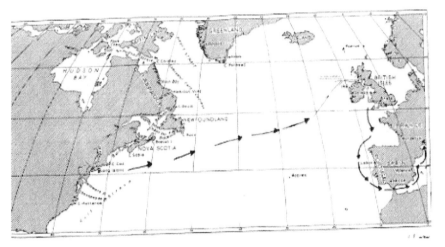

De Sudeley Return Voyage

Passage 77

> *I have thus returned to the Cistercian Abbey at Castrum Sepulchri in three Moons. My shoulder has healed well but pains me a bit when the damp sets in. Father Abselem has sent us brother Antoninus to take down my story so that it can be added to the record by order of the Grand Master, Odon de St. Amand. He*

> *has informed me that the map and instructions to the treasure of the Alpha scroll shall be my reward for the valuable service I have provided and having received the Sacraments and been given Absolution I shall be given a Command of the Garrison at Petra. This is more than I can hope for.*

From Wales de Sudeley and his group have now sailed to Castrum Sepulchri, on the Mediterranean coast of northwest Italy. His log is *added to the record,* a clue that Castrum Sepulchri also kept other Templar records. Is it possible that these records remain in some hidden section of the abbey, lost for centuries?

Odon de St. Amand is the Templar Grand Master at this time. He gives de Sudeley his reward—the *map and instructions to the treasure of the Alpha Scroll.* De Sudeley is also given command of the Petra garrison, which readers may recall is the location where treasures of the Temple of Jerusalem were hidden from the Romans (see Passage 50). It is the Alpha Scroll, the one given to de Sudeley, which describes the Petra hiding spots. Apparently de Sudeley is to search for these treasures. Here is the relevant passage repeated again:

> *The second document ... told of a vast treasure in gold and gems and precious relics including parts of the tablets given to Moses from God and held in a golden chest feared taken by the Romans when they overran Jerusalem and it was hidden below in the tunnels cut for water in the ruined city of Petra.*

It is not just gold and gems, but also possibly the Ark of the Covenant and the Ten Commandments, which were secreted in Petra. We shall learn more of de Sudeley's adventures in Petra below.

Passage 78

> *We have returned with nine tubes many having several scrolls within but the marriage agreement Master Odon states is valued beyond measure. Unfortunately Hubert and his ship was lost at sea thus no disks remain.*

> *A quest is to be assembled to recover the ones with Altomara de Leon but I shall not be a party to it nor shall Ponce, he hated that name and always wanted to be called the Spaniard.*
>
> *However, the new Grand Master, Arnould de Torogo decides to delay it.*
>
> *I state that all of the above is as I remember it and to so place my sign and name below to so attest this by the Grace of God in the Year of our Lord 1180. (MCLXXX)*
>
> *Ralp De Sedley.*

Grand Master de St. Amand declares that, of all the items brought back from Hunter Mountain (nine tubes, each with many scrolls within), the *marriage agreement is valued beyond measure.* This is one of the most extraordinary statements of the entire record. We have speculated as to identities of the parties to this *agreement of union between one Hasmonian princess, Myriam of Migdal and Yeshua ben Yosef of the Royal House of David at Cana*—Jesus and Mary Magdalene.

We know that important documents and writings were hidden during the years of the first century CE, when Rome ruled Judea. Desperate measures were taken to preserve and hide both ancient and current writings. For example, the Dead Sea Scrolls list hiding places of treasures which have never been found. Other documents were hidden below the South Wall in Jerusalem. Apparently, as we have just read, another group of clay tubes with scrolls were transported across the Atlantic Ocean to Onteora in northeastern America. These nine clay tubes containing scrolls apparently are similar to twelve other clay tubes containing scrolls found in an ossuary (along with gold bars, four navigation devices and a decoder, and the bones and separated skull of a man found in other ossuaries) by the Templars beneath the Temple Mount in the first part of the 12th century. All these treasures, and likely others, were deposited in Castrum Sepulchri in Seborga, the place de Sudeley referred to as the "Temple." Castrum Sepulchri is pictured below; note the Templar cross in the mosaic in the courtyard:

Castrum Sepulchri

No disks remain. Hubert's ship was lost, along with the disks he was carrying. The loss of the disks/decoders is a huge setback, as the writing on the scrolls was in Theban and the decoding device was needed to decipher the coded texts. Plans for another voyage to recover the disks left in Altomara's cave on the mountain are in the works, but the incoming Grand Master Arnoud de Torrojo decides to delay the voyage. Why there is a delay, we do not know.

Hunter Mountain—Modern Day Search

Later we will return to Ralph de Sudeley and examine his activities post-journey. Before we do so, there is some modern-day research being conducted on Hunter Mountain which is relevant to our story.

In a compelling excursion that validated many details of "A Year We Remember," a team of researchers ascended Hunter Mountain in June, 2009 to follow up on the 800-year-old clues left by de Sudeley and his team of Templars. The team consisted of Don Ruh, David Brody, Steve St. Clair, Scott Wolter, and Scott's son Grant. Don had found an odd sketch in the Jackson papers; the sketch had a note on it referencing

"the one remaining tube in the cave on hunter mtn," with the date of 1984. The sketch featured what looked to be a Masonic compass and square, squiggly lines which Don believed were a stream, three Theban letters, and a directional arrow pointing north:

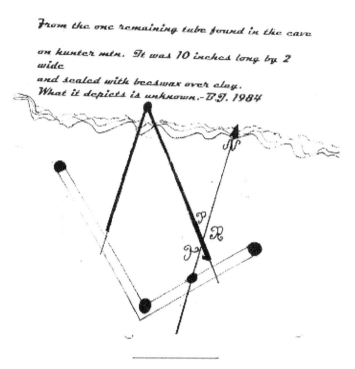

Hunter Mountain Map/Sketch

Don had a hunch that the sketch could be a map of Hunter Mountain and that there may be more artifacts to recover. I suggested that the copper objects found inside the mysterious brass device inside the Bannerman Island garden ornament were clues that would help in searching the mountain. I also suggested that three of my friends and fellow researchers accompany him in his search. The team started at the small pond off Route 214. The mountain was very imposing and the trail leading up was steep and rugged, roughly following parallel to the stream marked on Don's sketch. The team looked for the markings on the sketch—roughly a hundred yards from the stream, they found a triangle carved into a sandstone rock outcrop. Scott Wolter, a geologist, took several photos and carefully studied the carved symbol with his hand-lens. He wrote, "The grooves appeared to be weathered and even though I couldn't determine how old they were, I could definitely say they were not recently cut."

Triangle Carving

As the team continued up the trail, following the map on the sketch, they found the next carving they were looking for, a carving of the Theban letter, 'B':

Theban 'B' Carving

The team was unable to find the Theban 'A' shown on the map sketch, but they did locate a massive outcrop opening which they believed it had once been carved (the carving may have worn away, become covered with lichen/moss, or spalled off).

The group also located so-called Table Rock, a large outcrop with a flat ledge on top. Readers may recall Table Rock, along with the stream and the depiction of Hunter Mountain, were drawn on the L-shaped copper device found in the Bannerman Island garden ornament (see Chapter 1).

About twenty minutes later, the team came to the next carving near the bottom of a massive block of sandstone further up the mountain. This carving was closer to the ground but was still clear and distinct—an outline of a bird (perhaps a dove) as depicted on the sketch, approximately eight inches in length:

Bird/Dove Stone

Scott concluded that the Theban 'B' and the bird/dove, like the triangle, all "had grooves that exhibited weathering and were not recently carved." The bird, especially, showed signs of significant aging, as evidenced by the lichen and moss having grown over and into its carved areas.

Both the triangle and the dove are symbols long associated with ancient Mediterranean cultures. And, of course, it was very unusual to have Theban letters carved on stones in America. (Readers will recall the Theban letters on the brass device and the Theban letters in the 12th century Templar Document.)

The sketch indicated that the carvings and Table Rock should be used as positional markers, and that from these markers a point of interest could be triangulated. Using a tape measure and string, the team performed what Don believed to be the directed calculations and placed a red flag in the ground at the point Don believed was indicated in the map sketch.

After a short rest, Steve, Scott and Grant decided to search for another cave they had been told about called the "Sand Cave." Dave stayed with Don to dig where the red flag was. They found a void under the surface about two feet deep. Don, lying on his stomach, reached down, pulled stones from the void and handed them to Dave, who cleaned them off and examined them. Dave noticed that one of the stones had markings on it. It was an axe-head sized flat stone. One of the flat sides of the stone was carved with Roman numbers and it had the words "In Camera" carved across the bottom. On the back of the stone was what looked like a hand and also a figure of the Carthaginian goddess "Tanit," with a triangle base, a dot in the center of the triangle, upraised arms and a head. This appears to be a blessing pose, based on other known depictions of *Tanit* found of the ancient Near Eastern goddess. Recall the words of Passage 15 discussed above, which state that the de Sudeley team boat is adorned with the *symbol of the goddess.*

"In Camera" Stone, Front and Back

The latitude and longitude numerals are clear:

X L V X X X 45⁰ 30' N

L X X V L I I I 75⁰ 53' W

[Note that Scott examined the carving and determined the final numeral in the second line was an "I" rather than an "L," the horizontal line being a natural fault in the stone.]

We thus end up with **45⁰ 30' North** and **75⁰ 53' West.** The letters below the numbers clearly spell, *IN CAMERA.* Dave, an attorney, explained that "In Camera" was a phrase used in the legal profession when a judge wanted to privately review a document or have a private meeting in his chamber or "in secret." The obvious inference is that the latitude and longitude were meant to be a secret. But where was the location of these coordinates? What was the secret?

Using Google Earth, the latitude and longitude coordinates revealed a location in a forested area near Ottawa City. That didn't seem to make sense until Dave realized that the Templars of the 12th century would likely have used Paris (where their headquarters were) as a prime meridian and not the Greenwich, England prime meridian used today. When Dave made the adjustment (Paris being 2°, 20' east of Greenwich) and typed the adjusted coordinates of 45° 30' North and 73° 33' West into Google, an image of the Notre Dame Basilica in Old Montreal popped onto his screen.

How were Notre Dame Basilica and Old Montreal connected to a stone found on Hunter Mountain? They now had a fascinating mystery on their hands. Scott recalled that he had read the *The Templar Legacy in Montreal,* by Canadian author, Francine Bernier. Ms. Bernier said that the Sulpicians, a religious Order from France (believed to be comprised of descendants of the French noble families who had originally founded the Knights Templar), had built the earliest parts of the "Notre Dame de Bon Secours Church." The early structure had some very interesting carvings—Templar crosses!

Templar crosses in Old Montreal in the early 1600's opened up an intriguing question. Were the Sulpicians in the early 17th century following a Templar tradition dating back to the 12th century? Ms.

Bernier had also written that the Notre Dame Basilica contained a "fabulous clue" that indicated an esoteric tradition tying the structure to nontraditional Christian beliefs. In October, 2009, Scott and Dave visited the Notre Dame Basilica to learn more about this "fabulous clue." They saw what Bernier herself had seen and described—a beautiful golden triangle surrounded by sunrays, on the ceiling high above the main pulpit:

Notre Dame Basilica "Tetragrammaton"

It was difficult to see the details as it was thirty feet high in a poorly lit area. Ms. Bernier had referred to it in her book as a Tetragrammaton, which she described as "the four Hebrew letters that spell the unspoken, sacred name of God." We know this name as Yahweh. However, this triangle has only three Hebrew letters, not four. The three Hebrew letters—He, Vav, He—spell "Chavah" in Hebrew, or Eve in Latin. (The first letter, Yod, or 'Y,' was missing; it should have been on the far right, Hebrew being read right to left.) Ms. Bernier concluded, after consulting various experts, that there was an esoteric tradition present during the time of the construction of the early Notre Dame Basilica. Whoever carved the triangle was sending a secret message: They had replaced the traditional portrayal of the divine and replaced it with a feminine counterpart. In other words, they had changed the name of God to Chavah (or Eve), meaning "mother of all life." Whoever carved this knew and understood the ancient tradition carried down from the ancient Goddess-worshipping cultures, a tradition later adopted by Bernard of Clairvaux and the Cistercians/Templars.

A second clue is contained in a mural on the left side of the Basilica as one enters. At first glance, this appears to portray the Virgin Mary with her son, Jesus:

Notre Dame Basilica Mural

But a more careful look leads to a different, startling conclusion. Traditional depictions of the Virgin Mary show her clothed in blue, always with her hair covered (to depict her modesty). This woman has red hair, uncovered, and is wearing orange and green, the colors traditionally associated with Mary Magdalene. As Ms. Bernier noted in her book, "[A]s absurd as it may seem from a Catholic point of view, this painting may represent ... the child of the beloved apostle, Mary Magdalene." Here we are again, back to the rumored marriage between Jesus and Mary Magdalene—recall the marriage contract naming these two discussed in Passage 51.

So why is a carved stone on Hunter Mountain directing us to Old Montreal, with its hidden Goddess symbolism and apparent acknowledgment of the Jesus/Mary Magdalene marriage? More research needs to be done here, but clearly the two sites are somehow related.

On a less esoteric level, Don and Dave removed a second interesting object from the hole on Hunter Mountain: an angular, clear, quartz-like stone which Steve suggested and Scott confirmed was gypsum. Gypsum was used by Norse and other ancient navigators on overcast days because gypsum, which polarizes the sun's rays, is able to pinpoint the sun's location even on the cloudiest of days. When used for this purpose, it is referred to as a sunstone or *sólarsteinn*.

These recent discoveries, along with other objects and evidence Jackson located on Hunter Mountain in the 1970s, further corroborate this story. As we turn back to Ralph de Sudeley, we find additional corroboration.

Post-Journey: Ralph de Sudeley

Recall that the historical record in England reflects "missing years" for Ralph de Sudeley during the 1175-1185 time period. We have just accounted for the first half of those years, when de Sudeley was preparing for and making his journey to Onteora. We can now fill in the final five years: He was made the commander of two Templar fortifications (named Al Habis and Al Wu'eira) in Petra and commanded there from 1180-1185. This command was as a reward for the successful mission and the return of the scrolls. Of course, his reward was more than just command: He was given the map and instructions to the treasures described in the Alpha Scroll. The ruins of the two Templar forts can still be seen today in Petra.

De Sudeley spent approximately five years in Petra. During this time he almost assuredly searched for the treasure of the Alpha Scroll. Recall that the scroll described *tunnels cut for water,* a fact which modern archaeologists have verified.

The record of his return to the Shropshire, Herefordshire area is documented in the "Annals of Winchombe and Sudeley," and it gives the date of 1185. Upon his return, he gave some of his lands to the Templars and built a Benedictine Priory in Alcester in honor of St. Mary and John the Baptist. We can deduce that this generosity was made possible by treasures he may have found in Petra. In fact, an intriguing clue is found in the *Warwickshire Records Department,* which houses a medieval document entitled the *Feet of Fines.* The document contains a short record of de Sudeley, including a sentence regarding ancient relics being brought back to England.

An interesting clue that de Sudeley may have confided in others upon his return to England is found in the writings of Roger of Hereford, Written in 1187, the chronicle *La Chronique a Roger de Hereford et Environs a Onteora* ("Environs of Onteora") makes specific mention of Onteora in its title. Hereford is located in the county of Herefordshire in southwest England near the border of Wales and not far from Herefordshire and Gloucestershire where de Sudeley lands and estates were. This is a potentially crucial piece of evidence proving the veracity of this journal, as how else would a man in England know about Onteora in northeastern America in 1187? I have been unable to obtain a copy of this book, but clearly it will be an important next step.

In 1192, de Sudeley returned to the Middle East to fight in the Crusades with Richard the Lionheart and died, perhaps in a battle in Cyprus. Though de Sudeley died, the repercussions from his journey were felt for centuries. His maps and charts led to further explorations of the northeast by explorers in the 14th century including, most famously, the Prince Henry Sinclair voyage in 1398.

[Research done by my friend Steve St. Clair uncovered a potentially important link between the de Sudeley family and the Scottish Sinclairs, and from these families to the founding of Freemasonry in Scotland. Readers may recall that de Sudeley's brother, William de Tracy, was one of the assassins of the Archbishop of Canterbury; one of his co-assassins was a man named Hugh de Morville, brother of Richard de Morville who gave land in Scotland to the Sinclairs in 1162. Recent research indicates their descendants built the famous Rosslyn Chapel. One wonders if more than just land (perhaps maps?) was shared between these families. In addition, the father of both de Morville brothers was also named Hugh de Morville (married Beatrice de Beauchamp). He became constable of Scotland under King David I and founded Kilwinning Abbey, which later became the Masonic Order's Lodge No. 0, the Mother Lodge of Scotland.]

Templars in Portugal (later known as the Knights of Christ) also knew of de Sudeley's voyage, which may have ushered in King Henry the Navigator's "Age of Discovery" of the early 15th century. Likewise, knowledge of the mineral wealth of Loango (see Passage 14) may have been what spurred Portugal to explore the west coast of Africa.

The report of what de Sudeley found in Onteora became known to a core group of Templar-related families in Italy and France. Its value was inestimable, for it was to pave the way to the opening up of new lands and wealth. Secrecy was of the utmost importance. From the 12th to the 15th centuries there existed a close connection between English and Italian royalty, cemented through intermarriage. By the 15th century, Milan/London banking connections existed in London and bankrolled John Cabot, the Venetian who sailed from Bristol to northeastern America.

In fact, the repercussions of this adventure are still being felt today. For Onteora was not the only sight of treasures found by de Sudeley. Maps and other compelling evidence indicate he and his group may have found gold and other treasures along the coastline of maritime Canada. Readers may recognize the name of one of the islands identified in these maps. Not by the name de Sudeley used, but by its modern name: Oak Island, home of the Money Pit.

PART IV

Templars on Oak Island
Maps, Gold and Epilogue

Templar Search for Gold
Two Mysterious Maps and a Cipher

It wasn't until my research (and this book) was almost complete, in 2016, that I happened to watch an episode of the History Channel's *The Curse of Oak Island*. In the finale of season 3, a descendant of the original Oak Island discoverer Daniel McGinnis appeared on the show and displayed a gold cross that was found on the Oak Island treasure site in 1795.

History Channel's, *The Curse of Oak Island*

As fascinating as the gold cross was, it was the name of the original discoverer that caught my eye: *Daniel McGinnis*. It was similar to the same surname I had seen on a document which had been found back in 2011 hidden in a book belonging to Dr. Jackson. I also remembered one of the maps in the Templar Document, showing Nova Scotia. Suddenly this Nova Scotia map, and another map also found hidden in a Dr. Jackson book, came into sharp focus and I began to study them as I had never done before.

Could the Oak Island treasure mystery help explain why the 12th century Templars made the voyage across the North Atlantic?

Three Important Documents

First I want to focus on three important documents that I showed when I appeared on the November 22, 2016 episode of *The Curse of Oak Island*.

The Three Documents Shown on *The Curse of Oak Island*

These three documents present an unknown history of Oak Island well before the 18th century. Two of them are maps which evidence that Oak Island was visited in the 14th century and in the 12th century by the Knights Templars. The implications of these two maps are far-reaching, involving ancient treasures carried to the island and hidden there. Further, the Nova Scotia map shows the Templars knew of the gold mines and marked off a section in Nova Scotia showing where the gold mines were. A third document, entitled the *La Formule* cipher, opened a new area of investigation.

Readers have already seen one of the Nova Scotia maps, as part of the Templar Document. The map was part of a series of maps showing northeastern America. The Nova Scotia map was bound in the original Templar Document with three other maps (below on left): a map of Connecticut/eastern Long Island (below on right), and maps of Cape Cod and Narragansett Bay (not shown; to be discussed in future book). It is the map of Nova Scotia that demands our attention now.

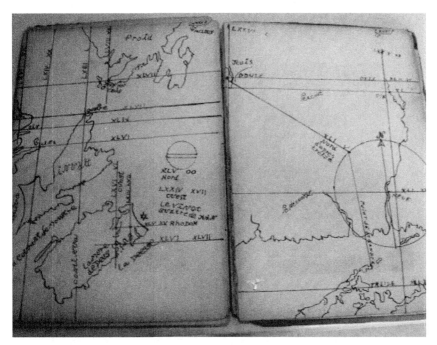

Photo of Maps Bound in Original Templar Document;
Nova Scotia Map on Left

Two Mysterious Documents Turn Up

Two documents, the *La Formule* cipher and an Oak Island map, were found by accident, hidden in the back of a book belonging to Dr. Jackson. During Christmas, 2011, two friends were visiting me, Harry Weymer and Don Ruh. We were examining two books that had belonged to Dr. Jackson which had been forwarded to us by a member of the Spartan Agency; Dr. Jackson had a habit of often hiding clues in his books.

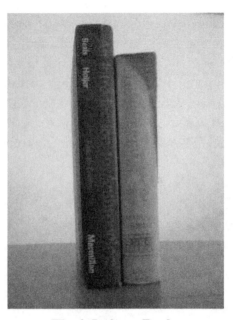

The 2 Jackson Books

In *An Introduction to Anthropology* (left book above), we found a strange handwritten note in the back of the book written by Jackson and dated 1996.

Jackson Note in Back of Book

We quickly transcribed this:

Annati holds the key now. That's why I use this page. The Frenchman was right. They wanted the info about the tunnels so they bought the document from me. But they didn't get it. Who has it now? I think it was broken up into 8 parts. I have 4 what happened to the rest? 1996.

La Bella Roma Rollo Mia Monte le Ostrica.

The mention of "Annati" was a clear reference to the other of the two books we were examining, *Palestine Before the Hebrews*, by Emmanuel Anati. Don was sitting in my kitchen and was leafing through this book and felt something thick in the back; using a knife, he sliced open a sealed back pocket. Inside were two objects: a map depicting some islands, and a folded, jagged piece of paper entitled, *La Formule*.

We examined the map first, which was written in French:

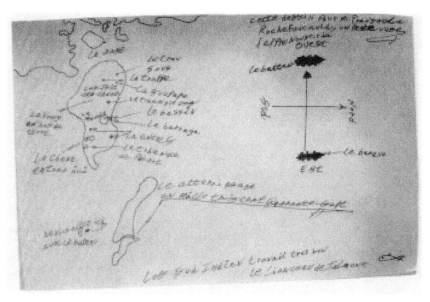

Map Found Hidden in Anati Book

Harry, a French teacher, quickly translated the words *La Chene* as "the Oak." We thought nothing of it at the time, as in 2011 we were not familiar with Oak Island.

Nor were we able to decipher the *La Formule* document. The page was covered by strange shapes and marks:

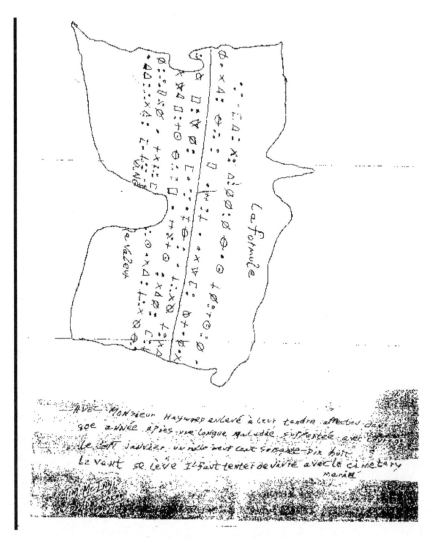

La Formule Document

As I said, I found the Oak Island Anati map and the *La Formule* document in 2011. I put them aside at the time as I was involved in researching and writing the book about the Templar Document. I knew that in 1994 Dr. Jackson had relocated from Long Island to Ireland. Sometime after Jackson moved to Ireland he sold the Templar Document—probably in 1996, the date on his note (see below for discussion on this). As the years went by, I found myself thinking about his note and began to connect certain dots. The mystery was the last five sentences—particularly the word "tunnels," something "broken up into 8 parts," that "he had 4," and his question, "Who has it now?" These few sentences were difficult to unravel. Who bought the document from him because it had information about tunnels? Who were the "they" who "didn't get it?" And what did they not get? (The postscript, "La Bella Roma Rollo Mia Monte le Ostrica," translates to, "The Beautiful Lady Rollo is Cleaning the Oyster." This too remains a mystery.)

As the years progressed, more of Jackson's papers became available to me, including another strange document Jackson found in a cave on Hunter Mountain in 1978 (see below for a full explanation). Things were getting very involved and it was becoming increasingly time consuming for me to track everything down.

The *La Formule* page was some type of code, and the page upon which it was written was shaped like a puzzle piece torn in a deliberate way. The one thing I could read was a faint note at the bottom left (not visible on this copy), reading: **Tim McInnis to W. David Jackson undesett**. It was difficult to read on the dark-edged copy, so I used a magnifying glass to make sure I read it correctly. The last word, *undesett,* was problematic—finally Harry translated the word after several tries as "one of seven." Again I was faced with more mysteries. Did "one of seven" mean seven men or seven items? More than that, who was Tim McInnis? And what did he have to do with Dr. Jackson?

In 2014, *The Curse of Oak Island* series began and I remembered the map and the strange symbols on the *La Formule* document. I made a copy of the Anati Oak Island map and the *La Formule* page and began to research the names on the map. What I found convinced me that the map was authentic. One French name mentioned on the map, *M. Francois La Rochfaucauld* was an important piece of evidence—he lived in the 16th century. Another name was *Neustria,* a French kingdom in the 6th to 8th centuries. Another name at the bottom of the map, *Talmont,* was a castle Richard the Lionheart stayed at during the Third Crusade. These names and places grounded the map in history, but why were they were on this map was a mystery. One thing did not remain a mystery: It soon became apparent that this map identified places on Oak Island and also showed two other nearby islands, Frog Island and Apple Island in Mahone Bay. Frog Island turned out to be a clue helping to date the map, thanks to Doug Crowell.

In the meantime my friend and fellow researcher Judi Rudebusch was helping me try to track down the name Tim McInnis from the *La Formule* document. Judi uncovered an article by Danny Hennigar (an Oak Island expert) which mentioned the name "Jim McGinnis," who lived in Florida. Judi tracked down the man from Florida and gave me his phone number. This was in 2011-2012. I was so involved in researching and writing the book on the Templar Document that I never reached out to him. But it turns out Judi had indeed located someone who knew the mysterious "Tim McGinnis." He was Phil Bayley, USAF Colonel (Retired). He had known Jim McGinnis for several years in Tampa. Jim McGinnis was ill at this time from his service in the Vietnam War. But he was obsessed with information he had about Oak Island and shared it with Phil Bayley. They were supposed to go to Oak Island but Jim had to move to live with his sister due to his illness. Before he died, he gave her the gold cross he always wore around his neck. This was the gold cross shown by his sister on *The Curse of Oak Island* which came from the original find on Oak Island. The gold cross has been found to be authentic and dated to the 16th century, as seen on *The Curse of Oak Island* episode which aired February 21, 2016. Jim McGinnis was a direct descendant of the original Oak Island discoverer, Daniel McGinnis. Phil Bayley shared all he knew about Jim McGinnis and revealed that he had worked for the CIA and was often in the New York City; this, I believe, is how he and Dr. Jackson first crossed paths. This path led to them sharing information with each other about Oak Island, sometime in the 1970s (it would have been after Jackson bought the Templar Document in1971 and translated it from 1971 to 1973). I now believe that Jackson found information about Oak Island that was part of the Templar Document. Certain people wanted this information and this connects to what he wrote in his mysterious note: They wanted information about the tunnels. Were these tunnels on Oak Island?

Mayan Gold?

Over the years of writing this book I kept on thinking about the two Jackson books I had, the anthropology book with Jackson's strange note in the back and the Anati book with the hidden Oak Island map and the *La Formule* page. I began going through every page in both books, wondering if Dr. Jackson might have hidden something else. I was shocked to find in the anthropology book that Jackson had pasted two pages of typewritten comments reduced to fit the pages in the book. When I read the first page it all seemed very mysterious, like some spy thriller with names that I vaguely remembered I had read about in the newspapers. Below is a photo of one of the inserted pages in the anthropology book:

Jackson Notes Inserted in Anthropology Book

The type was so small that it was difficult to read. But I soon recognized that he was writing about the Templar Document and the men who escaped from the British prison in 1914. Much of what Dr. Jackson wrote in these notes is contained in my discussion and analysis set forth in earlier portions of this book. But one new reference intrigued me: He made frequent references to the Mayans. In particular, he referred to a "Maya connection," to "Maya treasure hoards," to "copper and the Maya," and to a necklace he found on Hunter Mountain which he believed to be Mayan:

Necklace Found on Hunter Mountain by Dr. Jackson

But what really shocked me was this passage:

Through this contact the Maya learned of the area north of Hunter and utilized it when the Spanish discovered their gold. They hid this by depositing it in several locations; New Mexico (Doc Noss), Illinois, New York and Nova Scotia (Oak Island).

This bears repeating: Dr. Jackson's research led him to conclude that the famous gold treasure of the Mayan people had been hidden in Hunter Mountain and Oak Island (in addition to New Mexico and Illinois). The mention of both Hunter Mountain and Oak Island in reference to the Mayan gold was a shocker. Jackson knew about Oak Island! But he had to get this information from someone. Who? I had many questions and few answers at the time. Was it possible that the Mayans came to Hunter Mountain and to Oak Island? I continued looking for clues.

A French phrase written across the bottom of the Anati Oak Island map jumped out at me: *Les sud Indien travile tres bon*, meaning, "The south Indians work very good." Who were these "south Indians?" Could they be Mayan, Aztec or Incan? Interestingly, the subject of Incan gold came up on one of the episodes of *The Curse of Oak Island*. South America and Mexico were the source of vast amounts of gold and silver taken by Spanish conquistadors Francisco Pizarro and Hernán Cortés. The Incans, Mayans and Aztecs were all known for their gold and silver treasures.

But this possible connection to the Native Americans and their gold, as fascinating as I found it, was nothing compared to what came next: In his notes, Dr. Jackson revealed that the Vatican had become a major player in this mystery.

The Vatican Connection

The details and motivations of the parties are sketchy, but the end result is incontrovertible: Sometime between 1994 and 1996 (when he moved to Ireland), Dr. Jackson sold the Templar Document to a high-ranking Vatican official, Archbishop Paul Marcinkus, one of Pope John Paul II's closest advisors. (A longtime President of the Vatican Bank, Marcinkus is most famous for his role in the Vatican banking scandal, of which more will be discussed later.) Recall that Dr. Jackson, as a member of the Spartan Group, had a long history of dealing with shady characters. He also likely had a finely-tuned survival instinct. From reading between the lines of his notes, I wonder if Dr. Jackson did not want to sell the Templar Document to the Vatican official, but understood that it would have been dangerous to himself and his family to refuse to do so. In other words, they may have made him an offer too good to refuse.

The question, of course, is why was the Vatican so interested in this information? Readers will recall from Part I that Dr. Jackson bought the Templar Document from Gustaveste Benvenuto in 1971. Later he asked Father Piccirillo to check Vatican archives to see if there was another copy of the Templar Document there. Based on his correspondence with Dr. Jackson, it is reasonable to conclude that Father Piccirillo believed in the authenticity of the Templar Document (which Jackson had shared with him). Because of the correspondence between Jackson and Father Piccirillo, a respected scholar who was the director of the Studium Biblicanum Franciscan Institute in Jerusalem, I wrote to the Institute asking if I could get copies of these letters. Unfortunately, Father Piccirillo had recently died and the documents were not available (see response letter from Institute in online appendix).

I believe that what occurred was that other documents existed in the Vatican archives which detailed the 1179 voyage and the existence of treasures on Hunter Mountain and/or Oak Island, but that the Vatican records were incomplete. They needed the documents Dr. Jackson had purchased to fill in some blanks. Whatever their motivation, it seems to me that it is reasonable to conclude that the actions and behavior of top Vatican officials indicate they believed in the authenticity of the Templar Document.

The Swagger Sticks

The Dr. Jackson sale of the Templar Document to Archbishop Marcinkus culminated a long history of dealings between Vatican officials and Dr. Jackson. The purchase of an artifact called the Swagger Stick illustrates the complexity and importance of these dealings to this mystery.

The Swagger Stick was obtained by Jackson from Marcinkus via the workings of a Spartan operative. The story of this artifact reads like a spy thriller. It begins with Lewellyn Deloros, whom we met in Part I; he was one of the two outside men in the escape from the Brittish prison by Roche and MacDonald in 1914. He reappears in this story over thirty years later in India, where he buys eighteen swagger sticks (a swagger stick is a short cane; some swagger sticks have hidden swords inside, as these did). Here is the exact paragraph from one of the Spartan Agency reports that documents the details of this purchase:

✗ * These swagger sticks were two of fifteen purchased from a company in Deli, India in 1948 by a Mr. Deloros as a purchasing agent for members of a select group within the Roman Catholic Church and serialized as 3000 through 3014. Of the recipients were a Mr. Licio Geli, Mr. Parde Frassico, Mr. Roberto Calvi, Mr. Paul Marcinkus, Mr. Juan DeCristo, Mr. Donato Santiago, Mr. Salvatore San Jiemao, Mr. Alberto Vignes, Mr. Carlos Bratfeld, Mr. Umberto Ortolani, Mr. Olaf Palme, Mr. Michele Sindona, Mr. Victor Emmanuel, Mr. Pietro Musumeci, and Mr. Ciril Natas a.k.a. Eduarnd Duchane.
The two in possession of Mr. Marcinkus had diferent carvings on them. All of the others were only carved with the name of the recipient. This information supplied by Mr. Arrimas of Interpol.

Spartan Agency Report re Swagger Sticks

Note that these swagger sticks were purchased for "members of a select group within the Roman Catholic Church," including Archbishop Marcinkus. We will return to this group later.

Of particular interest for us now is that one of the swagger sticks given to Marcinkus contains carvings on the sword blade that appear to be an encoded map of Hunter Mountain, showing many of the same symbols on the map used by the Hunter Mountain climbing team to make its discoveries in 2009 (see Part 3):

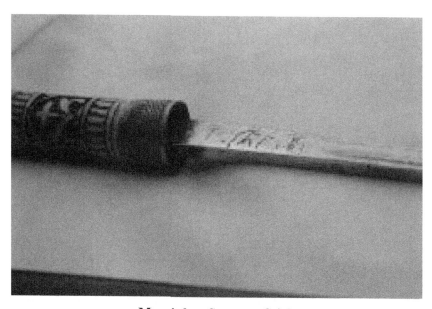

Marcinkus Swagger Stick

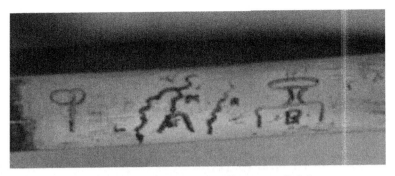

Carvings on Marcinkus Swagger Stick

The carvings depict Table Rock (shown with a 'B'), wavy lines (which is the stream on the map), and a cave.

In 1978, Dr. Jackson used this swagger stick map to search on Hunter Mountain. It is unclear how Dr. Jackson obtained the swagger stick from Archbishop Marcinkus, though a note in the Spartan Agency records indicates some subterfuge was involved, stating that the swagger stick was obtained "nefariously from Marcinkus." The details of this 1978 exploration are laid out here, in a 1992 letter from Spartan operative Bob Terrance, who accompanied Dr. Jackson:

Terrance Letter

TERRANCE Doc.   EAGLE WITHIN CIRCLE

BADGE

August 1992

Grafton, Vermont

This document testifies to the authenticity of the find made in my presence by William David Jackson on March 12, 1978 at a mountain location in the area of Diamond Notch in New York State country of America. Having acquired through Our Father's friend Professor Hiram Gorman who knew Bill Jackson in College and just prior to the Father's death one ebony and ivory headed swagger stick embalmed with a lions head from Mr. Quentin Arrimas of the Masonic order of Christ to which he was a member. It was nefariously obtained through Paul Marcinkus in December of 1979 a long time before his leaving the Instituto per le Opere de Religione and his relocation to Arizona in 1990. As I am sure you are aware Mr. Marckinkus and Mr. Arrimas were both members of the Masonic Lodge P2 whose grand Master Licio Geli was involved with Mr. Roberto Calvi in the death of Don Albino Luciano on September 29, 1978. We ascended the mountain by a steep path marked with blue blazes nailed to rocks and trees as are those upon the Appalachian trail that I maintain a section of in Vermont for the Green Mountain Club. After several hundred yards of this transverse and when themarked trail led to the left we continued to ascend straight up following the left bank of a small stream till a large rock with a triangle cut into it was reached. At this point we bore more to the right still rising in elevation and crossing the stream near a small water fall. Here we found a rock with a carving of a bird on it. To the left and slightly uphill we observed a large stone formation in the shape of a table with a flat top and a small cave at its base that resembled the engraving on the sword blade within the swagger stick. Now proceeding father afield to the right we came upon a right angled cliff of rock with a large crevasse in it. In this did Bill Jackson climb and with compass in hand, referring to the sword took some bearings unexplained to me. Then we proceeded to his left seeing a large rock pointing North and following the point along a steep ledge using a rope tied to a piton driven into the rock face we come upon a small cave some five or six feet deep by six feet high and wide. At the back of this was a pile of stones forming a flat stone seat. Below this we began to dig, I with a shovel and Bill with a small mattocks. About three feet down I hit something with the spades blade and Bill got on his hands and knees and using gloved hands scraped away the remaining soil to reveal a clay tube that I had shattered cutting through the rolled document within slicing a section of it off. We continued to dig but found nothing else and so replaced the earth and sstones replacing the stone seat and retired to our hotel in Phoenician, New York where we used scotch tape to restore the document to its near original condition. It had a reddish backing and some lines on the back that excited Bill exceedingly. The lines formed an odd outline like a coastline on a map and there were the words in French. "Comment est ce que on procure de l'eau partie de tunnels." At the bottom edge of the document is said also in French, "Trois, ouvre le tran." He then copied them using some sepia paper andpassed me

I read it but he said that the contents were of no importance. It is herein enclosed as I have found it among some stuff I am throwing out as we are moving again. If it is of any use to you that is great as it is of no interest to me and I feel I owe you for your help in the problems with the Carpenters Institute of America. The swagger stick I don't know what happened to it. Yours truly, BT

Terrance Letter Retyped

In the letter, Terrance summarizes the 1978 climb, following the clues on the swagger stick. His description largely matches what the 2009 Hunter Mountain climb team (Don Ruh, Steve St. Clair, David Brody, and Scott Wolter and his son Grant) saw during their search—a stream, a small waterfall, a triangle carved on a rock, a carving of a bird, and a table-like rock formation. Dr. Jackson and Terrance dug inside a cave, finding a clay tube. Within the tube, they found a document with French writing. We will examine this in more detail later, but for now suffice it to say that it is ragged-shaped, torn in such a way that it fits together perfectly with the *La Formule* document.

Turning back to the Vatican officials' interest in this matter, Dr. Jackson sheds additional light on the swagger stick and its importance. He wrote:

> **This is where the swagger stick came into play and Marcinkus in Rome got it. He also thought the secret to the Maya treasure hoards was still in the cave. That is why he bought the Benvenuto documents [i.e., the Templar Document] the asshole.**

This explains the Vatican official's involvement: According to Dr. Jackson, Archbishop Marcinkus believed the maps of Hunter Mountain led to a Mayan treasure buried in a cave. We do not know if Marcinkus found any treasure on Hunter Mountain, but the conclusion is inescapable: Marcinkus and members of his Vatican group were searching for something on Hunter Mountain. They clearly believed in the authenticity of the Templar Document.

Rogue Group: P2

The spy novel aspects of this mystery were only heightened when I began to examine the names of the "members of a select group with the Roman Catholic Church" who received the swagger sticks. Many of them were members of a rogue fraternal group called P2 (for 'Propaganda Due'). This P2 group was essentially a shadow government which had taken over *de facto* control of the Italian government. The P2 group was heavily involved in the Vatican banking scandal which rocked Rome in 1982. Note the name *Robert Calvi* on the list of swagger stick recipients; he was the Chairman of Banco Ambrosiano, the bank behind the scandal. The sensationalism of this scandal was only heightened when Calvi was found hanging from the Blackfriars

Bridge in London one morning in 1982, a death ruled a murder by British authorities (it remains unsolved).

I could not help but wondering how and why Dr. Jackson had come to be involved with these men (note the passage above, in which Dr. Jackson referns to Archbishop Marcinkus as an "asshole"). But it occurred to me that a shared belief in the existence of a hidden treasure could forge together some odd alliances. We might never learn if the Vatican group recovered any treasure on Hunter Mountain. So we will instead refocus our attention on another treausre, to the north.

The Oak Island Map

We turn our attention back to the Oak Island map, reproduced again here:

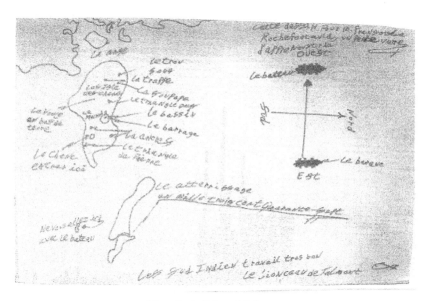

The Oak Island Map

My first task was to translate the various French words and labels (translations courtesy of Harry Weymer). I will begin with the general notes on the map, then move to the specific labels of the three islands on the left side of the map:

Upper right: *Cette dessun pour M. Francois La Rochfaucauld un pette verre d'appre Neustria*

Translation: *This drawing for M. Francois Rochfaucauld a little drink learned from Neustria*

Across bottom, line 1: *Le sud Indien travail tres bon*

Translation: *The south Indians work very good* [discussed above]

Across bottom, line 2: *Le Lionceau de Talmont*

Translation: *The young lion of Talmont* (with a fish symbol)

Below small island in upper left: *La Anse*

Translation: *Small Bay*

Along right side of middle island (which is clearly Oak Island):

La trou sous la trappe
Translation: *The hole under the trap door (or hatch)*

La soupape
Translation: *The valve*

Le triangle Le Dieu
Translation: *The triangle of God*

Le bassin
Translation: *The pond*

Le barrage
Translation: *The dam*

La ancres
Translation: *reeds (in a wet land)*

Le Triangle de Pierre
Translation: *The Triangle of Peter*

In center of middle island:
  Les isle des chene
  Translation: *The island of oaks*

[A second label, beginning with "Le M," is illegible]

Along left side of middle island:

  Le Voute en Bas de Terre
  Translation: *The Vault Beneath the Earth*

  La Chene entre ici
  Translation: *The Oak enter here*

  Bottom island, right side: *Le atterrissage; Un Mille trois cent quarante sept*
  Translation: *The Landing 1347*

  Bottom island, left side (words surround a small island): *Ne vous allez ici avec le bateau*
  Translation: *Do not go there with the boat*

There is a lot to examine here, obviously. The label in the center of the middle island, *Les isle des chene,* meaning *The island of oaks,* is self-explanatory. And a label identifying *The Vault Beneath the Earth* is sure to send any treasure hunger's heart racing. I will address other intriguing passages in order of relevance.

The 1347 Date

The label on the bottom island, which we have identified as Frog Island, jumped right out at me: *The Landing 1347.* (Note how the map shows water between the larger and smaller portions of the island; today, a swamp separates the island at this point.) The 1347 date obviously is after the 1179-80 Templar voyage described in "A Year We Remember." Is the date 1347 significant? Researcher Doug Crowell found a compelling answer. The cornerstone in the famous Royston Cave, a Templar repository in Hertfordshire, England, has the 1347 date carved into it. The bell-shaped artificial cave was cut out of the chalk bedrock and used as a secret hideout and repository by the outlawed Templars:

Royston Cave Drawing by Joseph Beldam (note 1347 date)

According to many historians, the Templars occupied Royston Cave from 1307 (when they were outlawed) to 1347, during which time they carved hundreds of images on the walls of the cave. I believe that in 1347, when the Bubonic plague swept across England, the Templars planned their escape. They knew about Oak Island from Ralph de Sudeley's 12th century visit, gathered their treasures, and set sail, landing on Frog Island. Recall that there are three possible sources for the Templar treasure (whatever it may have been): 1) the treasure found under the Temple Mount in the early 12th century; 2) the treasure found by Ralph de Sudeley in Petra upon his return from Onteora in 1180; and 3) the treasure accumulated by the Templars during their 200+ years of power and influence from the early 12th to early 14th centuries. There is also a fourth possible treasure in play: the Mayan treasure, believed by Dr. Jackson to have been buried at Hunter Mountain (and perhaps also somehow connected to Oak Island, based on the reference to the "south Indians" on the Oak Island map). (A fifth possible treasure—whatever treasures the Jews fled Jerusalem with in 70 C.E.—was, according to the Templar Document, brought to Onteora, not Oak Island.) Whatever the source or content of these treasures, when the Templars arrived on Oak Island they buried their hoard in an elaborate *Vault Beneath the Earth* (as identified on the map). They then booby-trapped the vault with sophisticated flood tunnels to thwart would-be treasure hunters, booby-traps that continue to stymie searchers ev8en to this day.

But as I studied the Templar Document Nova Scotia map, a sixth possible source for the Templar treasure came to mind. Was it possible the reason de Sudeley and his team spent so much time in the Oak Island area, and devoted so many men and women to the mission, was because they were not only *hiding* gold, but *mining* it as well?

The Templar Document Nova Scotia map (cropped) is reproduced again below (note that the western half of Nova Scotia is shown on the bottom middle of this map while the eastern half is shown on the top left. The two halves join where the star symbols are marked):

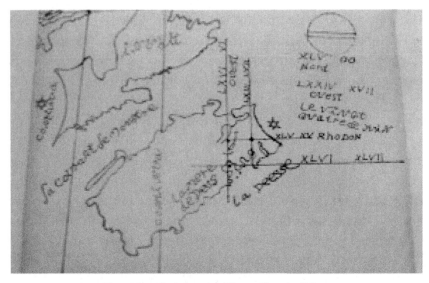

Templar Document Nova Scotia Map

Two things jumped out at me on this map. First, four lines intersect to make a box just north of Mahone Bay, where Oak Island is located. Second, one of these four lines (the northern horizontal one) is labeled, *Rhodon*.

The main natural feature of the area in the box is the Gold River. Aptly named, the Gold River played a prominent part in the Nova Scotia "gold rush" on the 1860s and 1870s. Though not as well known as other gold-producing regions, Nova Scotia has produced over a million ounces of gold since mining began in 1861. There are 365 known gold mines located on Nova Scotia, many clustered along the southern shoreline not far from Oak Island:

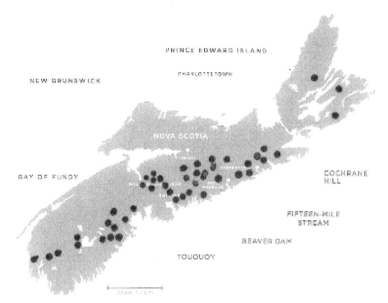

Red Dots Show Gold Mines in Nova Scotia
[Credit: Art Gallery of Nova Scotia]

Note the cluster of gold mines corresponding to the boxed-off area on the Templar Document Nova Scotia map (boxed-off area is due south of the 'N' in 'Nova Scotia' on above map).

Turning back to the Gold River, this river originates north of Mahone Bay, in the town of New Ross, close to the upper left point of the box on the map. Interestingly, there exists a stone in New Ross amid some castle ruins which features a faded Templar Cross.

The word *Rhodon* also intrigued me. This word is almost phonetically identical to the modern-day *Rawdon* gold mine located not far from the upper right point of the box on the map. Could the modern name be a vestige of what once had been a medieval Templar gold mine? If so, the likely source of this name is *Rhodon,* a 12th century English village in West Yorkshire. Could one of de Sudeley's men have named the gold mine after his home town?

More research will need to be done on this, but I believe it is entirely possible that the Templars and their descendants were mining gold on Nova Scotia in the area around Mahone Bay near Oak Island.

The Hole Under Trap Door On Oak Island

In 2014, I began watching *The Curse of Oak Island* show on the History Channel. The show caused me to reexamine the Oak Island map. As I studied the map in more detail, cross-checking the map references with other research and known history, I became convinced that the map was authentic.

It took me two years after 2014 to get someone from the show to look at the map. Judi Rudebusch referred me to researcher Doug Crowell of Nova Scotia and I sent him the map and the *La Formule* document. Doug contacted Rick Lagina, one of the two brothers who star in the show. Doug began working on the *La Formule* cipher as he has a background in cryptography. In June and July of 2016, I showed Rick and members of the television production team the evidence I had which was presented in a thirty-page report. Eventually the show producers interviewed me for the show, both over the phone and then in person. Portions of these interviews have appeared throughout season 4 of the show (airing in late 2016 and early 2017). In particular, *The Curse of Oak Island* team focused on the location on the map labeled, *Le Trou Sous la Trappe*, meaning *the hole under the trap door*.

I will recount these events as they occurred on-air, as I was not told beforehand what (if anything) the team would find. Jack Begley overlaid the 1347 Oak Island map with a modern map of Oak Island, thereby confirming the accuracy of the older map. The team searched the area marked on the map. They found a strange depression cut into the ground exactly where the map had marked it. They called this depression, "the Hatch." Rick Lagina asked, "Could this opening lead to a tunnel system?" The photo below shows Jack Begley examining the opening.

The team returned a second time, probed below and found that there was a shale bottom beneath the opening. Nothing remains today of whatever trap door might have existed, but the opening remains a tantalizing clue. [Flash! Feb. 28, 2017: See below for what was discussed on the last episode of Season 4 about the "Hatch" with the team at Traverse City, Michigan.]

**Jack Begley and Oak Island Team Examining Hatch Opening
(back to front, Rick Lagina, Dave Blankenship, Marty Lagina,
Charles Barkhouse)**

Will there be another investigation of this strange site in another season of *The Curse of Oak Island*? Have they found something that has triggered their interest? My curiosity is intense but I have to wait until they present their findings. In the meantime, I can only speculate that the Oak Island map could possibly show some kind of tunnel system where none was expected. One must be judicious and thoughtful, but our imagination can carry us into unknown areas.

The research on this map has thus far proven the map to be remarkably accurate. With that in mind, I turn to one name that has focused me on an early medieval kingdom and the legend of its king of semi-divine birth. The name *Neustria* on the map opens an extraordinary story.

Neustria

The message in the upper right of the map is translated as, *This drawing for M. Francois Rochfaucaulda little drink (message) from Noustria.*

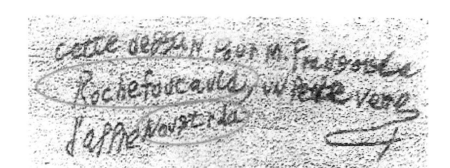

Message in Upper Right of Map

The reference to "Neustria" is an important clue. Neustria was a historical kingdom in northwestern France during the 5ᵗʰ to the 8ᵗʰ centuries, ruled by thirty Merovingian kings with many descendants of the royal families. Readers will recall the legend of the Merovingian king and how the kingdom became linked to the symbol of an octopus with five arms. Like so much in cryptology, the number five is significant. Readers will also recall that the five-armed octopus symbol was on the objects found in the brass device.

The Kingdom of Neustria

The second historical reference in this message is the name, *M. Francois Rochfaucauld.* There were several Rochfaucaulds in the historical record, some as far back as the 12th century. Rochfaucauld Castle still stands in France. Was the Rochfaucauld on the map the famous French cardinal living during the 16th century? I believe so. I could not figure out how Cardinal Rochfaucauld was connected to this mystery until I learned that when Rochfaucauld's father was killed when the boy was three, the family lived in the household of Caterina de Medici, Queen of France. Readers may recall that the Medici family played a prominent part in this mystery. The fact that Rochfaucauld is a 16th century figure indicates to me that either: 1) this map was drawn in the 16th century (during Rochfaucauld's life) to depict events (a landing) from 1347, or 2) the note in the upper right was added to a 1347 map centuries after it was first drawn. Research continues on this cryptic note.

Unexplained Circles on Coins

As often is the case in this mystery, the reference to the Merovingian homeland led me to stumble upon another important Merovingian/Templar connection. The kings of Neustria minted coins, as most royalty did. Some of these coins feature a cross similar to that later adopted by the Templars; the cross also features distinctive circles called "pellets" around the four arms.

Merovingian Coin

The distinctive "pellets" around the cross are also found on other Templar crosses of the 12th century.

Templar Coin Dated to 1163-1174
(From Crusader/Templar Fortress of *Dor* on the Coast of Israel)

What caught my eye is that the famous Hedden Stone (also called the H & O stone) on Oak Island, believed to be a clue to finding the treasure, has a similar design, with four "pellets" surrounding the cross in a box-like shape:

The Hedden Stone

A cross on a Templar carving from Royston Cave features the same distinctive "pellets." And, to further support my belief that these "pellets" are not merely random markings but are instead some kind of symbol used by the Templars, coins minted by Richard the Lionheart, King of England from 1198-1192, feature the Templar cross with at least one "pellet" (another may have faded) in the upper left quadrant of the cross area of the coin:

Silver Denier of King Richard the Lionheart

Readers may recall that one of the notes written on the Oak Island map in the Anati book (across the bottom) translates as, *The young lion of Talmont.* This is a known nickname for Richard the Lionheart, who resided in Talmont Castle sometime during or after the Third Crusade which began in 1189 and ended in 1192 with the siege and capture of Acre, thereby giving the Templars control of that strategic harbor until 1292.

In conclusion, we have a Templar Cross with distinctive "pellets" around it carved on the Hedden Stone on Oak Island, which matches not only Templar coins from France and Jerusalem but also a Templar carving in Royston Cave, England. And we have a note on the map referencing a medieval king who minted these matching coins. The weight of evidence continues to grow.

Sea Levels

According to a paper published by the Geological Society of Canada in 1970, the sea level around Oak Island was lower in 1450 by about 2 meters. Thus a beach of that time would now be under water.

Frog Island was identified on the Oak Island map by researcher Doug Crowell. I noticed that it is shown on the map with water separating the lower and upper sections of the island. I was told that there is a swamp there today. Likewise, the map of Oak Island depicts *reeds in a wet land,* yet there are no wetlands there today. As per the oceanographer who appeared on one of *The Curse of Oak Island* shows (confirming the Geological Society of Canada paper), the sea level was lower by approximately two meters three or four hundred years ago. I believe based on the above that the Oak Island map was drawn centuries ago, at a time when ocean levels were much lower.

The Templar Document Nova Scotia map shows a land mass where the Strait of Canso is today. The strait divides the Nova Scotia peninsula from Cape Breton Island by a long thin channel about 3 kilometers wide and extremely deep (about 200 feet deep); it connects Chedabucto Bay on the Atlantic to St. Georges's Bay on the Northumberland Strait. On the Nova Scotia Map this area is clearly shown as a single land mass with no separation between Nova Scotia and Cape Breton Island, which is labeled "inuit."

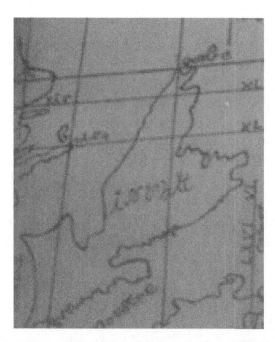

Land Bridge Connecting Nova Scotia and Cape Breton ("inuit")

The medieval map maker was very accurate in identifying places. He or she took care to mark "quatre" and "XLVII" just north of Cape Breton, identifying St. Paul's Island. He/she identified two groups of islands off the coast of Newfoundland and also marked an island off Prince Edward Island. This was a meticulously crafted map, and its sea level representations further speak to its centuries-old creation date.

Revisiting the *La Formule* Document

As I said at the very beginning of this book, there is much research still to be done. One of the most promising clues is the *La Formule* document. Can it be translated? Are there other pieces of it that can be found?

Doug Crowell has been working on this document and has come up with some intriguing results. Rick Lagina decided to send the *La Formule* page to Professor Kevin Knight at the University of Southern California, whose work in cryptography is well known (he is the author of several books and papers on machine translation and decipherment). A thorough summary of Doug's research can be found here: www.Oakislandcompedium.ca/blockhouse-blog/the-La-formule-cipher-investigation . Doug was also interviewed on *The Curse of Oak Island* and presented his findings on air.

To repeat, this is what we know about this document:

1. The *La Formule* page was given to Dr. Jackson by Jim McGinnis, a direct descendant of the original discoverer of the Money Pit.

2. Translated, the note scrawled across the bottom of the *La Formule* page reads, *Tim McInnis to W. David Jackson, one of seven.*

3. The *La Formule* page is ripped like a jigsaw puzzle piece and fits together with a document recovered from a clay tube on Hunter Mountain by Dr. Jackson in 1978.

4. The cipher on the *La Formule* document is the same cipher used on the famous "90 Foot Stone," the stone found in the original hole dug on Oak Island in the 1790s. The message

on the stone has been translated as, "Forty Feet Below, Two Million Pounds are Buried."

The Curse of Oak Island team interviewed Professor Knight and his decipherment was presented on air. He concluded that the cipher was likely a substitution cipher used by secret societies and believed that it was created by someone knowledgeable in ciphers. It's important to note that the *La Formule* translated into French. Below is Professor Knight's decipherment (with some words apparently missing):

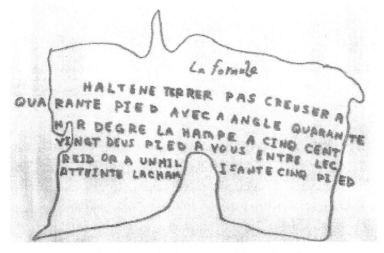

La Formule Document Translated

In English it reads:

> *Halt. Do not burrow/dig to forty foot with an angle of forty-five degree the shaft of five hundred twenty two foot you enter the corridor of one thousand sixty-five foot reach the chamber.*

Onteora Defined Again

Readers may recall that in Chapter 7, I described how Dr. Jackson found reference to the name *Onteora* in a 1715 pamphlet, which translated the name as a Native American word meaning "Land in the Sky." I had always accepted this as an accurate and appropriate translation, until I began to learn more about the gold (Templar and/or Mayan) buried on Hunter Mountain and Oak Island. Then an alternative translation came to mind.

If we break down the name into its two halves, we begin with *onte*—could this be the prefix *ante,* meaning "in front of" or "before?" *Ora,* meanwhile, is the Spanish word for "gold," with the Latin root being "or." Putting these together, we have a possible meaning, *In Front of Gold.*

So, which is it? Does Onteora mean *Land in the Sky,* named by the Native Americans or other early inhabitants for a Temple standing, literally, high in the mountains? A place where, figuratively, the highest aspirations of humankind were honored and took root?

Or, instead, does Onteora refer to Oak Island, a place *In Front of Gold,* describing either Hunter Mountain or Oak Island itself, where treasures and secrets were deposited by Templars fleeing the close-mindedness and tyranny of medieval Europe? Like so much else about this mystery, we may never know the answer.

But I'd like to think it could be both.

Conclusion

Researching and writing this book truly has been a labor of love for me. I have always considered historical research to be a kind of intellectual challenge, and this has been an undeniable trial of my research skills and stamina. As I said at the beginning—and repeated many times—there are many questions still unanswered in this mystery and much work still to be done, even after a decade of research. But at least, going forward, other researchers will have something to build upon.

I invite readers to keep up with developments in this ongoing saga by visiting my website: www.zenahalpern.info . I also plan to continue with Volume 2 of this work, which will contain a more detailed account of documents found by the Templars in Jerusalem as well as updates on my research.

Finally, I have a request: If you are out in the woods, especially around Hunter Mountain or in the Neversink River Valley, please keep your eyes open and let me know what you find. Somewhere out there, the past is speaking to us.

The End
(But See Epilogue)

EPILOGUE

As this book was undergoing final edits, a question arose about two numbers and two letters inscribed on one of the inserts Dr. Jackson found in the brass device. (Readers will recall from Chapter 1 that Dr. Jackson found garden containers on Bannerman's Island in 1968 and that, a year later, he found the brass device inside one of these garden containers. Inside the brass device were four metal objects.) These two numbers and their explanation have opened up a new line of inquiry that needs to be brought to the reader's attention. This book ends with this unplanned epilogue, revealing a breakthrough which extends the Oak Island history beyond what was known.

The two numbers and two letters on side 2 of the rectangular object found in the hollow center of the brass device are "312," "356," and "SW," as shown here on the left of side 2:

Copper Rectangle Found in Brass Device

I assumed these numbers had something to do with direction and navigation, but did not know what the numbers stood for. I again consulted Richard Moats, who had helped me previously with my questions about astronomy and navigation. What he has found is a major discovery. The numbers/letters—which refer to azimuths and celestial navigation—point to the mouth of the Hudson River and

Hunter Mountain, to the Saugus River on the coast of Massachusetts, and to Nova Scotia. This is nothing short of amazing.

Two of the three other objects found in the brass device are also relevant to this discovery, and are pictured again, below. The triangle, which Dr. Jackson called a "nail," is inscribed with the words *Angra Pequena* on one side and *Quetzlcoatl* (sic) on the other:

Triangular Metal Object (Photo and Drawing)

The round copper disk is also pictured below. Note how, on side 2, the dotted line goes to a circle with an X and a small island, possibly Nova Scotia or Oak Island.

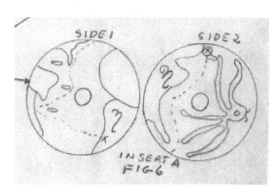

Round Copper Disk

Richard Moats' analysis, completed in late February, 2017, follows:

* * *

Zena asked me the following question: "What is 312 and 356 on side two of the metal tab pictured in figure 9 on Jackson's mechanical drawing of the device?" I did not have an answer and that bothered me greatly. We had worked so hard to find some answers as to the use of this enigmatic object we called the "device," but still did not have the answer to such a seemingly simple question.

312 and 356 could be azimuths, I thought. But the "SW" inscribed on the tab likely refers to "South West" and 312/356 are azimuths toward the North West. It doesn't make sense. We knew the coordinates inscribed on side 1 of the tab had been intentionally reversed. If this is true, then there is likely a deception in the inscriptions on side 2.

The inverse of azimuth 312 is 312 minus 180 which is Az132. The inverse of 356 is 356 minus 180 which is Az176. Az132 from the coordinates on the Saugus River noted on side 1 is to the South East and to Africa. Impossible, I thought. Az176 from the location on the Saugus River also heads to the South Southeast and intersects the Dominican Republic. At that time, it made no sense at all.

I asked Zena if she could tell me anything that may be a clue. Her reply referenced the name inscribed in the top corner on side one of the tab: "Quetzlcoatl." Impossible, I thought. Quetzalcoatl, as properly spelled, is the name of a Mayan god. How in the world could this device, or more specifically the items placed inside the device, have anything to do with a Mayan god from a Mesoamerican culture going back to the first century, post classically 900-1519 AD and the Aztecs? It makes no sense; but there it is in black and white. Or better stated, inscribed on a piece of metal stashed inside a 15th century navigation device.

As I studied the device diagram, I noticed the misspelled word "Quetzlcoatl" again on the "nail" depicted in figure 8. The nail was one of several like objects used to anchor the device to the ship when it was used as a navigation aid. Also on the nail in figure 8 are the words "Angra Pequena." Angra Pequena is Portuguese for "Small Cove." Small Cove is a port that exists today on the west coast of Namibia, Africa. Africa? Small Cove was first mapped in 1487 by the Portuguese and is referenced today as Luderitz Bay.

Is it possible the items placed in the "Brass Device" were done so by a Portuguese navigator sometime after 1487 or into the 16th century? This is at the end of the post classic period which ended about 1519. Is the metal tab a sort of "crib note" to extend the memory of the navigator? Is it possible the azimuths of 312 and 356 begin at Small Cove?

I ran the azimuth of 312 from Small Cove to the northwest. (Angra Pequena will be referred to as Small Cove). This azimuth intersected the Cape Verde Islands. As I extended the azimuth further on, I was shocked to find it ended within .75 degrees of intersecting the coordinates on the bank of the Saugus River on the coast of Massachusetts as noted on side one of the metal tab. As the hair stood on my neck, I realized a Portuguese Navigator had logged the route from Small Cove to a location on the Saugus River in what we now call Massachusetts sometime in the late 15th or 16th century.

But what about 356? I ran azimuth 356 from Small Cove and found it went nowhere. I then studied the device diagram again and focused on the small disk found inside the device depicted in figure 6 (Insert A). On side one is a map showing what appears to be Africa, South America, and part of the South Eastern coast of North America. A dotted line seems to indicate a travel route from what may be Namibia west to South America and then north, through the Caribbean Islands, then along the South East coast of North America. Side two of the disk depicts the route extending north and ending with an "X" at what appears to be Nova Scotia. But again, where does Az 356 come into play?

On the metal tab, (Fig 9 Insert B), 312 is separated from 356 with a box. This joins 356 with the words "Altomra De Leon's Tomb" and the image of an Octopus with five arms. Zena had told me about Altomara's tomb being at Hunter Mountain in Southeast New York State. She also told me the device had been found on Bannerman's Island in the Hudson River. I ran Azimuth 356 from the mouth of the Hudson and found that it comes within .40 degrees of intersecting with Hunter Mountain. In my opinion, the "SW" inscribed on the tab was a reminder to go to the south west from the Saugus River to the Hudson River, then follow the Hudson River North West on azimuth 356 to Altomara's tomb at Hunter Mountain.

Azimuth 356 from Hudson River Mouth to Hunter Mountain

Still not satisfied, the travel route depicted on the disk in figure 6 (Insert A) troubled me. I reasoned that a navigator only needed to travel from Small Cove to the Cape Verde Islands then to the Caribbean Islands. From there, they could travel into Central America or northward to reach the "camp" at the Saugus River. If the navigator was as skilled is I believe they were, then if he left Small Cove on Az312 to the Cape Verde islands then go west with the trade winds to the Caribbean. The first island encountered would be Barbados. This would seem to be a better choice to reach the Saugus River than to travel directly on Az312. The distance was much shorter to Barbados from Small Cove making the journey between land falls shorter and the risk of having trouble in the open sea much less. I ran an azimuth from Barbados northward on Az356 and expected it to come to the mouth of the Saugus River. But it does not. It makes landfall on Nova Scotia within 3 degrees or within 90 miles of Oak Island.

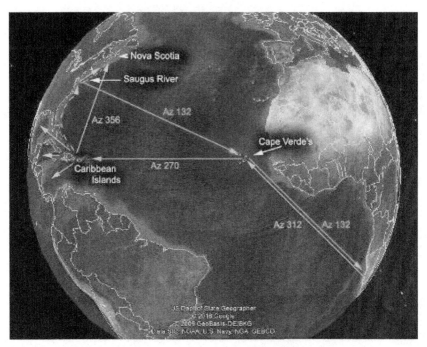

Overview of Azimuth 312 Travel

Since Barbados could be the first island encountered on the safe western route from Small Cove to Nova Scotia, it is plausible Az356 is a reference for the navigator to make final landfall at Nova Scotia using the Gulf Stream to decrease the travel time. I ran an inverse of Az356 from Oak Island to the southwest. Az176 from Oak Island comes within .04 degrees of Monserrat. Monserrat is right in the middle of the Caribbean Island cluster. Az356 from the Caribbean Islands passes very near the island of Bermuda. Az356 from Bermuda arrives on the south end of Nova Scotia.

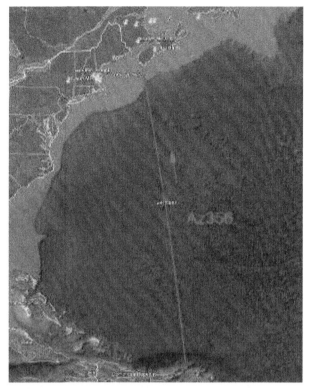

Azimuth 356 from Bermuda to Nova Scotia

A stop at the Saugus River camp would be easy when land marks on the east coast of North America from memory were applied.

The three islands pictured on disk (insert A) in figure 6 are not to scale or in proper spatial relationship. It is most probable that these three islands represent the three largest island of the Caribbean group, Cuba, Dominican Republic, and Puerto Rico. This is logical in that without highly accurate mapping, it would have been very difficult to differentiate one of the smaller islands of the group from the other. With this in mind, it is most probable that the navigator only needed to reach one of the three large islands and then go north northeast to find the Gulf Stream current, the "fast track" north to their destinations. It was better to make a series of shorter trips than to make one very long one. Considering all the evidence, it is most probable Az356 was a reference to Altomara's tomb and possibly the route from somewhere in the Caribbean Islands to Nova Scotia.

When the navigator needed to return home to Small Cove from Nova Scotia, the route into the North Sea and then down the coast lines of the British Isles, to the Iberian Peninsula, Northwest Africa, to Small Cove is possible. But the North Sea is fraught with potential disaster due to weather. Piracy would have also been a major deterrent along the western shores of Europe and Northwest Africa. A route reversing the trip down the Northeast coast of North America would be safer. A stop at the Saugus River camp would allow them to renew supplies and prepare the ship for the long trip. They would be pressing against the Gulf Stream but it was not impossible. Logically, the best route from Nova Scotia to Small Cove was to travel back down the coast to the Saugus River camp then cross the Atlantic on the reverse of Az312; Az132 to the Cape Verde Islands and on to Small Cove. The west wind would be quartering at their stern. And just as the coordinates of the "Saugus Camp" were intentionally reversed, so was 312. Reversed to protect their cargo and sources thereof. Az312 is also Az132, the route home.

What a trip... for those early sailors, Zena, and myself. In many ways as rewarding for us as it was for those who sailed into the Dark Continent and back home using a device made of brass with the navigation reminders in code, hidden inside a "garden container" found on Bannerman Island, NY.

The more research I do, the more evidence I find that proves transoceanic travel to North and South America long before Columbus in 1492. I am not addressing the peopling of the Americas that occurred thousands of years ago, but crossings into the Americas by cultures from the Iberian Peninsula and the Mediterranean area. There were cultures and people with ocean going vessels and sailors with navigation skills beyond what history has previously told us. The reason they came was to exploit resources and for profit.

I cannot wait to work with Zena on Volume 2 of this journey. The new discoveries on Oak Island related to astronomy and navigation are proving to be breakthroughs. It is going to be quite a ride.

It was an honor to help my dear friend Zena.

Richard D. Moats, Archaeoastronomer/Researcher

* * *

This analysis by Richard Moats explains a number of previously unsolved mysteries. First and foremost, it explains the "312," "356" and "SW" markings on the brass device. More fundamentally, it shows how ancient navigators crossed the Atlantic and were able to locate sites like Hunter Mountain and Oak Island. The Moats analysis also helps explain the coconut fiber found at Smith's Cove as shown on various episodes of *The Curse of Oak Island.* The coconut fiber was carbon-dated to between 600 and 800 years ago, which places it sometime between the 14th and the 12th centuries. And coconut fiber is not indigenous to the northeast; it is only found in south Florida, Puerto Rico, the Caribbean, Bermuda, Trinidad and Mexico. Based on the Moats analysis, I believe the coconut fiber was collected during a Caribbean stopover of a cross-Atlantic voyage.

The Moats analysis is also consistent with the map drawings on the round copper disk.

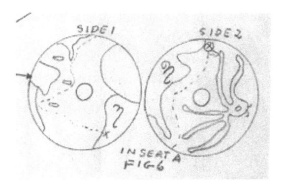

Round Copper Disk

These drawings show a journey beginning in western Africa and crossing the Atlantic at an easterly heading to some islands, and then a second leg progressing north along the eastern seaboard of America to a spot marked with a circled X. I believe the circled X represents Oak Island.

Slowly we are beginning to unravel this Templar mystery. The Nova Scotia map is one of four maps in the Templar Document. The other three maps will be discussed in Volume 2. Much of this story is still unwritten. Oak Island is part of a larger, unknown history going back at least a thousand years which involves maritime technology and engineering. This history is not limited to Oak Island and Nova Scotia, but includes the entire coastal area of northeastern America. We find it in Newfoundland, in Maine's Spirit Pond Rune Stones, and in Quebec, as seen in inscriptions and evidence of a Templar presence found by researcher Gerard Leduc. New Hampshire features the America's Stonehenge site (formerly Mystery Hill) with its intriguing astronomical alignments. Massachusetts boasts the Westford Knight carving and related sites, evidencing the Prince Henry Sinclair journey. Rhode Island is home to the Newport Tower and the Narragansett Rune Stone, and Connecticut the Gungywamp site, all of which add to the growing body of evidence that ancient explorers visited northeastern America. And, as Rich Moats has shown, eastern Long Island was the gateway to the return voyages across the Atlantic Ocean. Along this virtual ancient highway stretching from Newfoundland to the waters of eastern Long Island, we find ancient inscriptions, stone structures, calendar sites and more. It is there for the viewing. We just need to open our eyes.

End of Epilogue

Index/Appendix/Bibliography

These can be viewed online at my website: **www.zenahalpern.info**

020 3440 8390

TRAFALGAR

Printed in Great Britain
by Amazon

22729588R00178